PARENTING
ADOLESCENTS

PARENTING ADOLESCENTS

KEVIN HUGGINS

NAVPRESS

A MINISTRY OF THE NAVIGATORS
P.O. BOX 35001, COLORADO SPRINGS, COLORADO 80935

The Navigators is an international Christian organization. Our mission is to reach, disciple, and equip people to know Christ and to make Him known through successive generations. We envision multitudes of diverse people in the United States and every other nation who have a passionate love for Christ, live a lifestyle of sharing Christ's love, and multiply spiritual laborers among those without Christ.

NavPress is the publishing ministry of The Navigators. NavPress publications help believers learn biblical truth and apply what they learn to their lives and ministries. Our mission is to stimulate spiritual formation among our readers.

Library of Congress Catalog Card Number: 89-62657

ISBN 08910-96973

Cover photo: Deano Mueller

Some of the anecdotal illustrations in this book are true to life and are included with the permission of the persons involved. All other illustrations are composites of real situations, and any resemblance to people living or dead is coincidental.

Scripture quotations in this publication are from the *Holy Bible: New International Version* (NIV). Copyright © 1973, 1978, 1984, International Bible Society. Used by permission of Zondervan Bible Publishers. Another version used is the *Revised Standard Version Bible* (RSV), © 1946, 1952, 1971, by the Division of Christian Education of the National Council of the Churches of Christ in the USA, used by permission, all rights reserved.

Huggins, Kevin
    Parenting adolescents / Kevin Huggins.
        258 p. ; 24 cm.
    ISBN 08910-96973
        1. Parenting. 2. Parent and child. 3. Teenagers.
    4. Parenting - Religious aspects - Christianity.
    649.125 H891p

Printed in the United States of America

9 10 11 12 13 14 15 16 17 / 00 99 98 97

FOR A FREE CATALOG OF
NAVPRESS BOOKS & BIBLE STUDIES,
CALL 1-800-366-7788 (USA)
or 1-416-499-4615 (CANADA)

Contents

*To those parents of adolescents
who have the courage
to face life as it really is.*

Author

Over the past ten years Kevin Huggins has presented numerous seminars across the United States and in several foreign countries for both parents and youthworkers. For several years he led a two-year training program for parents of teens at the Chapel in Akron, Ohio, which ministered weekly to over 200 parents of teens. He has also led various counseling ministries to troubled adolescents.

Kevin currently serves as professor of Christian counseling at Philadelphia College of Bible. He is active in training Christian workers for counseling ministries in the local church. He operates a counseling practice for troubled adolescents and their parents in Langhorne, Pennsylvania.

Kevin is the author of two books, *Parenting Adolescents* (NavPress, 1989) and *Making Peace with Your Teenager* (Discovery House, 1993). He holds the Master of Divinity and Master of Arts Degrees from Grace Theological Seminary. Over the past twenty-two years he has served as a youth pastor, college and prison chaplain, family therapist in both inpatient and outpatient settings, and writer of Christian curriculum for high school students.

Kevin is married to Vicky, and they reside with their five daughters near Philadelphia, Pennsylvania.

Acknowledgments

There are so many whose contributions have been vital in developing the ideas and material found in this book. Certainly my thinking about parenting and family issues has been heavily influenced by the teaching and writings of Dr. Larry Crabb, my mentor and intern supervisor in graduate school. I will also always be grateful for the instruction and encouragement of Dr. Charles Smith, who is now at home with the Lord. As a professor and colleague at Grace Seminary Dr. Smith was instrumental in teaching me to apply the Bible to the everyday problems of living.

I am also indebted to the numerous parents and teenagers who gave me an opportunity to learn and grow with them as I served them as a youthworker, pastor, and counselor. Many of the insights in this book are truths we struggled together to capture and understand as they gave me the privilege to be part of the real struggles they faced.

Of course, the ultimate place where my ideas and teaching about parenting adolescents came to face the acid test was in my relationship with my own teenage daughters. Their love, patience, and struggles have provided me many opportunities to experience firsthand the joys and agonies of growing in my own parenting skills and maturity.

However, most importantly I want to thank God for giving me the strength and guidance to write this book. Writing it perhaps was one of the loneliest and most grueling tasks of my life. Without His ever-present love and encouragement I could have never finished it. It was in an attempt to further His purposes in the lives of parents and teenagers that I have written it. This is how I pray it will be used in the lives of all those who read it.

Foreword

In the last twenty-four hours, two sets of parents (each close friends) have told me of current struggles with their teenagers. One family has a son who is in jail. His parents have to decide whether to pay bail and get him out, or to let him sit there. The decision is difficult, the emotional agony deep.

The other family is dealing with a teenage girl who has been the source of preoccupying concern for years. Recently her life turned around; she found the Lord and changed into a delightful daughter. But just yesterday they found out she had lied to them about serious matters and is slipping back into old patterns.

As a father of two sons (one twenty-one, the other eighteen), I know something of the empty feeling that comes over problems you are powerless to change. Frustration sometimes breeds anger that leads to overreaction, then to a sense of failure that makes you want to quit. Proverbs speaks often of the deep sadness children can bring. But there is equally clear mention of joy, verses about full quivers and wise sons.

Every parent with much-loved teens longs to taste more of that joy. When it's present, nothing comes closer to Heaven on earth. But when it's absent, the pain (for those who are willing to admit that they still really care) can be indescribable.

We parents of teens must be encouraged to do more than just "hang in there." We need to know what to do. Do my friends pay their son's bail or not? Do my other friends confront their daughter with evidence of her deception? Or should they wait for an airtight case before they speak? Perhaps improving communication would solve everything and eliminate the need for a potentially nasty confrontation.

Parents want answers to specific questions like, "What's going on?" and "What should I do?" But we don't want formulas. There must be a simple way of thinking about parenting that is not reducible to a few simplistic steps.

Fifteen years ago, being a father seemed rather easy—challenging but not terribly complicated. Fairly regular devotions, rules about finishing spinach before dessert, lots of wrestling on the living room floor, an occasional spanking for definite infractions of clear boundaries, some good family outings, and a weary but noble patience seemed quite enough.

But in fifteen years the stakes have risen considerably. Misbehavior then meant an unmade bed or perhaps a tantrum. Now it may involve drug abuse, anorexia, or a lifestyle of angry retreat. And the decisions parents must make seem so much more complex.

My blood boils when I hear an expert presenting "six steps to producing responsible teens." Any honest parent who is after more than outward appearances knows that formulas don't work. They don't take into account so much that must be dealt with. Detailed instructions are good for assembling toys; they're useless for raising kids.

I also don't want platitudes. Delivered at the wrong time, they can be devastating. When your daughter has just told you she's pregnant, advice like "Let the Lord do it; you just do what you can, then step out of the way" does not help much. I know there is truth in most clichés, but I'm usually too irritated by the condescending tone in which they are spoken to hear the good that may be there. Platitudes stay on the surface of things, but people, especially teens, don't live there.

The years between twelve and twenty offer staggering opportunities for life-molding choices. Those choices emerge out of innumerable influences that can never be fully sorted out. I want help that takes seriously the complexity of my child's world, both internal and external, and gives me confidence that I'm not missing something crucial in my efforts to respond. I don't want to recommend bed rest when the patient needs surgery, but neither do I want to cut deeply when a Band-Aid would do.

Then, beyond all that, I want help that lets me relax a little. Most parents are just too uptight. None of us wants to evaluate the rightness of every word we say or decision we make. It's nice to be natural, not completely of course — until Heaven, spontaneity is not always best — but still we'd like to simply enjoy our kids without worrying about heavy things. Even during hard times, it would be good to know where the green pastures and still waters can be found. I really don't want the kind of help that makes me wonder if I've ever done anything right as a parent and that pressures me to be more careful next time. I want to face my shortcomings and work on them but not at the cost of depression and ulcers.

What parents want is help that is

1. specific but not expressed in formulas,
2. biblically accurate but not irrelevantly pious,
3. sophisticated and rich but not discouragingly confusing,
4. confronting in a way that makes me feel hopeful and relaxed rather than pressured and inadequate.

And I'd like it all in one book.

Kevin Huggins has not written that book. But no one has come closer. After you've read the best book available on any topic involving relationship, you still face situations that require a courage and trust that can come only from a personal walk with God. I think that's what I like best about Kevin's book. He makes it clear that one central point underlies everything he teaches: *The key to becoming a more effective parent is to become a more godly person.*

But he doesn't leave it there. To do so would risk leveling a rich truth into a bland (and well-worn) cliché. He looks carefully at what godliness looks like in a parent who is struggling to understand, love, and guide a teenage son or daughter. And he supplies content for the struggle. Here's what may be going on in your kid when his grades drop. This is what it could mean to love him. Consider why it's so hard to relate to him without anger when you bring up the topic of homework. It's practical, it's biblical, it's clear, and it's challenging.

I must admit, however, that I finished the book feeling a little tired. It's really too much for one sitting, or even two or three. And you need to be spending time in Scripture and in prayer as you read it; otherwise, you may lose sight of the simple truths on which Kevin's thinking is squarely founded.

I wish life could be simpler, or to put it more honestly, I wish life required less of me. I wish my lawnmower always started and weeds never grew and rain never fell on afternoons set aside for yard work. And I sincerely wish all I had to do was pray with my family before meals, put in an honest day's work, and never miss church on Sunday and, as a result, my kids would be guaranteed to turn out well, thankful to God for the life He gives and appreciative of me for all my efforts.

Kevin's book reminded me how much I sometimes wish for what can never be. Sin has made such a mess of things. Lawns have weeds, kids forget to say thanks, and I sulk over not being appreciated.

We live in a fallen world. But God has told us what we need to know in order to relate to Him as loving worshipers and to others (including our kids) as loving servants. And information from God is always relevant to all that matters. It's never off the mark. It goes into things as deeply as needed without ever becoming unnecessarily complex. And it points up our failures with a redemptive gentleness that draws us to joyfully expend efforts to do better.

I feel especially privileged to write this foreword for two reasons. One, Kevin likes the model I've developed for understanding people. He does a brilliant job of taking a simple framework for thinking about the insides of people and coming up with a penetrating discussion of adolescence that rings true to me, both as a counselor and as a parent.

Two, I know Kevin well. He is a man worthy of respect as a counselor, youthworker, teacher—and more importantly—husband, father, and friend.

Few books will make you think more profitably about dealing with adolescents than this one. It may not become a ground-breaking classic, but then again it may.

LARRY CRABB

Introduction

I am writing this book because I love teenagers. I have spent the past seventeen years working with youth toward one principal goal: to see a personal faith in Jesus Christ become the controlling reality in kids' lives. According to some standards for measuring success, my seventeen-year investment may be viewed as relatively ineffective. Although it's impossible to know what the long-term impact of my involvement in kids' lives really will be, at this time I can point to only small handfuls of kids and young adults with whom I have worked that bear the marks of being controlled by a personal faith in Christ. Though the personal rewards and joys of working with kids have been tremendous, these seventeen years have made one thing clear: Personal faith in Christ cannot be mass produced in adolescents' lives.

When the Apostle Paul composed his final three letters at the close of his life and addressed them to Timothy and Titus, he was occupied with one burning concern. What would prevent the gospel from dying with the aging apostles? How could a personal faith in Christ continue to be cultivated in the hearts of each successive generation until Christ finally returned? This is the same concern Christian parents and youth workers must share today.

It is certain that, as Paul addressed this concern in his letters to

Timothy and Titus, he recognized the task of discipling young people as a very personal and painstaking one. Paul intended to pass down to the churches his relationship with Timothy as a prototype of the kind of relationship necessary for transmitting personal faith from one generation to the next. The best, and perhaps the only, context for transmitting such a faith is through an intimate relationship of the kind that Paul offered Timothy.

Just before starting this book manuscript, I spent three weeks touring the western United States by minivan with my family. It was a vacation my wife, Tina, and I had planned to give our family extended time together. It seemed like the prescription we needed — the five of us traveling forty-five hundred miles together and experiencing some of the most breathtaking scenery God ever created.

The two months prior to the trip were a whirlwind of activity for our family. Church activities, visits from relatives, sporting events, and work commitments filled our schedules to the point that we were starting to lose touch with each other. Although no major problems seemed to be brewing at the time with any of our kids, Tina and I both looked forward to getting away with them to deepen our relationships before another busy school year started.

The trip, unlike many we had taken before, seemed at first to come off without a hitch. We followed our itinerary and observed all the beautiful sights just as we had planned. However, something did begin to happen to Tina and me that we hadn't anticipated. It was something we could and should have predicted because it happens whenever time or attention is given to improving relationships with others. Let me just call it an "uncomfortable awareness" — a certain despair that emerges when we see what lies beneath the surface of our lives and our kids' lives.

Thousands of years ago the prophet Jeremiah observed under inspiration from God that the human heart is desperately wicked. There is no better context in which this "wickedness" can be observed (and, incidentally, combatted as well) than in intimate, family-like relationships. More than likely this is what Solomon was getting at when he wrote that a man's "malice [lack of genuine love] may be concealed by deception, but his wickedness will be exposed in the assembly" (Proverbs 26:26).

As our family spent those many hours together (many of them very pleasurably), it became obvious to my wife and me that we still had a long way to go as a family. At home as we stayed busy and interaction time remained limited, it was often possible to imagine ourselves as the ideal Christian family, even though occasional crises or outbursts brought us back to reality. Normally, as these were settled, it was possible to retreat again to the delusion that all was well at the Huggins' household.

In reality, a kind of cancer is alive in each member of our family (as well as in each member of your family). It is that cancer in the human heart that Jeremiah diagnosed as "wickedness." As long as it's allowed to grow unnoticed in a heart, it goes unchallenged and eventually spreads to destroy any possibility of genuine love or service for Christ in the person. It is quite difficult to detect it, even in its advanced stages, except in personal relationships. This accounts for both the indispensable and painful nature of family relationships in God's design for Christian growth. He uses families or family-like relationships to expose the obstacles (known in Scripture as "wickedness") to pure love and to provide opportunity for them to be acknowledged and combatted.

On our vacation, the long hours at close quarters in the van and motel rooms made it quite apparent that our love for each other was incomplete in many ways. As Tina and I observed this in our kids' behaviors and in many of our own reactions, we tried at first to lightly dismiss it with comments like, "The kids are just tired of riding in the van," "We're all hot," or "We just need a good meal or a good night's sleep." However, by the end of the first week both of us were feeling very disappointed and even angry that our vacation didn't seem to be working as we had hoped.

I've observed that most families, when they are honest enough to admit it, experience similiar kinds of disappointment and irritation when they spend time interacting. That same "uncomfortable awareness" is aroused—an awareness that there is still a lot beneath the surface of each of our lives that is very unloving and selfish.

Too often parents react to these unpleasant revelations by trying to change the circumstances or surroundings. They say, "We need some time apart from each other," "We just need to get out of the house," or "We need a new toy that will enable our family to enjoy each other better." They assume that the culprit is extended time together or certain topics of conversation or conflict. The solution then becomes avoidance. To have strong or healthy family relationships, any touchy subject, conflict, or intense conversation must be dodged. In the end, this strategy weakens family relationships even more and blinds family members even further to the real problem—the "cancer" in their hearts.

I recently heard one newly married couple comment, "Marriage just doesn't work. Since we came home from the honeymoon all we do is talk about each other's faults. It's as if marriage has brought out all the worst things in each of us."

I thought to myself, "Their marriage is working for them exactly as it's supposed to. It's bringing out the worst things in each of them so that they can be dealt with." That is what parent-child relationships are supposed to do as well.

In counseling I often ask families to tape-record several hours of their conversations with each other around the home. When we play these tapes back and study them in counseling sessions, most families are shocked at how they treat each other. Studying family patterns opens a new window to get an honest glimpse at what was previously undetected in their hearts.

Living in a family and being honest about what you experience (especially in yourself) is always a source of pain. However, it is a pain that, if faced, can be one of the best tools Christian parents can use for building a godly home environment for their kids. One of the main objectives of this book is to help parents of teens learn how to use this tool.

When my wife and I looked objectively at the disappointment we were experiencing on our vacation, we had to admit that nothing really was going wrong with our family's time together. It was working just as God had intended, and as we had planned. *Our goal was to deepen love in our family. God's was to develop the kind of pure character that generates love.*

Love cannot be deepened without first deepening our awareness of who we really are as people. Purity cannot be developed without first exposing impurity—how a person refuses to trust Christ. Both occurred in our family because we were spending time together and were honest about what we were experiencing. It gave us the opportunity and motivation to shift our focus in the middle of our vacation to the real problems within our hearts that kept us from loving.

Kids need help to recognize and combat the problems in their hearts—the destructive beliefs and attitudes that are especially prone to be formed and reinforced during adolescence. That help can come only from those in a position to offer them the kind of intimate relationship the Apostle Paul offered Timothy. It is the parents of adolescents who most naturally fill this position, and therefore have this responsibility.

For parents, however, to be able to offer their sons and daughters this kind of help, they first need help themselves. Just like Tina and me. Our own fears and misguided assumptions too often keep us from loving our kids and diagnosing the real problems in them and ourselves. We need help using our relationships with our kids as tools for taking an "inside look" at ourselves and our teens and making sense of what we see. We need help knowing what to do with what we find inside—first in ourselves and then in our kids. And we need help knowing how to offer a new kind of relationship to our kids—a relationship that gives them their best chance at developing a personal faith in Christ and providing a foundation for their lives.

Many parents of teens may read this book with the hope of finding specific steps or formulas to follow that will guarantee that their teenager will turn out godly. My hunch is that they will be initially disappointed. I have purposely attempted to avoid giving such formulas or recipes for three reasons.

First, God seems to refrain from giving these kinds of formulas to parents. In Scripture He has given broad boundaries for parenting and left a lot of room for the exercise of individual parental judgment and discretion. His plan seems to be for parents to focus on attaining a level of spiritual and relational maturity in which they can start to trust their own parental instincts (which in itself requires a lot of trust in God). Giving formulas to parents can short-circuit this plan and breed a dependence in parents on those who give the formulas (if not on the formulas themselves) instead of on God.

Second, formulas can be very destructive to kids. To give specific steps for parents to follow with every kid who has a problem would be tantamount to prescribing the same medicine to everyone who complains of a headache without first investigating the cause. Similar problem behaviors in kids (e.g., suicidal threats) can be caused by very different internal and external factors. There are a few general principles that might guide parents in dealing with a suicidal adolescent (e.g., ridding the house of all firearms), but in the end how parents respond to a suicidal teen depends primarily on what is going on inside that adolescent and his or her unique environment. Instead of giving parents hundreds of formulas that attempt to cover any conceivable situation they might face, the approach of this book is to teach parents how to think through the situations on their own and form their own convictions about what is best for their teen. When parents do this, their teen feels far more like a person who is loved, instead of like a problem that needs to be solved.

Third, I believe formulas tend to lock parents into becoming "externalists." The indiscriminate use by one parent of techniques that worked for another parent is always aimed at achieving immediate, measurable results. Parents who depend on these techniques typically focus only on their teen's obvious behaviors. The implications of the behaviors and the subtler realities of what might be going on inside the teen too often get ignored. *Parents who are handed formulas for raising an adolescent, without first being equipped with the maturity and insight to wisely use them, will in the end stand little chance of cultivating any genuine form of godliness in their adolescent.*

While parents who read this book to find formulas will be initially disappointed, my hope is that in failing to find formulas they will succeed in discovering something much more valuable: *a model of parenting that shifts their focus from that which they really can never control (the kind of person their adolescent decides to be) to that which they really can control (the kind of parents they decide to be).* I believe that will be a shift to a biblical model; a model that can give parents new strength and hope, but in a way they would have never guessed.

PART ONE

WISDOM
What a Parent of an Adolescent Must Know

ONE

Understanding How Parents and Their Adolescents Are Alike

W hile loving my kids is often as natural as breathing, sometimes loving them as God intended is the most serious challenge I've ever faced. Recently I found it necessary to intervene in a quarrel between my two oldest daughters as we were riding in the car. I decided both of them needed to learn a lesson about controlling their tongues when angry. As I used to do on occasion when they were younger, I calmly informed them that they had lost their privilege to speak another word for the next fifteen minutes. My adolescent daughter, however, did not respond the way she had when she was younger.

Christi's response went something like this: "This is a free country and I will speak whenever I want."

Her words triggered all kinds of emotions within me. I felt angry, afraid, and ashamed all at the same time. Few people have the power to evoke the strong emotions within me that my teenage daughter does.

The angry part of me wanted to make her regret her words. I had the urge to stop the car and let her see what it was like to walk home in a free country. My anger called for a response that would restore the power or control I felt I'd just lost.

The fearful part of me wanted to make her take her words back and say she didn't really mean them the way they sounded. I felt the need to assure myself that my daughter wasn't really challenging my authority. My fear did not want to accept the reality that inside my daughter there might be some real problems developing.

The part of me that felt ashamed wanted to react like I used to when I was taken out of a game for throwing the ball away in Little League. I wanted to retreat and forget the event ever happened. Her response signified to me how poorly I must be doing as a dad to be addressed in such a disrespectful way by my daughter. I felt an urge to just give up. A sense of failure overwhelmed me.

In that moment my responsibility as a father called for me to respond to Christi out of love, in spite of everything I was feeling. And I failed her. I chose to let the angry part control me, and I lashed out at her with some threatening words. As soon as I did, I knew in my heart that my words had been destructive. I was the one who needed a lesson in controlling the tongue.

"INCARNATIONAL" PARENTING

Adolescents have an incredible ability to stir strong emotions in their parents. This is not a twentieth-century phenomenon at all. From the earliest scriptural records, the parents of young adults experienced an array of very strong emotions over their children's behavior (Judges 14:1-3, 1 Samuel 2:22-25, 2 Samuel 13:21-22, Job 1:5). Then and now the parents of young adults face the same great challenge: offering a relationship to their kids that draws them to God in spite of strong forces within the parents that prompt them to do otherwise. Careful study of the scriptural examples cited above (i.e., Manoah and his wife, Eli, and David) reveals how difficult this task is and how easily parents, even good ones, can allow the strong feelings their children stir within them to dictate the character of their response. Manoah and his wife allowed their fears to lead them to compromise God's standards in order to keep their son happy. Eli permitted his shame to keep him from making his sons experience the public consequences of their sin. David let his anger with his children create a distance between them and him so that he wouldn't have to deal with the ugly realities in their hearts. These kinds of responses are inevitable when parents allow internal pressures to dictate how they respond to their kids.

In Ephesians 4:29, the Apostle Paul wisely advises his readers that one basic principle should govern what comes out of their mouths. This same basic principle should govern the responses of parents as well. A paraphrase of this principle for parents of teens might go like this:

> Do not let any response motivated by personal need come out of your heart, but only such a response that is directed at the strengthening of your adolescent according to his need at the moment, that it may be beneficial for his relationship with Christ.

One prerequisite for applying this principle to parenting an adolescent is a personal understanding by the parents of their teens' needs at any given moment. This is possible only for parents who are in touch with their kids enough to know what they are experiencing in their world and in their hearts. It is only when parents can look at the world through their adolescents' eyes that they can understand them enough to know which response would be constructive and which would be destructive.

We might call this the "incarnational" approach to parenting. We read in the Scriptures that Christ is approachable to His children and qualified to help them in their time of need because of His incarnation (Hebrews 4:14-16). He became a man and experienced the world through human flesh. He actually looks at people through eyes that reflect a personal understanding of what they have experienced. His empathy and grace make a relationship with Him irresistible.

Parents certainly cannot become adolescents again by incarnation in the same way that Christ became a man. If this were possible, however, it might be valuable for two reasons. First, parents would remember very quickly what it is like to be an adolescent. And second, because the world changes so much between each generation of teens, they could see their teens' experiences as unique from their own.

In reality, however, parents can come to understand how their adolescents look at their world, and why they react to their environment the way they do, without becoming a teenager again. It requires the painstaking process of developing an awareness of what is going on inside their adolescents as well as inside themselves. Such an inside look at adolescents and their parents exposes many ways they are alike and many ways they are different. Being aware of both is a prerequisite to effective parenting. How they are alike will be the focus of this chapter. How they are different will be the topic of chapters 2 and 3.

UNDERSTANDING THE HUMAN PERSONALITY

To understand how adolescents and their parents look at their worlds, it is necessary to understand how people in general do. The Scriptures are the only reliable guide in providing a basic model for understanding people and adequately explaining why they function as they do. Investigating just what the Bible says about the human heart must be the starting point for this understanding.

Solomon made a point to study the human heart and record his observations in the book of Proverbs. Written under inspiration from God, Proverbs contains some of the most penetrating insights into the nature of the human personality found in Scripture. From Solomon's observation we can draw biblical conclusions about what parents and adolescents have in common in their personalities.

Solomon identifies four aspects of the human personality as central to the way people (parents and teens alike) approach life. Human beings, he asserts, have the God-given capacities to think, to desire, to choose, and to feel.[1]

Plans of the Heart

> Many are the plans in a man's heart,
>> but it is the LORD's purpose that prevails.   (Proverbs 19:21)

The Scriptures, here as elsewhere, are careful to portray people and God as alike in one very important way. Both are thinking beings who operate by self-chosen purposes; neither operates arbitrarily. In their hearts both have plans that give purpose to all their choices, behaviors, and words. Parents can be sure that beneath every one of their adolescents' actions is a plan. Even the most seemingly illogical behavior teens may choose (e.g., risking death by starvation in order to be thin) will begin to make sense when the underlying plan or strategy is exposed.

This is not to say that adolescents are always conscious of the plans they have chosen for themselves. Recently I spent several months working with a high school guy who was arrested for shoplifting seven dollars of merchandise. At the time he was arrested, he had fifty dollars in his wallet still left from his last paycheck. He had no conscious idea of why he stole the merchandise when he could have easily paid for it. It was not until we thoroughly came to understand what his experience at home and at school had been over the past several years that we began to understand what purpose the shoplifting (or rather, getting arrested for shoplifting) could have possibly accomplished for him. As it turned out, the adolescent designed the shoplifting, almost unconsciously, so that he would get caught and cause public embarrassment for his parents. He was furious at them for not letting him go out for football. Football had been the only place he had felt truly accepted or respected by an adult man. When this was taken away, he wanted his parents to hurt as much as he did. He wanted them to give up on him and leave him alone. His relationship with them did not allow for angry feelings like these to be expressed directly. So he chose to express them indirectly.

Generally adolescents are not very aware of the purposes that guide them. They usually form their plans in the midst of rather traumatic pain or disappointment, often involving a loss or blow in one or more of their most important relationships during childhood. Because of this there is a lot of pain associated with the plans themselves. To numb the pain, the kids often block out any conscious recollection of the event itself until they are older or more equipped to deal with it. As the events and accompanying pain are kept out of conscious thought, so too are the strategies that have been formed to prevent future disappointments. The Scriptures explain that "the purposes of a man's heart are deep waters" (Proverbs 20:5). They are hidden beneath the surface.

Parents can be equally sure that underneath their own actions and words are hidden purposes. These plans or strategies account for the ways in which they choose to relate, not only to their kids, but to other adults as well. Although parents are considerably more equipped as adults to be aware of the plans that are controlling them, it is also not unusual for them to be operating with little or no awareness of their inner purposes (Proverbs 14:8,15; 16:2).

Recently I was talking with the father of a sixteen-year-old boy. The father, Dick, was in a lot of anguish over the harsh way he'd been treating his son David, so much so that he had come to the conclusion that he needed professional help for himself. He told me how much he loved David and how much he wanted to be a good dad for him. After each blowup or cruel remark he would always beg his son's forgiveness and promise that it would not happen again. But it always did.

As I listened to him, I wondered what hidden purposes could drive a dad, who obviously loved his son, to abuse him. As we discussed Dick's own childhood and adolescence, he recalled that one of his greatest fears as a boy was that someone would think he was a homosexual. He had an older brother who had been accused of being a homosexual at that time and was the object of much scorn and ridicule in their high school. He remembered that he had decided, while in early high school, never to give anyone a reason to attack his mas-culinity like they attacked his brother's. As a result, he chose a plan to live by that called for constant demonstration of the proof of his manhood. He equated manhood with being good at sports, mastering the things a man should be good at, and coming out on top in whatever he tried.

As a father, he passed the same expectations on to his son. As David grew older, however, he became a threat to Dick's purposes. He was not very athletic. He showed very little interest or ability in the manly arts of hunting, woodworking, or mechanics. He had a much slighter build than his dad and at times seemed to walk like a girl. Dick was terrified that he was seeing other effeminate gestures in David as well. Dick was starting to be embarrassed to even be seen with his son in public. Even the sight of David was starting to trigger angry and cruel remarks. Somehow Dick believed that his own manhood de-pended on his son's virility.

When these facts were finally brought out into the open, the distraught father became aware for the first time of the plans of his own heart. He was shocked to see where the pressure and anger were originating. This self-revelation became the first step toward real growth for him as a dad who was able to love.

Although being purposeful is a characteristic people have in common with God, it is important to note that God's plans are always different from people's in one important way: His plans are never blocked. He has sovereign control of everything and needs to depend on no one else to accomplish His purposes. In contrast, all parents and adolescents experience frequent frustration of their plans, because people's plans are characteristically dependent on using others to accomplish their purposes (Micah 7:5-6).

Parents often have purposes or plans in their hearts that require their adolescents to act or be a certain way for them. Adolescents more times than not have plans in their hearts that won't work unless they can get their parents to respond to them in a certain way. When both approach each other with these kinds of intentions, conflict and resentment are inevitable.

I remember once working with a parent and her teen whose purposes came to diametrically oppose each other. The mother's plan for living required her to maintain a sense of "moral superiority" in every relationship. In one way or another she needed to make herself appear in every context (family, church, ladies' Bible study, PTA) as more concerned or obedient to the standards of God than anyone else. However, to make this strategy work as a Christian mother, it required her to be able to display ideal Christian children. This resulted in a home environment in which the kids felt a lot of pressure to make their mother look good to others. The adolescent daughter had learned at an early age that parental approval depended upon performance. However, the older she got and the more that was expected from her, the less able she was to perform well enough to earn her mother's approval. Although her childhood plan for getting approval and love required her to do whatever it took to meet her mother's expectations, she changed it during adolescence, when it no longer seemed to work. Her new plan demanded that she get away from people with high expectations and find approval from those who accepted her without the pressure. This resulted in behaviors that threatened to sabotage her mother's strategy (e.g., dropping out of church; picking nonchurch kids as friends; avoiding time around the house). The mother responded by stepping up restrictions and expectations. The daughter viewed her mother's response as an attempt to rob her of the little acceptance she had been able to get from her friends. She responded by running away, which seemed at the time like the only way she could make her new plan work.

When people have their plans blocked, they will initially respond by strengthening their efforts to make the plans work (Proverbs 21:22). Even if the plans keep working only a little, people may stay committed to them for life. *But during adolescence, when people face more changes in themselves and their worlds than at any other time of their lives, they are most likely to conclude that their old plans will never work.* This is when major new plans are conceived, making adolescence an opportune time for building healthier plans in kids' hearts. Children's teen years can be just as critical for the parents' lives as well. *Nothing causes parents to question the direction and purpose of their lives quite like the presence of an adolescent in the family.* As with the mother above, the true nature of parents' purposes can often best be seen in the way they respond to and impact their adolescent children.

Desires for Relationship

What a man desires is unfailing love.   (Proverbs 19:22)

People do not easily give up the plans they have fashioned for themselves. There is something behind these plans that fuels them and makes them in a real sense a matter of life or death to people. In the book of Proverbs that energizing force is referred to as "desires" or "longings." According to Proverbs 19:21, there are many plans in the human heart. In 19:22 the core motivation behind these plans is identified as a deep desire for a certain type of relationship. A relationship of unfailing love! *It is this desire that both parents and adolescents share. And it is this desire that all their plans are ultimately designed to either fulfill or numb.*

Every person has been built by God for relationship (Genesis 2:18). As soon as God created man, He also created a support system to meet his basic needs. From the very beginning man was dependent by nature. He could not exist without the resources that only God could provide. The environment God created for him not only met his need for food, water, and air to breathe, but for relationship as well. At first his only relationship was with his Creator, but later he developed relationships with his own kind (Genesis 2:20-24). It was as if man and woman could not function as God intended without having a certain kind of relationship with other thinking and choosing beings like themselves.

Then the fall into sin occurred (Genesis 3:1-7), and relationships became corrupted. Adam became afraid of his relationship with God and turned on Eve (3:12). The woman became threatened and changed the way she related to her husband (3:16). Their son Cain, probably as a teenager, became jealous of the relationship his brother Abel had with God and murdered him (Genesis 4:3-8). The environment created by God that offered pure relationships to mankind became polluted, so much so that the prophet Jeremiah could record these observations about the quality of relationships that are now available:

> "Beware of your friends;
>> do not trust your brothers.
> For every brother is a deceiver,
>> and every friend a slanderer.
> Friend deceives friend,
>> and no one speaks the truth.
> They have taught their tongues to lie;
>> they weary themselves with sinning.
> You live in the midst of deception;
>> in their deceit they refuse to acknowledge [any need for
>> relationship with] me,"
>
> declares the LORD.
> (Jeremiah 9:4-6)

In this lies the dilemma that every person faces. Every parent. Every adolescent. Although the availability of pure (unfailing) human relationships ceased at the Fall (Proverbs 20:6), the human appetite for pure relationships did not (Proverbs 19:22). *Each person's deep desire for a relationship that is unconditional and unfailing remains. And it is this desire that he brings into every one of his relationships.* In one way or another the behaviors and plans brought into these relationships reflect a person's desire for others to stop failing him. When and if a person ever comes to the realization that these desires will never be met by others, he experiences perhaps the deepest kind of pain known to the human soul. Many, in order to avoid ever experiencing this kind of pain, will refuse either to acknowledge that they have really been failed by others, or that they have any desires for relationship at all. This denial serves to numb the pain of their unmet desires.

More times than not, by the time a person emerges into adolescence he has already learned to deal with his unmet desires by numbing them. One of the healthy and natural functions adolescence has in a kid's life is to awaken him to the existence of these desires. *As long as his desires for a relationship of unfailing love are allowed to remain asleep, he will never be motivated to passionately hunger and thirst for anything.* He will experience apathy and boredom. As an adult he will not be motivated to pursue deeper relationships (with God or with other people) and will lack the ability to develop intimacy with others.

Often when these desires are awakened in an adolescent, parents misinterpret them and respond in ways that encourage the teen to hide or deny them again. This obstructs one of the most important developmental tasks an adolescent has to accomplish: *to come to the realization that his deepest desires cannot be met anywhere except in a relationship with Christ.* Unintentionally, many parents become their adolescent's greatest obstacle in accomplishing this. Since parents are the primary source of relationship for their kids prior to adolescence, a teen's first expressions of unmet desires for relationship usually take the form of complaints against his parents. This tends to stir up strong emotions in the parents themselves. It may awaken some of their own unmet desires for relationship, especially if they feel their kids are failing to appreciate them or return their affection. This can easily lead to parental responses that teach the adolescent that it is unacceptable and unsafe to express his unmet desires. Such responses short-circuit a kid's search for a relationship of unfailing love. If the search is short-circuited, so is his awareness of his deep longings, and in his numbness, it is unlikely he will be motivated to investigate a deep and fulfilling relationship with Christ.

I remember how my own desires were first awakened during adolescence, and how the opening they created allowed me to seriously consider a relationship with Christ. It happened during my senior year of high school. My parents worked for the government and found it necessary to transfer several times while I was in junior high and high school. By the time my senior year came I had attended four different schools. I was just beginning my senior year at a high school in a Chicago suburb when my parents informed me that another move was necessary, this time to Washington, D.C. After several long discussions, my parents agreed to let me stay behind and finish my senior year where I had already begun to get established the year before. They arranged for me to live with the parents of one of my friends who had an extra room.

In October the day arrived to say goodby to my parents. As I arrived back at the house after school, the moving van was just pulling away with all of our furniture. My parents were making a final check of everything. This was a moment I had not been dreading at all. I was looking forward to the adventure of being truly on my own.

My parents and I had enjoyed a pretty tranquil relationship together. We had had very little conflict over the years. Both of them worked outside the home ever since I can remember. My brother and I had learned pretty early how to take responsibility for ourselves and seldom got into anything that would have alarmed my parents. My mother commented years later that she regretted I'd come so early to the conclusion that I didn't need other people. Especially as a teenager I had become accustomed to making friends without becoming dependent on them. The moves had conditioned me to minimize the pain of leaving friends by not allowing myself to get very close to anyone.

That day, as I arrived at the house to give my parents a sendoff, I was feeling very self-reliant. I had my own place to stay (at least it seemed like my own place), I had my own car and job, and I had two parents who trusted me enough to move a thousand miles away and leave it all in my hands. Desiring something more in the way of relationship from anyone was the furthest thing from my mind.

My parents were on a tight schedule and had to hastily get on the road. As we said our goodbys, I'm sure my parents felt a lot more pain than I did. I waved from the front yard as they pulled out of the driveway and watched their car drive out of sight. I still was not aware of feeling anything except a mild sadness at seeing my mother cry.

After my parents left, I walked one last time through the house and made sure everything was turned off. As I did I started to feel very heavy with emotion. Before I knew it my eyes had flooded with tears, and I dropped to my knees in the living room and began to sob. The thought kept running through my mind that my life was just like this empty house. I really didn't have anyone but myself. And that was the loneliest, most depressing feeling I'd ever felt. My unmet desires for someone who would never leave me, and for someone I would never have to leave, rolled over me like a tidal wave.

I am convinced that the unmet desires I tasted that day were what stirred my heart to begin looking for someone who could love me in the unfailing way I'd never experienced. *No amount of good parenting could have satisfied these desires. In fact, good parenting tends to do the opposite in adolescence.* It creates the atmosphere where unmet desires are allowed to surface and be expressed. Very often this occurs in mid-to-late adolescence when kids are permitted to draw far enough away from mom and dad that they can get a glimpse of their own relational poverty—an inevitable reality in a fallen world. This doesn't happen for many kids until their first year or two at college, or even their first year or two of marriage.

Approximately one month after my parents had left, someone at the YMCA where I worked as a lifeguard must have noticed I wasn't myself. After work that night he invited me out for a coke. For the first time I shared with another person about the lonelines and desires I was experiencing. Slowly over the next several weeks this man helped me to understand what I really was looking for and then consider the possibility of finding it in a relationship with Christ. I had heard things about accepting Christ before, but it made no sense to me because I felt content (my desires for relationship were unaroused). But this time I was in pain. I now was aware of desires deep within me that were crying out. In this context a relationship with Christ took on a whole new appeal.

There is no question that it can be a dangerous thing to stir up desires in an adolescent. It has always been curious to me how Samson responded to being stirred up by the Lord. No doubt Samson was the equivalent to an adolescent in our culture when "the Spirit of the LORD began to stir him" (Judges 13:25). The very next verses (14:1-2) say he became attracted to a young Philistine woman and decided to marry her despite the Hebrew culture's prohibition against marriage to Canaanites.

I think the Lord was stirring up Samson to make him discontent with the type of existence his countrymen had chosen to settle for. Samson knew he wanted more out of life than servitude at the hands of the Philistines. But he didn't know what would really fulfill his longings. He experimented with excitement and immorality, as many adolescents do. But nothing he tried on his own seemed to quiet his restless spirit. Every relationship seemed to fail him, including the one with his parents, who were always too intimidated to give him the strong direction he needed.

When desires are awakened in adolescents, there is no guarantee they will not seek to satisfy them, as Samson did, through illegitimate means. However, the more help adolescents get in clarifying what their desires really are, the less likely they are to find immorality attractive. *It is when kids are left entirely to their own devices to cope with the disappointment and confusion of adolescence, that they are likely to direct their desires toward that which is evil.*

Once her desires have been aroused, an adolescent begins to subconsciously ask herself two basic questions: *"What kind of person do I have to be to get someone to want me and love me?"* and *"What kind of person do I have to be to accomplish something significant that others will value?"* These questions reveal what the human personality really longs to find in a relationship. The first guides the adolescent in constructing a plan that is calculated to win her love; the second moves her toward a plan that is calculated to win her impact. By the very nature of the questions, the plans require the adolescent to hide the person she really is and pretend to be the kind of person she thinks will win what she desires. *It is when a person's desires for relationship become married to plans that are designed to get those desires met apart from Christ, that the desires draw her foolishly toward evil* (Proverbs 13:19).

Left to themselves, adolescents will inevitably come up with their own evil plans for dealing with their unmet desires. It is imperative then that, as desires are stirred up during adolescence, kids are encouraged to openly ask the questions, "What kind of person do I have to be to get someone to love me?" and "What kind of person do I have to be to accomplish something significant?" Regardless of the words or behaviors kids use to ask these questions, parents should make it their goal to provide a home environment that can guide their kids toward finding biblical answers.

It is important to remember, however, that parents have unmet desires, too. It is not until parents have dealt biblically with their own desires — that is, acknowledging and directing them in healthy ways — that they will be free to deal biblically with their kids' desires. Parents of adolescents have long ago answered for themselves the two questions their kids are now asking. The answers they came up with as adolescents are probably determining their current parenting style. If a mother of teens decided during her own adolescence that in order to get someone to want her or love her she must always be "useful," then her parenting style will be that of a rescuer. Her greatest fear is to not be needed by others. As her children move into adulthood and express the desire to have their independence respected, she will feel like her whole existence is being threatened. She will not be free to deal biblically with her children's desires for respect until she first deals with her own unmet desire to be "wanted."

If a father of teens decided during his adolescence that in order to accomplish something significant in others' eyes he must never appear weak or wrong, then his parenting style will be that of a tyrant. His greatest fear is to appear incompetent to others. As his teens begin to express unmet desires for warm involvement and understanding, he will feel like his world is falling apart. He will not be free to deal biblically with his children's desires until he first deals with his own.

Deceptive Ways of Relating

> Like a coating of glaze over earthenware
>   are fervent lips with an evil heart.
> A malicious man disguises himself with his lips,
>   but in his heart he harbors deceit.
> Though his speech is charming, do not believe him,

for seven abominations fill his heart.
His malice may be concealed by deception,
but his wickedness will be exposed in the assembly.
(Proverbs 26:23-26)

Since people's unmet desires are for a certain kind of relationship, their plans to either fulfill or numb these desires are by nature directed at manipulating relationships. To carry out their plans, people take on false "identities," or "styles of relating," in their relationships to get others to respond in certain ways. Solomon was not the only biblical author to observe that the human heart naturally generates deceptive styles of relating. This was also observed by Jeremiah (Jeremiah 9:4-6), Micah (Micah 7:5-6), and the Apostle Paul (Ephesians 4:20-25), among others.

Two basic human traits make people's relational styles inherently deceptive. The first is the way people disguise what they want in relationships. Instead of directly asking another to meet an unmet desire, people feel compelled to "win" it from the other person one way or another. They seem to operate by the assumption that "since no one really cares deeply enough about me to give me what I desire, I will find a way to get it from them." This results in nothing less than manipulation.

Adolescents often learn in early childhood to be deceptive about what they want. As young children they were content to operate by simple requests like, "Mom, can I have a cookie?" Spoken by a three-year-old who is just beginning to astonish his parents with a growing vocabulary, such a simple request is eagerly rewarded. However, a child of four or five who has expectations to live up to may hear this response instead, "No, not until you have picked up all your toys like I asked you to." A four-year-old may easily conclude, "Mom really doesn't want to give me a cookie anymore. I have to find a way to make her." This could result in the invention of any number of new relational strategies. She may resort to throwing a temper tantrum, stealing the cookie when her mother isn't looking, or acting like no one in the world loves her—all behaviors that cause the child to take on a new "identity" with her mom. If rewarded by the parent, the child learns the lesson that deceit is the way to get what she wants.

As teens these children begin to experience much deeper desires—desires for love and impact in their relationships. By adolescence it is usually unthinkable for them to state any of these in the form of a simple request. It would be rare for an adolescent to approach his parents and say, "Dad, Mom, I feel very angry and frustrated with you. I don't feel any impact when I talk to you. You miss how I really feel. You have your minds made up before I even give my opinion. Could you guys start to be more sensitive to my need to feel like I have something important to contribute? Thanks for considering my request. I love you guys no matter what."

Putting such a heartfelt desire into a clear request is very risky. A direct request like this could result in much deeper feelings of rejection, loneliness, and even humiliation, especially if the parents respond defensively or critically. Instead, it is much safer for the adolescent to resort to manipulative ways to numb the pain he often feels around them. He may choose not to express his opinions around his parents anymore (avoiding the experience of being disregarded as a person), or he may defiantly announce his decisions and look away when they object (making them the ones who feel powerless for a change). Of course, parents have the same knack for disguising what they want in relationships. Many parents have the desire to know that they are having an impact on their teen.

Often as adolescents reach their late high school and college years they pull away from the family and spend less time with their parents, which can easily cause their parents to feel unimportant. Rare is the parent who takes his child aside and says, "Son, Daughter, I am really struggling with feelings of loneliness and worthlessness. I came to depend upon our relationship in some big ways. I'm proud of the way you're starting to really take on the responsibility for your own life and operate as your own person. But I feel left out. I'm working at adjusting to all of this, but it's not easy. Could you help me by trying to keep me a little more up on what's going on in your life? I would also like it if we could spend a couple of hours together every week. Take some time and let me know what you think."

Instead, parents typically hide these kinds of feelings from their kids (which, by the way, robs the kids of knowing what kind of impact they're having on their parents). Parents may choose to deal with the situation by relating to their kids coolly. Perhaps they'll play the "martyr" and try to use guilt to get their kids to stay home more. Or maybe they'll choose to "clamp down" and withhold privileges until they see changes. ("When you start to show some respect and appreciation around here we'll start to let you use the car again.") *Discipline or withdrawal of privileges are never appropriate responses when the parents' goal is to fulfill or numb their own unmet desires. Discipline under these conditions becomes deceptive and destructive.*

The second human failing that makes people's relational styles deceptive is disguise. Not only do people disguise what they want in relationships, but they also disguise who they are. They disguise the fact that they are hurting and confused. It seems like a shameful or weak thing to have one's desires, especially unmet ones, exposed to others. So people typically try to hide from others how they are really impacted by their world. Even when someone touches them deeply by fulfilling a desire, they are inclined not to let him know it. Early in life people acquire a basic assumption toward others: "If I let others get close enough to really know how I am impacted, they will use this information to hurt me." Recently one adolescent, the victim of a broken home, commented, "I'm afraid to let other people know how I feel about them. It seems every time I tell them I love them, they decide to leave me."

The relational styles that parents and teens typically use will be discussed in detail in chapters 4 and 5. What is important to recognize now is how the deceptive styles of relating that both parents and their teens use grow out of the plans and desires in their hearts.

Disappointment in Relationships

> Many a man claims to have unfailing love,
>   but a faithful man who can find? (Proverbs 20:6)

As people look to their relationships with others as the main source of finding fulfillment for their desires, they will inevitably be disappointed. Solomon observed that initially the claims of others can look very promising. What bride or groom does not approach his or her wedding day with great expectations for what his or her marriage partner vows to provide? And yet the very purpose of the vows and public ceremony are to hold the new marriage partner accountable. Why is this necessary for two people who say they love each other? Because of the nature of human love. God compared human love—the love of His own brides!—to "the morning mist . . . the early dew that disappears" (Hosea 6:4). Sooner or later (and usually sooner) human love falters. The prophet Micah observed that even the most sacred of human bonds (husband-wife, parent-child) is not enough to keep human beings from disappointing and hurting the very ones they are responsible to love:

> Do not trust a neighbor;
>> put no confidence in a friend.
> Even with her who lies in your embrace
>> be careful of your words.
> For a son dishonors his father,
>> a daughter rises up against her mother . . .
>> a man's enemies are the members of his own household.
>
> (Micah 7:5-6)

This sad reality makes people's relationships too often their main source of pain instead of their main source of pleasure.

What every parent and every adolescent has in common, then, is that each is a victim of failed relationships. Although some have been failed to greater or lesser extents, none have been able to find a human relationship that gives them more than just a taste of the love and impact they long for. Since the Fall, total fulfillment in another human being's love has not been available.

Perhaps the parent-child relationship carries with it greater potential for pain than any other type of human relationship. Children rightfully turn to their parents with all of their desires for relationship. Until they reach adolescence, it is difficult for children to even recognize or accept any deficiencies in their parents' love. Their dependence on their parents is too total to allow doubts or resentment to creep in and threaten the relationship. Children strive to remain naive to their parents' sins, and therefore maintain a sense of stability or security in their lives.

As a person reaches adolescence, however, something begins to open her eyes to her parents' current and past failures. This becomes the primary catalyst for arousing within the teen an awareness of her desires for a relationship with someone who won't fail her like dad and mom. Whether she acknowledges it consciously or not, she feels victimized and sets her heart toward avoiding further victimization. This has great impact on determining the type of relational styles she will carry into her dating and marriage relationships.

Many parents remain trapped in highly self-protective styles of parenting as a reaction to how their parents disappointed or failed them as children or adolescents. Very often they are unaware of how these styles were developed, or even of how they function to protect them from further hurt. It is ironic that as long as parents operate oblivious to this, the great probability is that their own styles of parenting are creating another generation of adolescents who will feel equally that their parents disappointed or failed them.

It's important to recognize the many ways children can be intentionally and unintentionally victimized by their parents. Of course, it's easy to view children who have experienced physical or sexual abuse, abandonment, alcoholism, or divorce in their families as victims. But children who have experienced lack of discipline, lack of focused attention, lack of physical affection, lack of verbal affirmation, overindulgence, overprotectiveness, overemphasis on achievement, or overexposure to adult tensions are victims, too. The writer of Proverbs observed the incredible propensity adults have to trouble their own families and children (Proverbs 11:29, 14:1, 15:27). This occurs in many different forms, but it affects every family.

There is a second reason, however, why parents and teens experience pain in their relationships. While it is true that a great deal of the pain people experience in their relationships is inflicted unjustly upon them, there is a way people add to their own pain needlessly. The plans they devise to avoid further victimization too frequently backfire and create an atmosphere that makes relationships even more disappointing.

As an adolescent, in an attempt to avoid further hurt from uprooted friendships, I devised a plan that went like this: "Life will work as long as I do not allow myself to need others." This strategy required me to keep up a "false identity" in my relationships. I did not allow anyone to see the "real Kevin," who was starving for friends and longing for relationship. Instead, I related to others as a person who could take people or leave people. Quiet. Aloof. Private. Self-occupied. Easily mistaken as snobbish.

When my parents observed this behavior, they were puzzled. They felt pushed away, maybe even unliked by me. They decided to back off and let me have my space. Kids at school and work figured I was not interested in friendship, so they ignored me. The natural reaction my relational style evoked in others only added to my loneliness and reinforced my assumption that I really couldn't count on others. My despair only deepened. *The victim, in an effort to escape persecution, had become his own persecutor.*

The writer of Proverbs recognized this to be a major source of pain in relationships (Proverbs 26:27, 30:32-33). A person who attempts to avoid pain in his relationships will, in the end, bring even more pain on himself.

As a parent, the same strategies still too often figure in shaping my response to my own kids. Recently I arrived home after a very long and disappointing day at the office. The events of that day had given my soul more than enough reason to reactivate my old strategy of playing the martyr. I'm sure my private thoughts echoed the theme from my youth ("I have nobody but myself. No one else really cares.") as I entered the house that afternoon. I decided to walk the pain off despite the fact that it was raining lightly. I thought it would help to have someone walk along with me and get my mind off what I was feeling. The only other person home at the time was my adolescent daughter, Christi, but she was on the telephone.

I decided it was my prerogative as her dad to interrupt her phone call. I motioned to her that it was time to get off. When I explained to her that I ended her phone call so she could go for a walk with me, she looked at me as if I had just suggested Chinese water torture.

Ignoring her objections, I threw her jacket over her shoulder and dragged her out the door. With every step we took down the street, Christi found a new reason why this was a dumb idea: "I'm getting wet." "My feet hurt." "I've got homework to do."

Finally it hit me. *I was trying to selfishly use my daughter to numb my pain.* And it wasn't working. In fact it was accomplishing the exact opposite. Forcing her to walk with me only added to my pain and built a wall of resentment between us that blocked a healthy relationship.

Suddenly I stopped and turned to Christi. "Christi, it really is okay with me if you want to go home," I said. "It was very selfish of me to make you go on this walk." My words took my daughter by surprise. There was almost a look of disappointment on her face. I think she was starting to enjoy the power struggle, and I had just ended it. She shrugged her shoulders, said, "That's okay," and with a puzzled look, turned back and started toward our house.

I walked on by myself and began to do in my heart what I should have done hours earlier. I began to talk to the Lord about my pain. I ached for a deep respect that had been missing all day long as I interacted with people. I also hurt over my own sin — the selfishness I saw in my relationship with my daughter. I confessed to the Lord how much I needed Him and how only He could satisfy the desires I had for unfailing love. As I walked, silently talking these things over with the Lord, a sense of calm and peace began to trickle back into my soul.

As I turned the last corner before arriving back in my own yard, I saw Christi walking hurriedly toward me with an umbrella in hand. "Dad, where have you been?" she asked in a concerned voice. "I've been looking all over for you. I got to thinking you shouldn't be out here walking by yourself. So I decided I would give you some company." Her words touched me deeply. Gratitude to the Lord welled up inside of me for giving me a taste of His love through my daughter's concern. It was something I was unable to instill in her on my own.

Parents and teens can have great impact on each other, for good and for bad. This is because both have complex personalities made up of deep parts (thoughts, longings, wills, and emotions) that are present every time they interact. If parents ignore these deep parts, their relationships with their adolescents will only inhibit the work of Christ in both their hearts. Learning to understand and deal with these deep parts is the key to effective parenting.

SUMMING IT UP

At this point you may start to conclude that I'm making parenting a teenager sound like quite a messy business. I am doing that intentionally for two reasons. First, because I believe it really is true! According to the Bible, understanding people and helping them grow are complex things that require an awareness of the deep parts in people's personalities that control what they do.

Second, I want to give you hope. Most parents know in their hearts that there are no simple answers to the challenges they face with their kids. When they are given simple explanations or formulas they are robbed of hope. They start to think that their family must be different or strange, since the simple answers just don't work for them.

Hope begins when parents recognize how complex it is to raise a healthy teen, and how confused all parents really are about how to do it. Hope grows when they bring their confusion and questions to the Scriptures and find direction. This is the kind of hope this book is designed to help you find. We must begin, then, by understanding what makes parenting a teen such a difficult and confusing task.

NOTE   1. For a more complete discussion of these four aspects and a fuller scriptural explanation of the biblical model for understanding people, see *Inside Out* (NavPress, 1988) and *Understanding People* (B.M.H. Books, 1987) by Dr. Lawrence J. Crabb, Jr.

TWO

Looking at the World Through the Eyes of an Adolescent

How painful is adolescence? A lot of debate is going on today about that question. Some have concluded, after studying the statistical increases in adolescent problems (depression, suicide, sexual abuse, sexual disorders, anxiety, violence, crime, broken homes, teen pregnancy, etc.), that adolescence is becoming more difficult for kids to weather.

Others who have surveyed typical cross sections of adolescents report that a relatively small percentage of kids indicate by their answers that they are plagued by trouble or turmoil. Over half in one recent survey conducted by *Psychology Today* seemed to be almost problem-free.

In light of such contradictory evidence, what are parents to conclude about their own adolescents? A scientific approach alone to understanding adolescence can lead parents to one dangerous extreme or another. At one time a scientific approach led many in the psychological community to conclude that spanking children was harmful. Extensive studies of children indicated that those who were spanked showed increased tendencies toward aggressive behavior. In light of these findings, parents were urged to refrain from using physical discipline with their children.

Of course this advice to parents directly contradicted the advice Solomon gave to parents in Proverbs: "The rod of correction imparts wisdom, but a child left to himself disgraces his mother" (Proverbs 29:15). If the biblical injunction is true — that correcting kids with a rod imparts wisdom — how should parents view the scientific research that states otherwise? Have those doing the research misinterpreted, or possibly even deliberately misreported, their findings? There is another alternative to explain the contradiction.

The Scriptures state that anything a parent does out of anger will achieve only destructive consequences (Proverbs 18:1; 29:11,22; 30:33). Could researchers have observed the effects of spanking when it was applied improperly (while the parent was either out of control or controlled by incorrect purposes)? According to the Scriptures, physical discipline, applied under those circumstances, would certainly stimulate aggression in the children. In other words, spanking must be applied in the same way one would apply a very potent medicine — with great care by a mature adult who is using it for the right purposes. Parents therefore should be instructed not to go to the extreme of avoiding spanking, but instead to be careful to learn how to use it properly.

Parents who allowed the scientific community to be the sole guide in parenting adopted a model of child development that viewed kids as ripening fruit. They were told to back off and not tamper with the fruit. Passivity in parents was encouraged. Spanking would only bruise the fruit and spoil the harvest, parents were told. In the case of clearly abnormal behavior, parents were advised that only a trained professional could intervene without disturbing the ripening process. Because the scientific data was limited and only detected the symptoms of a problem, parents were coached to unhealthy extremes in their relationships with their kids.

Years later, new studies conducted by behavioral scientists began to reveal a whole new slant to the subject. They observed that kids who received no physical discipline at all from their parents felt unloved and lacked internal impulse controls. Scientific data like this can be very helpful as long as parents recognize that it is piecemeal and doesn't tell the whole story.

The same is true when we look at adolescence. To understand

how this time period impacts kids, parents must remember to look at all the data through biblical eyeglasses. Parents must remember how the Bible says people respond to their worlds: with plans that are sure to be frustrated; with unmet desires; with deceptive ways of relating; and with pain and disappointment. Wearing these eyeglasses, we want to come to a better understanding in this chapter of just what it's like to be an adolescent. What are adolescents experiencing inside as they encounter life in the late twentieth century? How is their experience unique or different from that of their parents?

WHAT AN ADOLESCENT EXPERIENCES IN HIS WORLD

How an adolescent experiences his world is different from how an adult does for two important reasons. First, because of the sudden physiological changes triggered by puberty, *the adolescent experiences a drastic change in how the people in his world view him.* Second, because of the intellectual changes that occur during adolescence, *the teen begins to view his world in a whole new way.* Imagine how these changes, occurring within months of the onset of puberty, confront the adolescent with a set of problems radically different from what he faced as a child.

New Expectations from Others
The human body comes equipped by God with a time bomb. When the time bomb goes off, an electrochemical shockwave is sent throughout the body triggering in every cell a growth frenzy that transforms a childlike body into an adult-looking body within just a few short years. This growth frenzy is called puberty. Today the average male in the United States reaches this point between ages thirteen and fourteen, the average female, between twelve and thirteen.

Once puberty begins, the physiological changes in and of themselves are not normally as traumatic to the kids as the changes that occur in how others begin to view and treat them. As their adolescent bodies begin to look more like adults' every day, adults begin placing new expectations on them in three major areas.

Think as mature as you look! In 1 Corinthians 13:11, the Apostle Paul mentions that when he was a child he talked, thought, and reasoned like a child. But when he became a man, he put away these childish ways. Most parents are eager to see the same process take place as quickly as possible in their adolescents. However, when does a person reach the point where he is truly able to talk, think, and reason like an adult?

Many adults assume that kids reach this point when they begin to physically look like adults. They begin to expect adolescents to handle adult responsibilities, process adult information, understand adult problems, and live with adult stress or tensions. But are teens really ready to function like adults in these ways?

Much scientific research on adolescent thinking capacities sheds light on this issue. Research tends to verify that as kids enter puberty they begin to have access to "adultlike thinking capacities," or what one Swiss psychologist, Jean Piaget, termed "formal operations." By this he meant thinking in abstract symbols or principles versus merely thinking on the basis of concrete experience. In contrast, he termed thinking that was characteristic of children as "concrete operations." What really distinguishes "concrete thinking" from "formal thinking" is not the complete absence of abstract reasoning. Children do possess and use some abstract ways of looking at their world. They use the capacity to picture what they have never experienced (i.e., Abraham Lincoln, air molecules, The New York Stock Exchange, and God) and connect it to what they do experience (i.e., freedom to go to a certain school, the ability to breathe, the price of a candy bar, and a feeling of relief about a grandparent's death). They also possess the capacity to detect their own feelings and desires and communicate these in symbols (words and behaviors) that are directed at altering what they are experiencing (i.e., crying about bedtime, pouting over a spanking, or performing for a prize).

Children, however, do lack some very important thinking capacities that adults and adolescents have available to them. These capacities enable an adolescent or an adult to reevaluate all the ways he has been told the "unseen" impacts his world. He is able to perceive more intricate cause-and-effect relationships and attribute the events in his world to entirely different causes than perhaps anyone has suggested before. (For example, he may attribute his unpopularity at school and resulting loneliness to his parents' decision to move, which made him ineligible for the football team.)

The adult or adolescent is also more equipped to detect and reflect upon her own internal world of unmet desires, plans, and disappointments and choose a style of relating that will shape future events specifically. This chosen style of relating becomes much stronger in the adult or adolescent than in the child because it is held largely independent of what others say and do. Unlike the child's pliable nature that adjusts behavior to whatever those around her expect or reward (Ephesians 4:14), the adult or adolescent's behavior can become rooted in her private evaluations and assumptions about life. This frees her to relate to those in her world on her terms, selecting goals and behaviors that are designed to reap the rewards of her own choosing.

In essence, these "formal" thinking capacities equip a person to interact with others in her world as an active and free agent. The more an adolescent or an adult engages in honest reflective thinking about how and why she is impacted by, and makes an impact on, her world, the more she operates by a sense of personal choice and conviction. This of course enlarges her capacity to be either holy or evil, depending upon what course she chooses for herself.

Despite the huge advantages that "formal" thinking capacities give a person, the research findings show that many of today's kids choose not to use them very much until late adolescence (and some may choose never to use them at all). There are several possible explanations for this.

One appears to be lack of opportunity. Some of the best contexts for developing formal operational thought may be less available to today's kids. For example, the single most important catalyst to mature thinking is personal interaction with others who are thinking maturely. The condition and lifestyle of many American families today severely limits the amount of time a typical adolescent has with her parents, who could be modeling formal operations for her. Schools are structured so adolescents get very little opportunity to interact personally with anyone but peers who think on the same level.

Other contexts include activities that involve the adolescent in reading, problem-solving, or creative use of individual talents. Disciplines such as mathematics, music, writing, art, athletics, and experimental sciences provide some of the best opportunities to do this.

Unfortunately, in many schools such activities are too often optional or extracurricular.

A second reason is lack of motivation. Two great motivators to the development of formal operations are pain and problems. When confronted with circumstances that block plans and arouse unmet desires, many adolescents will start to use their formal operations to deal with the situation. However, when they find themselves in environments that fail to challenge, and even reinforce, their wrong strategies, they will find little need to engage in formal operations. Only when the environment changes (which may not be until college or even marriage) will the adolescent be motivated to give any kind of serious thought to deeper issues.

It has also been observed that adolescents show little motivation to expend mental energy in settings that are highly structured by adults. The traditional classroom setting that is built around lectures and objective test-taking is one of the best examples of this. In contrast, kids tend to register their highest levels of concentration and motivation in low-structured settings where they receive assistance from adults to think on their own and attempt tasks that require the utmost of their abilities. Art, music, and athletics may be some of the best examples of this kind of setting.

A third reason for delayed intellectual development in adolescents is anxiety-related stress. This is usually a greater factor for teens who are experiencing turmoil or conflict in their family relationships. When subjected to stress in the very relationships that ought to provide them with security and fuel to face life, many kids focus strictly on the concrete in order to survive. This enables them to reduce stress levels somewhat since only the immediate and concrete circumstances that confront them are on their mind. Kids who are subjected to sexual or physical abuse frequently resort to this tactic.

Although kids clearly have the potential to start thinking like adults at puberty, expectations that they will automatically do so are quite unreasonable due to the factors cited above. In fact, the pressure that results from these expectations on the kids may only compound the stress and make it that much harder for them to develop the intellectual capacities to handle adult responsibilities.

Once I was consulted by a concerned father who discovered that his high school son had been wearing women's underwear on occasion. He was horrified at the thought that his son might be turning into a homosexual. He was desperate to get his son some help.

In talking with the son, he revealed that he lived in constant dread of his dad's verbal criticism and ridicule. He felt like he could never please his dad. His father would often blast him with sentences like, "When are you going to start acting like a man?" "Why don't you ever use your head?" "You do that like a girl!"

In time he became convinced that he really didn't have what it took to be the kind of person his dad could be proud of. He began to withdraw from involvement in anything at which his dad might see him fail. He started seeking his mother's comfort and protection more and more. He expressed regrets that he had not been born a girl. "Because girls have it easy," he said. His younger sister was in many ways the apple of his father's eye.

The father's plan for helping his son face adult responsibilities was backfiring. It had resulted in terrorizing the son to the point that he was not only avoiding adult responsibilities but also anything that he perceived as a "male responsibility" as well. Terror in the boy's heart was channeling his mental energies into finding some way to avoid his father's angry words and stares. The only concrete solution he could find was to take on the identity of a girl. This was starting to become his style of relating.

Every adolescent is confronted with others who expect him to think as an adult. Seldom do they realize that he desperately needs help from the adults in his world to develop his intellectual capacities. However, if at the same time these very adults are becoming frustrated with him, he'll start avoiding them and lose their help. He'll keep his thoughts to himself and lose the opportunity of allowing adults to stretch his thinking. He may also begin to regard himself as "intellectually inferior" and look to others to do his thinking for him.

Love as mature as you look! Not only are adolescents expected to think like adults when they start to mature physically, but they're also too often expected to handle themselves like adults in relationships.

There are two basic roles people can take in relationships. They can be "fuelers" or "drainers." Children should legitimately be allowed the privilege of being predominantly "drainers," while adults are rightfully expected to fill roles as "fuelers" (especially in parent-child relationships).

In our home we have three drainers and two fuelers most of the time. As fuelers, my wife and I have the responsibility to fuel our three daughters. I like Ross Campbell's idea that children have emotional tanks, just as cars have fuel tanks. Children and adolescents, according to Dr. Campbell, need emotional fuel in order to function in healthy ways.[1] It is primarily the parents' job to provide this fuel through a loving relationship until the kids are mature enough to find fuel for living in their relationship with Christ.

Some days when I walk in the door after work, I can almost literally hear the gurgling sound of a bathtub draining. Then when I see my wife I realize it wasn't the bathtub that was being drained. It was her! That's what children do to parents. They are drainers.

Adolescents are drainers too! They haven't reached the maturity level to become fuelers yet. It's easy for parents to forget this, however, when their teen seems as strong and full of energy as any adult. Even so, it would be a mistake for parents to expect their adolescent to fill the role of a fueler to others.

The most common way kids are thrust prematurely into fueling roles is in their dating relationships. Imagine some high school guy who leaves for school each morning with his emotional tank on empty. He sees your bouncy, carefree, sixteen-year-old daughter one day in the hall. When they speak, she makes him feel alive, important, and even cared about, something his parents have had little time to do lately. He decides to make your daughter his primary fueler. She accepts. They call it going steady.

Soon, however, this high school guy has drained your daughter to the point of exhaustion. And he still wants more. She becomes grouchy and starts to demand a little fueling herself. Now the good feelings have stopped and the relationship has become draining for both of them. The boy decides to move on and find another fueler. He is on empty himself and doesn't have anything to give to your daughter.

Your daughter is left wounded. She feels a great deal of shame and guilt over her very first attempt to be a fueler. As she evaluates the experience, it's possible she'll conclude that she doesn't have what it takes to be a fueler for a man. She'll reason that a "real woman" can keep a man happy and content. She comes out of her first steady relationship committed to being less vulnerable around men because she doesn't want to be "found out" and thrown away again. Perhaps she'll resort to trying to be everyone's fueler from now on, or no one's. At any rate an experience like this can prompt her to question her adequacy as a woman.

Parents can do much to help a daughter like this, even after she has been hurt. However, it is far better that parents, as much as possible, take pains to prevent their adolescents from being thrust too early into fueling roles (e.g., by not permitting intense dating relationships until their kids are out of high school).

Many parents are guilty of using their own adolescent children as fuelers. This often happens during family crises or divorce. One or both parents begin to look to the adolescent for sympathy, understanding, or support. Parents cannot avoid draining their adolescent when they involve him in their own marital or emotional problems. This too can lead to serious damage to the adolescent's developing sexual identity, especially when he inevitably experiences failure at keeping mom or dad "pumped up." When talking with their teen about their own struggles, parents should always be guided by the Ephesians 4:29 principle, sharing "only what is helpful for building up [their teen] according to [his] needs," not according to their own.

During adolescence kids must be helped to get ready to become fuelers. Learning to fuel others in healthy ways is much like learning to swim. *The person who is immersed in fueling roles without instruction, practice, and supervision will end up drowning.* When adolescents are expected to automatically function as fuelers, they will encounter serious problems.

Look as good as you can! Adolescents face problems due to at least one more set of new expectations. As children experience their growth spurt during puberty, two things begin to happen. First, physiological differences between kids become much more accentuated. Height and weight variations increase. Unique facial features become more pronounced. Differences in sexual organs (breast size, penis size, etc.) become noticeable. Differences in athletic abilities become greater. Once puberty has struck, kids are much more apt to be unfavorably compared in their physical appearances to each other.

Second, kids discover that the physical proportions that are considered beautiful or admirable for an adult body (unlike a child's) are very narrow. Some have estimated that less than five percent of all American women are physically capable of attaining the body proportions of the average model or actress that have been held up by the media during the last decade.

This leads many American women to conclude that their body is deficient and must be regarded as shameful. An epidemic increase in eating and exercise disorders among American women certainly points to this. There is strong evidence as well to indicate that many men also struggle with deficient images of their bodies (e.g., steroid abuse, body-building obsessions, preoccupation with clothing and hairstyles).

Parents tend to grow much more alarmed over their children's physical proportions once they get a glimpse of what they might look like as adults. They have learned through personal experience how much more painful the adult world can be for people who are considered unattractive. In their minds, and sometimes even with their words, parents begin to make comparisons between the physical features of their kids and those of other adolescents, focusing on where their own kids don't measure up. As good-intentioned as this may be, it can often lead to magnifying even more the embarrassment kids feel about their own bodies.

Compared to what they sensed as children, kids find the expectations for their physical appearances in adolescence overwhelming. In order to live up to these expectations, kids compensate any way they can—often devoting obsessive attention to such things as clothing, hairstyles, dieting, body-building, and cosmetics. Some kids may rely on athletics, dating, or even sexual promiscuity to prove something about the adequacies of their bodies. Their bodies become a constant source of problems that never confronted them as children.

Adjusting to these three new sets of expectations are not the only problems that confront an adolescent, however. The physical changes of puberty cause people to alter their expectations toward the adolescent, but the intellectual changes that also accompany puberty cause the adolescent to view *others* in a whole new way. This creates a whole new set of problems.

New Insights into the World

While formal operational thinking may remain largely under-developed until early adulthood, adolescents will still make sporadic use of these new capacities from puberty on. These capacities give adolescents insight into at least six new dimensions of their world. In effect, everything in it changes for them. Imagine how overwhelming these insights can be to someone who is receiving them for the first time.

Things could have been different. Adolescents can begin to go back and reevaluate past events, especially painful ones. They can identify the causes that were responsible for their present circumstances and imagine how the present would have been different had things in the past not occurred. The adolescent girl living in a single-parent home can begin to visualize what life would have been like if the divorce had never happened. She can even reflect on the divorce and decide whose fault it was and how it could have been avoided. This of course begins to make the world a much more disappointing place to her. Living with only one parent did not seem so depressing until she started to realize what it would have been like to grow up with two parents. It was also a lot easier for her to admire her mom and dad, until she became aware of what their inability to get along actually cost her.

Before parents jump to the conclusion that this kind of insight is always destructive for an adolescent, they must remember that this same capacity is what enables their adolescent to become aware of her own unmet desires. And it is the awareness of unmet desires (especially in relationships) that is a prerequisite for adolescents to begin thirsting for a growing relationship with Christ.

Things should be different. Adolescents also begin to acquire the capacity to compare the actual with the ideal. They are able to look at the actions and attitudes of those around them, as well as at their own, and decide how they should be different. As children, they could do this only when a behavior violated a concrete rule that had been given to them. However, as adolescents, they are able to judge an action or attitude not only as right or wrong, but also as loving or selfish, just or unjust, prejudiced or impartial. This might be thought of as a whole new ability to spot problems.

It is not unusual for children from an alcoholic or incestuous home environment to regard the events that go on at home as "normal" until they get to adolescence. As adolescents these kids can begin to recognize, even without being told, that something in their family is not right! Their eyes start opening to the injustices that go on around them, and the world can suddenly become a much uglier, crueler place to them. This insight enlarges the capacity adolescents have to experience anger and shame, both toward themselves and their family.

Things could be changed. A medical doctor who works with chemically dependent adolescents recently told me of the comments he receives from kids as they are released from the rehabilitation program. One question he always asks is, "What do you think your parents could have done to have prevented you from becoming chemically dependent?" He said one adolescent girl's answer in particular seemed to typify how most of the kids answered this question. She said, "There ought to be a law that makes parents and their kids sit down and talk together for an hour every evening."

Her answer reveals real insight into how things could be changed. It also demonstrates that this adolescent girl is exercising a new capacity to visualize solutions to the problems that confront her. Unfortunately, such a capacity also often results in making the world a much more frustrating place for the adolescent. Imagine what feelings this new insight will trigger when she returns home and observes her parents continuing in the same negligent pattern of communication, even after she gave them her wonderful suggestion of spending an hour in conversation every evening.

As kids exercise their new capacity to creatively solve the world's problems, they often experience a great deal of frustration with the adults in their world who often fail to respond to their ideas. Nevertheless, this capacity does strengthen in the adolescent an awareness of her own volitionality. She begins to recognize that she has several options for solving a problem. In choosing one of these, she begins to accept responsibility for her own choices.

Things aren't as they seem. It is so much easier for parents to fool a child than it is to fool an adolescent. When children are small, parents can usually hide their feelings and thoughts from them. However, adolescents begin to develop a capacity to imagine what others are thinking and feeling. And often they are right in what they imagine.

As a youthworker, I received a phone call from a concerned mother. She wanted to know why I was mad at her daughter. Her daughter did not want to come to church anymore because she felt like I was giving her angry looks in my Sunday school class. I told the mother that I was not aware of feeling any anger toward her daughter, but I would be glad to meet with the girl and find out what was going on. I learned when I met with her where she got the idea that I was angry with her. She had recently attended a couple of parties where she drank alcohol with some of her friends for the first time. Since a couple of other church kids attended one of the parties, she was sure I was told about her drinking. She imagined how I would feel when I found out, so the next time she was around me she thought she detected those feelings. In reality, I had not heard about her drinking. If I had, however, I probably would have felt something akin to anger (e.g., concern, disappointment, worry).

As an adolescent, this teen was exercising her new capacity to read beneath the surface in her relationships. The more she uses it, the more accurate she'll become in not only picking up what others are thinking and feeling, but also in predicting what others will think or feel in different situations. As kids learn how their own actions impact the thoughts or feelings of others, the possibility of successfully manipulating others becomes greater.

This new capacity makes the world a much lonelier place for adolescents. As they come to understand to some degree what is in other people's hearts, they'll feel less loved and esteemed. Even as they come to understand more of what is in their own hearts, they'll feel like no one understands them.

Acquiring this new capacity to sense what is going on inside the human heart is absolutely essential to developing genuine love in the adolescent. It is not until an adolescent is conscious of her own needs and motives, as well as the deeper needs of others, that she will be able to understand what it means to "deny herself" and "lay down her life" for others.

Things could get worse. The world becomes a much more dangerous place for adolescents once they become adept at imagining what the future holds. A preadolescent can imagine consequences to a certain extent. She might consider what her parents' reactions will be that night when she brings a bad report home. Or a young guy might worry about what will happen the next day in gym class when he is the only one who can't do a pull-up for a physical fitness exam. The preadolescent might even experience physical symptoms over the anxiety that such prospects bring. However, the preadolescent's ability to foresee consequences is considerably shortsighted compared to the adolescent's. Seldom will the preadolescent see far enough ahead or have enough forethought to devise a plan that is calculated to ward off danger. This very practice, however, can come to occupy a great deal of the mental energies of an adolescent. *The adolescent develops a new capacity to visualize the future and foresee painful events on the horizon.* He or she is capable of mobilizing incredible energies for weeks or even months in an attempt to keep the events from happening.

I remember a high school girl named Sally, who was in my youth group. Her attendance patterns at church and youth group seemed to be cyclical. We would almost never see Sally during the summer or fall, but every winter, toward the end of January, she would come back and get very involved again through the spring. After this happened three years in a row, I became very curious. One day I made a point of getting together with her to ask her about it. She acknowledged rather sheepishly that this was indeed her pattern. She explained that every year, about two to three months before cheerleading tryouts, she would start to get worried about her relationship with God. Cheerleading was the most important thing in her life, and she was afraid that God might cause her to slip or mess up one of her routines during the tryouts. She figured she could prevent this from happening by getting her spiritual life back together each year before the tryouts came around.

Sally's insight into how things could turn out required a lot of foresight and ingenuity, even though her theology left much to be desired. Because of this new insight, Sally's capacity to worry about things also ballooned. The future came to be dreaded for the myriad of painful events she saw it potentially offering.

In spite of all the disturbing possibilities with which this new capacity haunts an adolescent, it is this very capacity that fuels a desire in an adolescent like Sally to learn self-discipline and delay her own gratification. It is only when an adolescent is finally able to visualize how certain rewards can be realized in the future that she will consider it worth the price to endure pain and hardship in the present.

Things can be hidden. Children often believe that their parents can read their minds. This serves many times as a deterrent to wrongdoing. They figure, "Why try it?" when it seems inevitable that their parents will find out about what they've done. This illusion, however, is quickly dispelled in adolescents' minds when they begin to think in formal operations.

As the adolescent grows in his awareness of his own thoughts and feelings, he also grows in his awareness of how easy it can be to hide them from others. Kids usually discover this when they are instructed to "quit feeling" a certain way or ordered "not to think" a certain thought. Children cannot do this. So, in order to comply, kids simply learn to conceal what they really are thinking and feeling and instead portray whatever demeanor others want to see. A kid can get so good at this, in fact, that when in desperation he wants to end the charade and really let his parents know of his pain, his parents won't accept that this is the "real" him. They might completely ignore his signals for help, figuring he's just messing around or making something up to get attention.

This was the case with one high school boy I worked with following a suicide attempt. It was strange how his parents insisted they had no clue that their son was feeling desperate, in spite of the fact that I could identify at least four ways the boy had tried to signal them. Three years earlier, their oldest son had died tragically in a motorcycle accident. At that time the younger son bottled up the grief he felt and attempted to be "strong" for his folks. For a couple of different reasons, the boy felt responsible for his brother's death, but he never expressed them. For three years he successfully hid his grief and guilt from his parents. When he finally couldn't cope, he sent several "SOS signals" to his family—he stopped coming to supper, left sad poems laying around the house, dropped out of his favorite activities, and started uncharacteristically to neglect household chores. But his parents missed the signals because they'd been lulled by the boy's passive and compliant manner into believing that "he didn't have a care in the world."

As kids discover how easily they can keep their feelings and thoughts private, it makes them much more apt to be deceptive. They can think about things that would upset their parents, even do what would upset them, and usually avoid betraying themselves. When teens choose this as a routine style of relating, they create immense problems for themselves.

This capacity can be harnessed for good, however, and used to give the adolescent a real advantage in his relationships. When a teen has insight into how things can be hidden, he is able to more readily spot truth and error in others and can become an accurate judge of character. As this skill develops, it presents the adolescent with a variety of new problems as well (e.g., knowing how to deal with the deception he sees in others).

Understanding how the world and its expectations change for an adolescent is only part of the challenge parents face. The other part lies in understanding how these changes and the problems they generate impact the heart of their teen.

WHAT AN ADOLESCENT EXPERIENCES IN HIS HEART

The great changes that begin to occur at puberty to an adolescent's body, mind, and eventually, his world, trigger in his heart three major crises. *Finding a way to resolve each of these three crises becomes the most important task the adolescent has to accomplish in preparing for adulthood.* Adults who emerge from adolescence not having accomplished this task, or having accomplished it without Christ, will lack the resources to genuinely love others.

In the first chapter, we observed how an adolescent approaches his world with desires in his heart, desires for things that only a relationship of unfailing love can provide. As a teen matures physically and intellectually, a realization grows that what he really desires is not being offered by anyone in his world. The world has changed for him in the ways described earlier in this chapter. And it appears to the adolescent that the changes amount to a refusal by everyone in his world to even partially fulfill his desires as they seemed to when he was a child. This precipitates some real crises. He is confronted with the task of finding the things he has lost. This is very difficult for an adolescent because his new physical and intellectual capacities do not allow him to find the same fulfillment in the things that fulfilled him as a child. Even if he could get the world to treat him like it did when he was a child (and sometimes an adolescent can do this for a limited time), it would be an empty experience. The adolescent's desires are much too deeply felt to be satisfied any longer by the concrete objects or experiences that delight a child. *The tasks that confront an adolescent require him to find a way to get his adult desires met in an adult world.* However, he must do it largely without the experience, maturity, or opportunities of an adult. Consider then what an adolescent must experience as he faces each of these crises.

The Longing for Security

The changes the adolescent experiences threaten her sense of security. So much of what she used to depend upon to be safe and reliable becomes suspect. Her parents' weaknesses and limitations become very noticeable. They are exposed for having less control of the world than she perceived them to have when she was a child. Almost nothing outside the home (school, friends, work, youth group) can be directly controlled by her parents anymore, and it seems that even less inside the home is controlled by them either. In the midst of such unsettledness, *the adolescent often sees no other recourse than to begin accepting the responsibility herself for creating her own sense of security.* In this, however, she often finds herself to be her own worst enemy.

Tammy was a high school junior when I began counseling her for depression and obsessive dieting. Her mother was most concerned about all the weight she'd lost and her refusal to stop dieting even though she was starting to look emaciated. It was interesting to find out that Tammy became depressed and started to diet at the same time her steady boyfriend broke up with her. Up until that time, according to her mother, she seemed to be a fairly well-adjusted, happy kid. Tammy's father had deserted her family five years earlier. Although it was a real blow at the time, Tammy seemed to handle it about as well as any twelve-year-old could. However, five years later when her boyfriend abandoned her, it was a different story. Tammy's mother could not understand how a girl who dealt with losing her dad so well could take losing her boyfriend so hard.

What her mother did not realize was that Tammy's whole way of looking at the world had changed. As a preadolescent she accepted the explanation she received from her mother about her dad's departure. She was told that he was a sick man and really could not help his actions. With the support and attention she received from the rest of the family, her sense of security was never seriously shaken. She was able to remain naive to the hostile and unpredictable nature of the world in which she lived.

Five years later, the rejection and loss of a boyfriend had a whole different kind of impact on her. This time the event represented so much more to her because she had new insight into how things were beneath the surface. She was able to independently come up with her own explanation for why he walked away. And this time no explanation that attributed it to a freak problem in him could console her. She was sure that if she'd just been a better person, she could have held on to him. After all, many of her girlfriends managed to hang on to their guys. "There must be something wrong with me," she thought. In fact, she now started to assume that her dad probably left for the same reason. Her! The more she thought about it, the more it hit her like a ton of bricks. There could be no guarantees anymore than any relationship, especially any relationship with a man, would be lasting unless she could become the ultimate person that no one would ever want to leave. The more she worked at being that ultimate person, the more impossible it seemed. That's when the depression began. She finally focused on at least being the ultimate "thin" person, hoping against hope that this would be enough. But in her heart, she knew it would not be.

It's so much more difficult for an adolescent to feel at home in the world or in her relationships than it is for a child. The adolescent cannot maintain a childlike naiveté about the world for very long. She must find a way to feel secure again in such a world. Her first inclination will often be to create an illusion that the world's hostility is really her own fault. This makes things more predictable. If she can only change herself, she reasons, then the world will become predictably less hostile to her. However, this illusion gets crushed when the so-called predictable does not happen. *No matter how much she works at self-improvement, she is never able to create a world that gives her that relationship of unfailing love she thirsts for.* The crisis will continue until she finds something that will!

The Longing for Impact

The second crisis an adolescent faces threatens his sense of impact on others that he has grown accustomed to since childhood. Most kids, by the time they have reached preadolescence, have figured out how to get their world to sit up and take notice. Usually this involves getting good enough at something so others will recognize him to have done something valuable. Whatever methods he used to achieve this as a child, however, begin to fail to evoke for him the same response from others in adolescence. This is primarily due to the increased expectations others have for him.

Recently I talked with one high school student named Darren. His father, Chuck, asked me to see him because of a lack of motivation he'd been exhibiting in several areas. Up until his seventh-grade year, he had been an excellent student and apparently was very well accepted by his peers at school. When he graduated to junior high, however, his grades slowly began to drop. And seemingly so did his popularity with the other kids. In junior high school the only strong interest that remained for Darren was involvement in a Boy Scout troop. In ninth grade, however, Darren's dad made him quit scouting until his grades improved. But his grades continued to plunge.

When Darren turned sixteen, he showed some initial interest in getting his driver's license. He was allowed to get his learner's permit, but after taking a few lessons with his dad he lost interest in learning to drive and failed to register in time to take a driver's education class at school. This was the final "straw" that led Chuck to seek counseling for Darren.

Apathy or low motivation in adolescents is often a warning signal that they have lost hope in making an impact on their world. In Darren's case, his main way of achieving a sense of impact as a child became blocked when he entered junior high school. In his small elementary school, Darren had become respected by the teachers and other students by being a first-rate student. In junior high school, however, this strategy began to fail him. A larger student body made it difficult to gain recognition as a top student. Changing classes and teachers every hour gave him little opportunity to develop relationships with teachers who could help him feel valued for his school work. Even Darren's old friends didn't seem to care anymore about who made good grades.

They were more attracted to the kids who had athletic, musical, or social talents, skills Darren lacked. The only place he continued to feel important or valued was in his Boy Scout troop. Eventually, however, even that avenue was blocked.

When his father urged him to learn to drive, Darren saw this as a new avenue for impact. However, during the first lessons Chuck got impatient and said cruel things to him. Darren started to avoid driving in order to avoid Chuck's anger. Darren believed the anger of others had to be avoided at all cost if any sense of impact was to be preserved.

Darren faced the same task every adolescent faces in one form or another—*finding a way to make an impact when he wasn't a child anymore, but really not an adult either.* He couldn't go back and get the world's positive regard again as he had as a child. Accomplishing that in junior high required abilities he did not have. Nor could he run ahead and master the things adults are respected for. Whenever he tried adult things (i.e., driving), he was only reminded of his limitations and inadequacies. Darren faced a crisis that had to be resolved if he was ever going to be ready to face adulthood with confidence.

The Quest for Love

As an adolescent begins to recognize selfishness and lack of love beneath people's actions in ways he never could as a child, he can start to feel unloved in spite of their verbal assurances to the contrary. *When the adolescent becomes disillusioned with the relationships he experiences at home, he'll often begin to regard relationships he finds outside the home (especially with peers) as the answer to the love he feels he has lost.* However, by midadolescence the teen experiences enough betrayal by his friends to create an even greater disillusionment toward relationships outside the home than inside. This constitutes another real crisis for the adolescent: he must find the love he longs for while stranded in a sea of relationships that offer more disappointment, rejection, and heartache.

This is the crisis that faced one sixteen-year-old adolescent named Marti. Marti grew up in a single-parent home, never knowing her father, who died when she was an infant. She was raised by her mother, Sandra, as an only child. Even with the absence of her father, Marti's recollection of her childhood was very positive. She and her mother enjoyed a very close relationship. By the time Marti was a preadolescent, she and her mother considered each other best friends. They liked to do everything together.

When Marti entered high school and began to develop a social life of her own, Sandra decided it was time to start looking around herself. She deeply desired to be married again and thought Marti was now at an age when she did not need her as much. She felt free to start building a life for herself again. Marti didn't seem to mind Sandra's decision to see men again until a serious relationship began to develop with one man in particular. Much to Marti's surprise, her mother fell in love with this man and married him in a matter of months. For the first time, Marti was forced to share her home and her mother with another adult. Even though Marti looked and acted like she was ready to be independent from her mother, inside she still felt like a little girl. She deeply resented Sandra's decision to remarry and chose to express it by spending as much time as possible away from home. This served only to confirm in Sandra's mind that Marti didn't need her as much anymore. She completely misread Marti's behavior.

Marti, feeling rejected and betrayed by her mother, turned to relationships at school for consolation. She quietly became involved in a series of serious relationships with guys. She started feeling very used. Finally when one boy she really thought she loved broke up with her in order to date a girl she considered much "thinner" and more attractive, she began to panic. She was confronted with the terrible possibility that she might never again find a relationship she could count on. Almost as a last resort, she decided to go on a starvation diet to lose weight. She reasoned that if she were thin perhaps she would be the kind of person others would want and love. After failing to stay on her starvation diet, she discovered she could still lose weight by forcing herself to vomit whenever she "messed up" and ate too much.

Although she failed to lose all the weight she wanted to, she did experience some satisfaction when people began to comment on how good she looked. This was enough to convince her, at least temporarily, that her new strategy would eventually regain the love she so desperately wanted. As a high schooler, she decided that a bulimic lifestyle would accomplish the task of finding love while in the mist of relationships with selfish people.

Left on their own, adolescents will eventually find ways to accomplish the tasks that confront them (or literally die trying). However, more times than not, the ways they find will lead to unhealthy and ineffective styles of relating in adulthood (imagine what Marti will face). This is why *kids desperately need help from understanding adults during adolescence.* Teens look to their parents to see what role they will play in their lives. Will they become their adversaries? Will they become their rescuers? Or will they become their allies in helping them find ways to deal with the crises of adolescence? *The role parents choose to play can have a great impact on the kind of adult their adolescent chooses to become.*

SUMMING IT UP

At this point it may be too late to warn you. Looking at the world through the eyes of your adolescent and realizing the deep ways it has impacted and hurt him can be a painful experience. It can be painful because you may see things you have never seen before: how your teen has been privately suffering; how he has been trying to cope with his pain by himself; how you have unknowingly been adding to his pain by the ways you've responded to him; or how you have failed him by not recognizing his pain earlier and doing more to help.

Guiltier parents do not necessarily make better parents. It has not been my goal in writing this chapter to inflict you with more guilt about the way you've been handling your kid. Rather, it has been to help you understand how to love your teen more deeply.

In order to accomplish this, however, it is necessary to first help you recognize how your kids are not being loved by their world. And this cannot be done without producing some guilt. But guilt can be constructive when you let it motivate you to understand your own failures to love and to seek help to love in better ways. Looking at the world through the eyes of an adolescent is a painful but necessary task if you want to deepen your love for your teen.

NOTE   1. Ross Campbell, M.D., *How to Really Love Your Teen* (Wheaton, Ill.: Scripture Press/ Victor Books, 1988), pages 27-28.

THREE

Looking at an Adolescent
Through the Eyes of a Parent

L ast fall our oldest daughter started junior high school. It seemed like a rite of passage for us as much as for her. For years Tina and I had worked with adolescents and their parents. But now, having a seventh-grader of our own gave us a whole new perspective. We started to look at Christi in a way we had not looked at any adolescent before.

Christi's first month of seventh grade came off without a major problem. Tina and I were starting to wonder why so many of the parents we worked with found raising an adolescent so difficult. Then a letter from one of our daughter's teachers arrived. It was a midsemester warning. Much to our surprise, Christi was failing language arts.

The letter had arrived while my daughter was at school, which gave my wife and me time to confer. As we discussed what to do, both of us felt sinking feelings in our stomachs. I look back and wonder if we couldn't have handled the news of cancer better than we handled this news.

We came dangerously close that day to overreacting to the situation. We considered penalties that ranged from permanent grounding to changing schools, things I would have recognized instantly as being inappropriate had I been dealing with someone else's adolescent.

Because of what I'd personally invested in my daughter, deep forces were stirred within me that were capable of producing responses that could have been very harmful to her.

Providing the kinds of relationships teens need to overcome the crises they face is very difficult for parents because of what they experience in their own hearts as they observe their children move through adolescence. Hidden forces are unleashed within the parents that hurt the way they relate to their teens. Even parents who have extensive knowledge of or training in family relationships can be unknowingly controlled by these forces.

THE FORCES THAT DETERMINE PARENTS' STYLES OF RELATING

The problem of hidden forces must have confronted people in the early Church. This concern caused one of the New Testament writers to ask, "What causes fights and quarrels among you?" (James 4:1). The question implies that the real source may very well escape people's notice. It is fortunate for us that James decided to answer his own question while still writing under the inspiration of God's Spirit. In doing so, he describes the forces within people that account for the destructive ways they choose to relate to each other. Understanding how these forces impact our relationships with our kids is imperative. Observe how James describes them:

> What causes fights and quarrels among you? Don't they come
> from your desires that battle within you? You want something
> but don't get it. You kill and covet, but you cannot have what
> you want. You quarrel and fight. You do not have, because you
> do not ask God.   (James 4:1-2)

James attributes the root cause of relational breakdowns to the human capacities to desire, feel, think, and choose that were discussed in chapter 1. In this chapter we'll examine further what role the first three of these have in determining the way parents choose to deal with their adolescent, especially in the added light of James' observations. In chapter 4 we'll look even deeper into how adults go about choosing the kinds of parents they become.

Parents' Desires for Their Adolescents

> Don't they come from your desires that battle within you?
>
> (James 4:1)

James identifies the unmet desires that battle within a person's heart as the place where trouble in relationships begin. In chapter 1 we saw that parents and kids alike have desires in their hearts for unfailing love. James indicates that *when a person turns to his relationships to meet these desires, he takes the first step toward creating destructive relationships* (1:14-15, 4:1). Many parents are tempted to use their relationships with their kids to quiet the desires that battle for relief in their own hearts.

By the time their children are adolescents, parents often have come to depend a lot on the relationships with their kids to give them a sense of love or impact. Their desires have already had the opportunity to be aroused and shaped in many ways by other relationships. Often their painful and disappointing relationships with other adults (particularly with spouses, in-laws, and their own parents) have led them to invest all their emotional energies into their relationships with their kids. Up until adolescence, children are often the least threatening source of relationships for parents because kids' behavior is usually far more predictable and controllable than that of adults. *When their kids become less predictable in adolescence, parents can experience a crisis that is just as great as the ones their kids experience.*

Sheldon is a good example of such a parent. I first met him when he sought help to deal with his defiant fourteen-year-old son, Jerome. Jerome had been suspended from school that week for bullying smaller kids on the bus and acting belligerently toward the driver. The first morning of his suspension, just after Sheldon left for the office, Jerome asked his mother to drive him into town to get some things at the hobby shop. She of course refused, thinking such an action would do nothing more than reward him for the suspension. He became enraged with her and stuffed her into a hall closet. All day he kept her locked in the closet because of her continual refusal to drive him into town. He finally let her out shortly before Sheldon arrived home from work that evening. When Sheldon's wife told him what had happened, he angrily went after his son. A brief wrestling match ensued. After his wife broke it up, Sheldon concluded he needed help in dealing with Jerome.

In chapter 10 we'll see how Sheldon and his wife finally decided to deal with their son's defiance. For now, what is important to understand is how Sheldon's own unfulfilled desires worked to fuel his son's defiance.

Sheldon grew up in a family with an alcoholic father. He said he could never recall his dad showing any affection or interest toward him. He remembered often being treated harshly and receiving angry looks whenever he came near his dad. Sheldon said he blocked out the pain of his father's rejection of him until he had a son of his own. At that time, he promised himself he would develop the kind of relationship with his son that he had wanted with his dad, but was always denied. At first it seemed to Sheldon like this promise wouldn't be hard to fulfill. When Jerome was young, Sheldon found it easy to spend time with him and do all the things he'd always wished his dad would do with him. However, things began to change when his son became an adolescent.

Jerome had several very disappointing experiences early in his adolescence. A learning disorder prohibited him from making better than C marks in his classes. Foot problems prevented him from making the junior high football team. Early physical maturation made him the largest kid in the school and often the brunt of jokes by other kids. A speech impediment also prevented him from developing necessary social skills with his peers. By the time he was a few months into his junior high career, he had already become exasperated with his world.

The only place he had to turn was to his parents. He began to express his anger to them by complaining about everything. Sheldon was unprepared to cope with this metamorphosis in his son. The angry look in Jerome's eyes reminded him of the angry look in his dad's eyes. In fact, every time he looked into the face of his distraught son he felt like he was looking into the face of his father. He saw nothing but glaring disapproval. His natural response was to pull away. He began to punish his son for his angry outbursts by taking away the activities they used to do together: hunting expeditions, Ping-Pong matches, football games. All of these were withdrawn, leaving the son feeling even more abandoned and less valued by his world.

Sheldon was blinded to Jerome's needs by his own needs. His dreams for a certain kind of relationship with his son were shattered. The unfulfilled desires that were aroused in Sheldon every time Jerome expressed anger were battling within Sheldon for relief—relief he could find only in avoiding his son. However, this only fueled Jerome's anger to even greater levels, making it impossible for Sheldon to keep avoiding him. And so the quarrels and fighting (of the kind James mentions in 4:1) erupted.

Three kinds of desires. In working with parents of teens over the years I have heard them express their desires toward their kids in many different ways. Not every desire they express is the kind that will trigger the forces James describes. I have found it helpful to think of parents' desires as falling into three basic categories: *casual, critical,* and *crucial.*[1] Only when parents try to get their crucial desires met by their children are *destructive patterns triggered.*

The *casual* desires of parents are those that are normally expressed to their kids as mere preferences, like how their kids should dress, how they should keep their rooms, and how they should spend their leisure time. When the final decision about these matters is left up to the adolescents, they remain casual desires of the parents. In other words, although the parents may have clear desires for their kids in each of these areas, they remain casual about them because they do not consider them critical enough to represent a serious threat to anybody's well-being. It is usually the mark of an unhealthy parent-teen relationship when parents go to either of two extremes: they view *every* area of their kids' lives as casual, or they view *no* area of their kids' lives as casual.

The desires of parents become *critical* when they are considered vital to the adolescent's well-being. Parents often consider such things as their children's schoolwork, choice of friends, choice of schools, choice of entertainment, and spiritual commitments as critical. In these areas the parents' desires are expressed as clear directives. Final decisions are rarely left up to the teen unless the parents are confident that the teen will make the same decisions the parents would. It is usually a mark of a healthy parent-teen relationship when the parents prepare the adolescent to gradually assume responsibility for the various critical areas of his own life.

Parents experience *crucial* desires when something they believe to be vital to their own well-being is at stake. When parents believe the fulfillment of these crucial desires actually depends on their children, most everything that happens to their kids becomes a crucial concern to them — almost a matter of emotional life or death. Sheldon regarded Jerome's anger as a threat to something that was crucial to his own well-being: a relationship of total acceptance. It is always a mark of an unhealthy parent-teen relationship when parents look to their adolescents to help meet the crucial desires only God can fulfill. Parents who come to depend on their kids for this level of satisfaction end up fearing their own children far more than they fear God.

Three ways parents depend on their adolescents. I have observed three ways in which parents come to depend on their adolescents to fulfill their crucial desires:

1. They look for responses from their kids that convey the sense of love and impact they long for.
2. They make their kids extensions of themselves in order to win a sense of love and impact from others.
3. They live vicariously through their kids in order to experience the love and impact they have never felt before.

When parents seek to fulfill their deepest desires through their relationship with their adolescent, they put incredible pressure on her. In essence, they *reverse roles* with her and force her to become the fueler in the relationship. One adolescent girl remarked to me, "We have an unwritten rule around our house: Always be up for Mom. If anybody gets the least bit down or angry, Mom starts to put them on a guilt trip. She'll walk around the house saying, 'From the way you kids act around here I must be a terrible mother.'" This mother was attempting to make her children feel responsible for her emotional well-being. The message her kids got was loud and clear: "It is crucial that you do nothing to make Mom feel unloved or unsuccessful."

Many parents don't look so directly to their adolescent to have their desires fulfilled. Instead, they make her a tool or an extension of themselves to get their desires fulfilled by others. As Tina and I reflected on our panicky feeling about our daughter's language arts grade, we had to admit that we were viewing her school performance as a threat to having our crucial desires met by others. Somehow we had subtly become dependent on our own adolescent's behavior to maintain the position of honor we enjoyed as family and adolescent specialists, perhaps even to maintain the level of respect we received from our own parents, who were so proud of their oldest granddaughter. Certainly, it would have been appropriate for us to consider our daughter's school performance as "critical" (i.e., a threat to her well-being), especially if it represented a deliberate choice on her part to neglect responsibilities. However, by making it a "crucial" issue, we made it a threat to our own well-being and took on a style of relating with our daughter that made it seem like our whole lives were at stake.

Other parents resort to yet a third way of fulfilling their crucial desires. They go beyond seeing their adolescent as an extension of themselves to seeing her as a younger version of themselves who has a chance to experience life in a way they never could.

One mother told me how painful her own childhood and adolescence had been as a result of her obesity. She remembered how her father had humiliated her because of her weight, calling her cruel names, making fun of her in public, and even withholding her meals.

As a young adult, she entered into a very short-lived marriage. Even though the marriage ended abruptly, she felt like it had at last given her the ticket she needed for happiness—a daughter. Early on she enrolled Marsha in dance, gymnastics, music, and even modeling classes. By the time Marsha reached adolescence, she was winning beauty and talent contests. With each of Marsha's accomplishments, the mother experienced a thrill in her soul like she had never known. Whenever her daughter was receiving the applause of hundreds of admirers, it was as if the mother were receiving the applause herself. As Marsha grew tired of the rigorous training and rehearsal schedules, she tried to talk to her mom about quitting. The idea evoked such a violent reaction from her mother that Marsha never brought it up again. A few months later she attempted suicide.

No matter how parents look to their kids to help them fulfill their crucial desires, the kids can never muster enough resources to deliver. In the end they become a source of great disappointment to their parents.

Parents' Disappointment with Their Adolescents

You want something but don't get it.   (James 4:2)

When we direct desires that only God can fulfill toward human beings, we experience profound disappointment. This disappointment usually hits the parents of an adolescent in waves. A wave hits with each new glimpse the parents get of a hidden reality in their kid's life. It is during adolescence that parents start to get a more complete picture of what kind of person their adolescent really is, with all of his liabilities—liabilities often perceived by the parents as threats to the fulfillment of their own desires.

Disappointment with their limitations. The first wave of disappointment often hits parents even before their child is an adolescent. It comes when the parents first become aware of one or more major deficiences in their child—intellectual, physical, or social. When parents who have a lot riding on their children encounter these limitations, they experience a great deal of disappointment, frustration, and even shame. They view the deficiences as obstacles to realizing their own personal dreams and desires.

One father viewed his son's inability to make the starting team in football as a personal embarrassment. The dad's brother had a son about the same age who not only made the team but also broke some school records. The father of the first boy wanted desperately for his son to do the same in order to make the grandparents equally as proud. He still felt like he was in competition with his brother for his parents' approval.

Another parent viewed her daughter's lack of popularity at school as a major threat to her own sense of worth. Since her daughter had only been an average student in junior high, she was unable to qualify for accelerated classes in high school. As a result, the kids in the "in-crowd" were not in her classes anymore. Her friends became a group of the very ordinary, unsophisticated kids. This frightened her mother. She desperately needed her daughter to marry well and "better herself." The mother saw improving her daughter's social standing as her mission in life. She felt this was the only way she could demonstrate to others that she'd been a quality mother. She'd struggled all her life with feeling inferior around her own family. Until her daughter became an adolescent, it seemed like the one thing she could excel at would be raising the perfect daughter. Now all of that was threatened by her daughter's academic limitations.

As children emerge as people who do not possess the natural abilities or talents to fulfill the expectations their parents have placed on them, it is the parents who often feel the loss—a loss in impact on others, a loss of self-esteem, and even a loss in relationships. The realization that their developing youngster will never have the talents or abilities to attain the most crucial things in life is one that can represent to the parents the death of all their hopes. This seems ironic when *it is this very reality—the child's inability to get his crucial needs met—that can lead him to consider Christ as the only One who can provide what is crucial to his soul.*

Disappointment with their depravity. A second wave of disappointment strikes when parents get a good glimpse at another frightening reality: their child's depravity. This reality usually hits them when their adolescent starts to speak out or act on what he really thinks and feels. When parents get a glimpse of the selfishness and immorality that characterize their kid's thinking and decisions, they once again experience a rush of despair and frustration. Until this time, parents are often able to convince themselves that their child is basically a good kid who is bound to turn out okay. However, by midadolescence parents start to seriously question this notion and try to assess what went wrong.

One father of a sixteen-year-old recently told me how surprised he was that his son kept challenging his authority. He felt he had been a reasonable and caring father and had always believed that this would ensure him against having problems with his son. *But he had failed to take into account the depth of his son's depravity.*

We'll discuss the problem of depravity in adolescents more extensively in chapter 5. Here it's important to see how depravity in kids tends to throw parents for a loop. Not expecting or understanding it, parents almost always assume that this is something very strange and very shameful that few families ever have to struggle with. As a result, parents too often respond to their adolescent's depravity in ways that are designed to quickly hide or deny its existence. This usually drives the problem underground and provides only temporary relief for parents who view their teen's depravity as the awful secret that can ruin all of their lives.

Disappointment with their view of their own family. At least one more wave of disappointment usually strikes parents when their kids' own disappointment with the people in their world, especially their parents, becomes obvious. In the last chapter we saw why this kind of disappointment is inevitable for an adolescent who starts to view the world with the insight of an adult. Adolescents also develop both verbal and nonverbal ways of communicating this disappointment to others. When parents begin to pick it up, they are struck by the frightening reality that they will never be enough or do enough to please their kids and satisfy their desires. This may become the hardest reality of all for parents to accept and live with because of another false notion about kids that parents want to hold on to.

This notion assumes that *the deepest desires in kids are more than adequately met by good-hearted, sincere parents.* Parents want to believe that as their kids get older, they'll come to recognize this and be grateful to their parents for all they have done. Parents come to count on their relationship with their kids as an insurance policy that will pay dividends when they need them the most. Then in mid-life, just when it seems that parents need the reassurance of their own purpose and worth as people the most, their adolescents revoke the policy. Teens begin to give parents much more reason to doubt their own worth as individuals when they start to complain that their own families are failing to meet their desires.

This was the case with one single mother I counseled. She was in a great deal of pain over her seventeen-year-old son's claims that she was too busy to listen to him and that she was a terrible mother. In reality, the mother had gone to great lengths to listen to and understand her son. He knew, however, that he could manipulate her with guilt by making these accusations. So he threw any complaint he could think of at her to get her to stay home and attend only to him. He, of course, was hurting over the absence of his father and was seeking to fulfill his unmet desires solely through his mother. She already struggled with questions about her worth as a person because she'd been deserted by her husband. Since he left, she'd tried to compensate for the shame she felt by devoting herself to fulfilling all of her son's desires. Now it all seemed to be backfiring for her. Her son's demands had become a "black hole" that she could never fill. She'd invested all she had in her relationship with her son hoping to get just a shred of self-esteem or respect back for herself. The reality finally struck. *She could never be enough for her son,* just like she could never be enough for her husband.

It's easy to see how parents who approach their adolescent with this strategy will in the end bear out the truth of James' words: "You want something but don't get it" (4:2). The result will be the kind of disappointment that creates in the parents some problems of an even deeper kind: problems in the way they think about their adolescent. This is the third factor James regards as a contributor to destructive patterns in relationships.

Parents' Thoughts About Their Adolescents

> You kill and covet, but you cannot have what you want. . . .
> You do not have, because you do not ask God.   (James 4:2)

Significant disappointment or frustration in relationships can trigger major thinking problems in people. James indicates that thoughts of "killing" and "coveting" are energized by desires that cannot find fulfillment in human relationships. Deep-seated anger and overbearing insistence begin to control a person's thinking toward those he's depending on to meet his crucial desires in life when they let him down.

These destructive ways of thinking too often characterize how disappointed parents view their teen. When parents' desires become angry demands toward him, the teen sees his parents as having hostile intentions. Parents' demands lead them to put destructive kinds of pressure on their adolescent in order to get their desires satisfied.

I remember the thinking problems that were triggered in me when I received that alarming midsemester report from Christi's teacher. The way I initially chose to look at the report made me feel anger, not only toward my daughter and her teacher, but also toward some friends at church whose adolescent daughters never seemed to have any problems. I imagined what they would think if they knew.

My plan to keep the respect I had come to so crucially depend upon called for having a well-adjusted adolescent daughter. When Christi's performance became a threat to that plan, my automatic response was to get angry and put my mind to work on how to make the plan succeed anyway! How could I shape this girl up? *At that point my intentions became hostile toward my daughter.* For a time I was blind to her pain and her needs, and I saw only my own.

Through experiences like these I've come to recognize three basic errors in the way I think about my adolescent daughter. These errors have a way of cropping up from time to time and affecting to some degree every serious relationship I have. However, I've discovered that these errors are prone to become more exaggerated and more destructive in my relationship with my kids, especially as they've grown older, than in any other relationships I encounter. They are errors that seem to affect the thinking of many other parents of teens with whom I work.

I believe the disappointment and frustration parents often feel in their relationship with their adolescent children reflect three common errors in thinking:

1. Misguided focus
2. Misdirected goals
3. Misplaced dependency

Misguided focus. Usually when a person encounters disappointment, the focus of her mental energies becomes fixed on what she believes will change the situation and relieve the pain. Rarely in the midst of disappointment does a person choose to focus on developing the kind of character qualities that will give her the strength to live with the disappointment. Any effort to change herself is focused instead on external qualities (behavior, appearance, etc), in order to stop the world from disappointing her.

In the parent-teen relationship, *the focus of a disappointed parent too easily becomes that of changing or controlling his adolescent's outward behavior.* This amounts to the same fundamental error that James warns against in 4:1-3. Essentially, James is instructing his readers to shift their focus away from others when their desires are blocked. By continuing to focus on changing people or their behavior in the midst of pain, the person comes to believe that controlling others is the solution to life's difficulties. This becomes a problem way of thinking for two reasons: it focuses his attention on what can at best only temporarily lessen his pain, and it diverts him from giving attention to what would ultimately bring fulfillment in the midst of his pain (the deepening of his own relationship with Christ). When a parent approaches his adolescent with a focus like this, he becomes an "externalist." The important things going on in the hearts of both his adolescent and himself will escape notice, and only those outward behaviors that evoke immediate pleasure or pain will receive attention. In working with parents of troubled teens *I always consider a shift in the parents' focus to be the first step toward bringing healing to their family.*

In the parenting teens course I teach in our church, I observed a father who struggled with a misguided focus toward his adolescent son. We were in the eighth week of the course when I got my first real glimpse of Steve's focus in parenting. The topic I was teaching that morning was "Making Sense of Your Adolescent's Behavior." We had just discussed how parents can open doors to their adolescent's inner feelings and purposes through the use of open-ended questions. Steve was the first one to raise his hand when I asked for a volunteer to come up front and role-play a conversation between a parent and his teen.

From the very first session of the course Steve had been eager to display his knowledge of kids and parenting. As a high school football coach and assistant principal, Steve fancied himself to be an expert on adolescents. He gave the impression that he saw himself as the unofficial "co-teacher" of the course and regularly took it upon himself to answer or correct the other parents during class discussions. Giving him a platform through the role-play to assume a position of superiority over the other parents made me uncomfortable. When no one else volunteered, however, I reluctantly allowed Steve to take on the role of the father of the sixteen-year-old guy I was going to play.

The role-play depicted the high schooler as having what counselors label an "oppositional disorder." Avoiding acts of outright defiance that could spark parental retribution, this kind of adolescent looks for subtle ways to oppose his parents' authority and make them miserable. He makes it very hard for his parents to catch him in specific infractions, and if he gets good enough at it, he can make his parents quite confused and frustrated.

As the role-play began, I explained to the class that Steve was to demonstrate how a concerned father could communicate acceptance to his angry and withdrawn son. His assignment was to invite his son to talk openly about his anger and deal with it in direct ways. As the son, I slumped in my chair and stared at the ceiling as Steve began to talk to me.

"Son, something is bothering you, and I want to know what it is."

"Nothing's bothering me, Dad. I'm fine."

"Son, are you mad at Mom and me for not letting you drive yet? That's it, isn't it?"

"No, Dad!"

"Is it because we wouldn't let you go out with your friends after the game last Friday?"

"No, I'm not mad! Okay?"

"Son, I'm not letting you leave until you tell me why you're mad!"

After a long pause of silence, I said: "Okay, I just wish you and Mom didn't treat me like a little kid all the time. I don't get to do any of the things my friends get to do."

"Son, you know that's not very fair. Just because we don't let you run all over the place like nonChristian parents let their kids do, that doesn't mean we don't love you. You know we love you, don't you?"

"I guess."

"That's better. Son, I want you to know anytime you've got a problem you can come right to me and we can talk it out like this. Okay?"

"Sure, Dad. Can I go now?"

As the role-play ended, I could see by Steve's expression that he felt pretty good about his performance. I felt sick. After eight weeks of class, I had hoped he would have avoided the fundamental errors he just committed. I decided to invite the whole group to give Steve some feedback on how he did. I was hoping he could get a glimpse at how his own kids might experience him.

I asked the group, "According to the principles we've been studying, how would you evaluate the dad in the role-play we just saw?" After several moments of awkward silence, one parent finally ventured a comment: "I think if I were the son I would have gone away more convinced than ever that I wouldn't open up again to my parents."

"Why would that be?" I inquired.

"I would have felt that my dad doesn't really care how I feel. He just wanted me to stop blaming him and making him miserable. He didn't care if I was miserable."

Other parents began to talk. Most echoed the same sentiments. Steve had only strengthened this boy's commitment to holding in his anger.

When I asked Steve to respond to the feedback, he expressed dismay. "I can't believe what I'm hearing. I really think everyone misinterpreted what I was trying to say."

"Let's try an experiment, Steve," I suggested. "This time you be the son, and I'll be the father."

In the new role-play I tried to play the dad in the same way Steve did earlier. As hard as he tried, Steve found it almost impossible to respond warmly to me. By the close of the role-play Steve's dismay had turned to revelation. "I can't believe I really come across that way to my son. I must!"

Steve left class that day for the first time openly troubled about himself as a parent. I found out later that his wife, Beth, left with more hope for her family than she'd had for a long time. Just seeing Steve's focus shift even a little to his own way of relating made her think that maybe some changes really were possible.

The basic characteristic of parents whose focus is still misguided is an insistence that the solution to the problems in their family involves changing someone or something besides themselves. They resist shifting the focus to their own actions and motivations because such a shift implies an admission on their part of personal failures, weaknesses, or sin. It means shifting their primary concern to their own way of relating with their family, something they are solely responsible for.

Making this kind of shift was very difficult for Steve. In his profession he was expected to have all the answers. He could never let himself appear weak or uncertain. Respect from his world carried the price tag of always staying in control. Always winning.

That Sunday morning as Steve returned home from class he tried to deny that he was failing as a parent. He worked hard for the next three days to dismiss these troublesome thoughts. He might have succeeded in shifting the focus away from himself if it hadn't been for the big fight.

On Wednesday night of that week Steve's fifteen-year-old son, Phil, announced he was quitting junior varsity football. Steve had never allowed himself to quit anything, and the thought of his son doing it was more than he could stand. Besides, many of Steve's own colleagues were his son's coaches. He could imagine what they would say.

Steve's answer to Phil was short and to the point: "You will finish the season. You're not quitting!" That ignited a scuffle on the living room floor. A bloody nose and screams by Beth finally ended the fight.

The conflict left Steve in more pain than he could remember ever having. It was not primarily physical pain, although the idea of beating up his son left him physically sick. It was, instead, the pain of exposure. He wasn't really the winner he wanted everybody to think he was. He had to admit he was even losing his own son. He saw how childishly he had behaved. And he couldn't deny it was because of his own selfish pride.

Steve came to see me in my office two days later. He described his son's spiritual disinterest in, and hatred toward, the church's youth programs. Steve complained that no one at the church had taken a personal interest in Phil.

Steve's focus troubled me because he still seemed to be looking for a change in circumstances—this time at church—to be the answer to his family's problems. After several minutes of exploring ways we could help his son better through the church, I gave Steve the opportunity to shift his focus. "Steve," I said, "could you tell me something about your own needs and what kind of help you could use as a dad?"

For the first time, Steve took the risk of bearing his private pain and shame to another. He wept as he told me about his fight with Phil. He admitted that the real problem was not with the church, but with him. He cried out for help for himself that day. Steve had become aware of the first major error in his thinking. However, there were two more errors he was yet to discover.

Misdirected goals. A second error that often characterizes a parent's thinking about her teen is that of misdirected goals. These goals divert her interest from developing her own character and deepening her own relationship with Christ. They are what James refers to when he explains why certain prayers go unanswered: "You do not have, because you do not ask God. When you ask, you do not receive, because you ask with wrong motives, that you may spend what you get on your pleasures" (James 4:2-3).

Even the prayers of a parent for her children can be misdirected — and go unanswered — because of the goals the parent has in her heart. When a parent believes her life and honor depend upon her children turning out okay, her prayers for her kids essentially become directed by selfish interests. If God were to answer these prayers, He would only be strengthening the wrong thinking in the parent.

A parent's goals can be considered misdirected when they are aimed at getting her desires fulfilled by people or circumstances in her world, instead of by her relationship with Christ. The most common misdirected goals found in parents of adolescents are aimed at denying, hiding, or eradicating any evidence of their kids' deficiencies, depravity, and/or disappointments in them. Since these realities most threaten the schemes and dreams of teens' parents, parental goals are often designed to escape them.

These goals are unhealthy for three reasons. First, they are directed at an impossible objective. The painful realities in kids can never be essentially altered or hidden. Parents who try to do either only end up frustrating themselves and communicating rejection to their kids. Second, they are based on a false premise. Even if parents could change the painful truth about their kids, it would still not provide the context parents need for experiencing wholeness or joy. Third, these goals are destructive. When parents attempt to change the painful realities in their kids in order to get their own crucial desires met, they are essentially teaching their teens to hide who they really are. This conditions the teens to become deceptive in the way they relate to others. A shift away from these goals is an absolute necessity to healthy parenting.

The Apostle Peter is careful to instruct his readers that a "sincere love" for others is possible only because of a pure heart (1 Peter 1:22). *Before parents can become skilled at really loving their teens, a change of direction in their hearts must take place.*

I knew as Steve left my office that day our responsibility to him had really only begun. Although he had become conscious of his unhealthy style of parenting, he was still unaware of the plans or goals in his heart that were causing him to relate the way he did.

As the initial course on parenting teens drew to a close, we encouraged Steve and Beth to join a small group for parents designed to promote deeper relationship and personal reflection. To the surprise of everyone, Steve concentrated a lot less on giving advice to others and a lot more on seeking answers for himself. Because of the continuing conflict at home, Steve and Beth both hungered to learn more about themselves.

One evening in our small group, I asked the parents to reflect on their own desires that are most often disappointed by their families. Beth brought up her heartfelt need to have someone listen to her. She talked with pain about her family as she was growing up. As the middle of five daughters, she felt no one ever took her seriously. Early in life she learned she could get people's attention only by "knocking herself out" for them in being useful. It worked pretty well for her in childhood and adolescence, but now as an adult she felt like it was backfiring. As a wife and mother, she felt taken for granted and ignored.

By the time Beth finished, some of us in the group had become irritated at Steve. He had interrupted Beth several times to correct details about the events she was recalling. I asked Steve to summarize what he had heard Beth saying about the pain she was feeling. After stumbling with his words, Steve finally answered my question by talking about his own feelings instead of Beth's.

I asked Beth to comment on Steve's answer. Her response shook Steve. "Oh, I know Steve wasn't listening to a word I was saying. He never does. He only hears what makes him feel like he's right. We've just learned to accept Dad being zoned out on us."

The next several minutes were perhaps some of the most excruciating ones Steve had ever experienced. He finally came face-to-face with some painful realities about his family and himself. His wife and kids were starving, and he had been ignoring their pleas for help. While his goal had been to feel like a winner, he had become deaf to their needs. As a result his family saw him as a loser. They didn't enjoy being around him. Their respect and love for him were dying. Steve began to weep over his own selfishness. He realized that as long as he approached his family with the goal of getting them to shore up his winner's image, they would all be losers. Steve's eyes opened for the first time to a second major error in his thinking—misdirected goals. There was still, however, a third major error that escaped Steve's notice.

Misplaced dependency. Goals that are directed at changing or controlling others reflect an even deeper problem in thinking: misplaced dependency. James identifies this as the core problem in relationships when he writes, "You do not have, because you do not ask God" (4:2). *When a person chooses not to ask or depend upon God to satisfy the desires that battle within him, his dependency comes to rest in his own ability to get people to come through for him.* In the parent-teen relationship misplaced dependencies make it impossible for parents to shift their focus or goals for very long.

Exactly one year after Steve's living room brawl with his son, Steve asked to share something with his small group. "One year ago I came awfully close to breaking my son's neck in the living room of our home," he said. "I asked God that night to help me change things. Tonight as I left our home to come to this meeting, my son stopped me at the door. In a teasing gesture he pulled my hat down over my ears and gave me a hug. He told me to drive safely. I feel as if I've got my son back. But it happened in a way I would never have guessed. Most of the change has happened in me, not in Phil."

The change Steve referred to was primarily a change in his own focus and goals. Over the intervening year Steve had attempted to consciously respond to his family on a whole new basis. He worked hard to pick up on their needs and made it his goal to love them by responding on the basis of their needs, not his own. Although difficult, it was now possible for Steve to begin learning new ways of relating to his family because the direction of his heart had changed.

This change proved to be only a temporary lull for Steve and Beth, however, as the eye of the hurricane passed over. Normally a person can't maintain a shift in goals for very long before he encounters a set of circumstances that totally saps his strength. This exposes the need for an even deeper shift, *a shift in the place he's looking to find the fuel for loving others.*

A few weeks after celebrating the one-year anniversary of the living room brawl, Beth called me from the hospital. Phil had tried to commit suicide by overdosing. He was in the emergency room.

Apparently, a disturbing breakup between Phil and his girlfriend had occurred during the week. The day of the overdose, Steve and Beth had a heated discussion with Phil. He was letting his homework and responsibilities slide in the wake of the breakup. As they related to me how they handled the situation, it seemed they had been very sensitive and reasonable. Although they wouldn't let Phil drop completely out of life because of his hurt, they did try to understand his pain and let him cut down on his activities. And yet, on the phone Steve and Beth were taking the whole blame for Phil's suicide attempt.

The next time our small group met, Steve shared with us a new decision he had made. "As I saw my boy lying in that hospital bed, I decided I was no longer going to get in his way. It's just not worth it. I want my son alive. I'll never do anything to endanger that again!"

Steve had decided to shift goals again. He lacked the strength to keep loving his son in the hard ways he knew were best if it meant taking the risk of losing him. *He didn't want to accept how little control he really had over what was crucial to him.* By backing off and pampering his son, he was pursuing the goal of regaining a sense of security and control over his own life. However, this false sense of security exposed what he was ultimately depending on to keep his son safe: his own efforts. He was looking to his new parenting style as the thing that would make him a winner. We decided to confront Steve on this later, after the shock from the suicide attempt had dissipated.

A few weeks later Rob, another of our small group members, told us about his struggle to deal with the death of his son in a car accident a year earlier. He said one of the most difficult things he had to face was learning how to trust the Lord with his other two adolescent children. Rob had come to see that one of his wrong goals, even before his son's death, was to protect his own sense of well-being by keeping everything in his life highly ordered and under control. The death of his son showed him how fruitless this strategy really was. Now in the wake of the accident, he struggled with the thought that maybe he could prevent future accidents by becoming even more controlling. He felt himself holding on so tight to his other two teens that they complained of being treated like children again. He realized that he could become free to relate to these kids as a healthy dad only by giving up what he had used his whole life to keep his worst fears from happening: his perfectionism. He knew it required shifting his dependence from his own goodness and power to God's.

Rob's words hit Steve like a bolt of lightning. By talking openly about his misplaced dependency, Rob helped Steve to get a glimpse of his own. Not long after that Steve informed the group of another decision he had made: "I've decided that no matter what the risk or loss, I want to be a godly dad for my son. If that means taking an unpopular stand or talking to my son about things that might get him upset, so be it. I can't control how he'll respond. I've decided to trust God with the outcome. I'm going to quit trying to make everything in my family turn out the way I want."

Steve's words signaled to us that he was not only well on his way to understanding his problem thinking as a parent, but also well on his way to altering it.

Without significant shifts in their focus, goals, and source of dependency, parents like Steve stay locked into some very problematic ways of relating to their families. No doubt this is why James carefully directs his readers to take an inside look at themselves when problems develop in their relationships. According to James, breakdowns in relationship can always be traced to hidden factors at work in one or more of the people involved. In parent-teen breakdowns, hidden desires, disappointments, and thinking problems can be found controlling the parents as often as they do the adolescent. By understanding these factors and bringing them under God's direction, parents can start relating to their adolescent in whole new ways.

SUMMING IT UP

Changing what kind of parent you are is never an easy task, but always a necessary one as your teen grows and changes. It usually requires a great deal more maturity to be a healthy parent of a teen than it does to be a parent of a younger child.

Be careful, however, how you go about trying to change. The problem ways of thinking and relating that control most parents are very resistent to change. If you try to change them by putting pressure on yourself to be the perfect parent, or by just trying harder to be a loving parent, you will no doubt only add to the frustration you already feel.

The first step to growing and maturing as a parent is to get to know yourself a lot better. Take some time to observe and understand the forces within you that cause you to relate to your kids the way you do — forces like James described in 4:1-3. As you understand yourself better and bring the deepest parts of yourself under submission to Christ, you'll begin to experience the freedom and strength to parent in healthy ways.

NOTE   1. For a more extensive discussion of these categories, see *Inside Out* (NavPress, 1988) by Larry Crabb, pages 80-85.

PART TWO
MATURITY
What a Parent of an
Adolescent Must Be

FOUR

How an Adult Decides What Kind of Parent He Wants to Be

My wife, Tina, is really good at helping me look at things in my life that I wouldn't look at on my own. She has a gentle way of getting me to ask hard questions about myself.

Recently, just in passing, my wife made this comment: "I wonder what's been going on with you, Kevin, that you've been choosing not to lead our family in Bible study lately?" When she makes that kind of comment, I hate it and love it at the same time. It always moves me to look at things in my life that are normally not too pleasant to look at. Afterwards, however, I'm usually glad because I grow as a result of what I see. It reminds me of what the writer of Hebrews said about the nature of God's discipline in our lives: "No discipline seems pleasant at the time, but painful. Later on, however, it produces a harvest of righteousness and peace for those who have been trained by it" (12:11).

Tina's question really got to me. I had let the fact that I was neglecting to lead our weekly Bible studies at supper conveniently escape my attention. A disruptive summer and hectic fall made it possible for the family Bible studies to be dropped without anyone really noticing. Except Tina, that is.

At first I wanted to attribute my neglect to factors that were completely outside my control. (That always helps relieve a sense of guilt for a dad.) The kids' schedules. Tina not having supper ready on time. Rushing from supper to evening activities at church. But somehow none of these explanations had the ring of truth to it. I knew in my heart that there was another reason — a reason I didn't want to admit to myself.

As I puzzled over Tina's question, I thought back over the past several months when I did lead the family Bible studies. I remember feeling very uncomfortable about doing them. The ages of our daughters span from first to seventh grade. The kind of response I would get from each of them as I took the Bible out and started to read was very predictable. Our oldest daughter, Christi, would usually put her head in her hand, look at the ceiling, and enter a state of suspended animation. Jessica, our third-grader, took it as a cue to draw pictures in her plate with her silverware, or give fresh attention to the ribbon or barrette that mysteriously fell out of her hair whenever we started to read the Bible. Our youngest, Alexis, always used the time to stage a retrieval operation by going under the table to recover whatever she had dropped during supper. Whenever I would glance over at my wife, she would be shooting a dirty look at one of the kids for not paying attention to the Bible reading.

I have a very hard time not being taken seriously. When I teach or counsel, I am used to having people sit on the edge of their chairs, taking notes, pursuing me with questions. It gives me a sense of impact. I feel very significant. When I teach at home, I encounter people that are sliding out of their seats, passing notes, and ignoring all of my questions. I suddenly lose all sense of impact. I feel very insignificant.

I must have decided while I was very young that my significance as a person depended upon holding people's attention. As far back as I can remember, I have always pursued activities that I could do well enough to capture people's attention, and I have avoided those in which my performance would meet with people's indifference or disapproval. This style of relating is automatic for me now as an adult. It is the automatic way I relate both inside and outside my family. It accounts for the kind of parent, teacher, and counselor I am whenever I operate nonreflectively by impulse.

When I finally got to the bottom of why I was neglecting family devotions, I had to admit it was because of my own wrong ways of thinking about what was crucial for life. There were deep parts within me that made my automatic style of parenting a very selfish and ungodly one. Unless I took deliberate steps to alter how these deep parts influence me, I would end up avoiding doing anything as a dad that did not feed my demand to be seen and treated as important by others.

Despite how critical styles of parenting are to adolescents' development, most parents do not deliberate about the kind of parent they want to be. Parents tend to be nonreflective about their parenting styles; that is, they allow their way of relating to their kids to be determined by internal and external forces of which they have little conscious awareness. Consequently, the parents' underlying problems in thinking go unchallenged, and the resulting problems in relating go unchanged. *This practice of operating nonreflectively as parents, with little or no awareness of the motivational forces within, is the single most important obstacle to learning to be effective parents of teenagers.*

To remove this obstacle, a parent must be willing to ask some hard questions about herself or himself: "What causes me to be a nonreflective parent?" "What kind of parent am I when I choose to stay nonreflective?" "What must I do to become aware of the deeper parts that automatically control me as a parent?" Helping parents answer these three questions will be the aim of the rest of this chapter.

THE CAUSES OF NONREFLECTIVE PARENTING

A parent remains out of touch with what drives him because he dreads facing three painful truths: (1) he is contemptuous, (2) he is wounded, and (3) he is defeated.

Perhaps the portion of Scripture from which we can glean the richest insights about nonreflective parenting deals with the life of David. In 2 Samuel 14:13-14, King David is asked a very pertinent question concerning his relationship with his son Absalom: Why hasn't he devised a way so that his banished son may not remain estranged from him? To understand the significance of this question and David's answer to it, we must understand the events that led up to it.

In 2 Samuel 13 the very tragic account of the lives of David's adolescent children begins. The first event recorded is the rape of David's daughter Tamar by her half brother Amnon. David's response to the incident is recorded in verse 21: "When King David heard all this, he was furious." Despite his anger, however, David evidently chose not to punish Amnon for the evil he committed.

Another of David's sons, Absalom, became quite enraged over the rape as well. Verse 22 tells us that "Absalom never said a word to Amnon, either good or bad; he hated Amnon because he had disgraced his sister Tamar." Apparently, Absalom bided his time for two years, maybe at first waiting for his father to take appropriate action, and later waiting for the perfect opportunity to take his own revenge on Amnon. During this time, however, Absalom evidently let everyone know about his intentions toward Amnon, except Amnon himself. Everyone in the royal household, including David, could have known what Absalom was planning if they spent any time at all tuning in to him (verse 32). Apparently, David was one of the few who failed to pick this up. Eventually, he allowed himself to be tricked into giving Absalom the opportunity he needed for carrying out his plan for revenge (verses 23-27).

After murdering Amnon, Absalom fled into self-exile. David was left grieving over the double loss of both his sons—one by death, and one by banishment (verses 36-37). In spite of what happened, David never lost the affection in his heart for Absalom. He longed to see him even after he had been gone three years. But, for some reason, David again took no action. His automatic response (as it was when Tamar was raped by Amnon) was to grieve in his heart, but to do nothing outwardly about it except remain at a safe distance.

When Joab, David's general, sent a wise woman to confront David about his behavior toward Absalom (2 Samuel 14:2-14), David's response was nonreflective. Instead of looking deeply within to discover the answer to the woman's question, David gave an "off-the-cuff" order to let Absalom return to Jerusalem, but with a stipulation that would maintain David's relational detachment from Absalom: "He must go to his own house; he must not see my face" (14:24).

As is normally the case with nonreflective responses by parents, David's response made matters worse. It addressed the problems with Absalom so superficially that it only served to allow anger and resentment toward his father to continue unchecked. There is no evidence to suggest that David had any idea about how his actions were impacting Absalom until it was too late (16:11-12). It is interesting to observe in David how out of touch a nonreflective parent can become to the needs of his own children. *Too often such a parent is ruled by no higher goal than that of lessening his own pain.* Ironically, parental goals like these only increase a parent's pain in the end (18:33–19:4).

I believe David's relationship with his son can provide some great insight into the causes behind nonreflective parenting. When I encounter parents of adolescents who take little time to reflect about their responses toward their kids, I often ask them the same kinds of questions Joab asked David through the wise woman—questions designed to get them to reflect. "What did you hope to accomplish by responding that way?" "What was your purpose in applying that kind of discipline?" "Can you tell me what was going on inside of you when you made that decision?" "What would prevent you from responding this way?"

More times than not I get nonreflective answers to these questions. One parent responded with this comment: "It's not what I'm feeling that's important, it's what works." The problem with this approach is that a parent's definition of "what works" is determined by the feelings in the parent's heart. David could have very well answered Joab's question by stating, "Look, keeping my son out of my sight and out of my hair works for me, okay? Even if it does make me depressed and him angry, it works!" And Joab could have very well retorted, "It doesn't look like it's working to me. He just burned up my field!"

David would have to go deeper into his own purposes to understand how such a style of parenting actually worked for him. Every adult decides what kind of parent he wants to be on this same basis. *Only by exploring his own purposes through personal reflection can a parent understand why he clings to the style of parenting he does.* Once the purposes of his heart are exposed, a parent can evaluate the health or appropriateness of his parenting style.

The question remains: Why are so many parents hesitant to do any honest reflection about why they parent the way they do? Some parents might offer lack of time as the reason: "With our schedule, we just don't have the time to think about what we're doing." Others might suggest lack of aptitude: "I'm just not a deep person. I never have been. I don't like to sit around and think about heavy things. I just like to keep moving." Still others might cite the lack of desire: "Look, I really don't care if I'm the perfect parent or not. When I was growing up my parents weren't around that much and I made it. My kid will too."

These kinds of excuses certainly wouldn't get at the real reason for David's nonreflection, just as they fail to expose the real reasons why most parents tend to be nonreflective today.

As a king and poet, David found the time and ability to reflect on politics, theology, and most any other topic that affected his kingdom. However, when it came to his own family, his reflective juices dried up. He certainly didn't lack desire. We're told his "heart longed for Absalom" (2 Samuel 14:1). It had to be something other than the lack of time, aptitude, or desire that made his relationship with his son one of the most difficult of all subjects for him to think about. It had to be something that made facing the consequences of continuing to exasperate and embitter his son seem less terrifying than the consequences of looking into his own soul to understand himself.

David, like many parents of adolescents, probably resisted taking an inside look because of his fear of the painful truths that must be confronted for the capacity of growth and love to be kept alive in the parent. *The parent-teen relationship is one of God's primary tools for putting an adult in the kind of situation where he can get a penetrating look at the truth about himself.* This is certainly what happened to David through his relationship with Absalom. (Some consider Psalm 55 to be a diary of David's anguished reflections during the time leading up to Absalom's final rebellion.)[1]

Had David reflected in the earlier years of his relationship with his son, he may have gotten at the painful truths in his heart while there was still time to turn his relationship with Absalom around. However, David's unwillingness to reflect really kept him frozen in a style of relating to his son that permitted the relationship to continue to deteriorate. Instead of growing in his capacities to communicate with and love his son, an unwillingness to face painful truths about himself stunted his growth as a parent.

In the accounts of David's life in 2 Samuel, clues are given as to what made personal reflection so painful and difficult for David. As I work with parents of teens today, I often have opportunity to observe similar kinds of things in them. Take a look with me at the inner realities that can make self-examination so difficult for parents of teens.

A Parent's Contempt

Notice how figure 1 below attempts to pick up on the imagery from Proverbs 20:5 ("The purposes of a man's heart are deep waters"). There are always hidden parts to the human personality that account for the relational style a person chooses to employ, even when it seems automatic or second nature to him. When a parent begins to look into the deep waters of his heart to understand himself, the first truth he often must confront is his feelings of contempt toward those who have disappointed him. This is one of the primary reasons why parents don't like to reflect. *They don't want to acknowledge that in their heart they often feel contempt for others, including their kids.*

FIGURE 1
THE NONREFLECTIVE PARENT

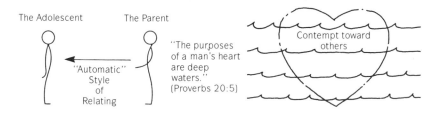

The fact that the contempt lies just beneath the surface means it usually lies just beyond the parents' conscious awareness. Parents can become suddenly aware of it when some event, especially one involving their child, threatens them in some way. However, just as quickly, parents can become unconscious of it again once the event or threat has passed. Very few adults are willing or ready to admit that a lot of anger and contempt lie behind the way they relate to their children. The implications of this are just too painful.

David's whole way of handling Absalom communicated real contempt for him. He allowed Absalom to stay in exile for three years without taking any initiative to restore him. Even many of David's countrymen viewed this as cruel and uncaring on the part of the king (2 Samuel 14:13-14). Then when David, under pressure, finally permitted Absalom to return, he was not permitted to see David's face for another two years (14:24,28). For Absalom, the underlying contempt came through loud and clear.

David gives us the clearest glimpse of himself as a contemptuous man in those situations where he encounters contempt from others. David started to answer contempt with contempt when Nabal refused to provide him and his men with food (1 Samuel 25). He answered contempt with contempt when his wife Michal belittled him for the way he celebrated the return of the Ark of the Covenant to Jerusalem (2 Samuel 6). When Amnon raped Tamar, David clearly harbored contempt in his heart toward Amnon (2 Samuel 13). Parents who harbor a lot of contempt in their hearts are usually unable to endure much contempt from others, especially their own children. It becomes virtually impossible for parents who have not acknowledged and dealt with their own contempt to respond in a healthy way when their adolescent shows some contempt back.

One might wonder whether the kind of contempt David experienced is a universal experience for parents of teens. I would argue that all parents harbor some degree of contempt and on some level (oftentimes unconsciously) will communicate that contempt to their kids unless they are engaged in ongoing personal reflection and repentance. I believe this is true of Christian as well as nonChristian parents. (Remember, although David was a man after God's own heart, he still had some real problems.)

To understand why contempt is something all parents experience, but only a few willingly acknowledge, we must first understand what function or purpose contempt serves. Contempt might best be understood metaphorically as *an emotional scab worn to protect a wound from further damage.* When people experience serious pain or loss in a relationship (which is a universal human experience in a fallen world), they form a protective layer over that wound in order to prevent others from hurting them in the same place or in the same way. The more they hurt, the thicker the emotional scab they wear.

The scab *contempt* functions to keep others in their place—at a safe distance or in a safe position—so that they can do no more harm. In effect, the contempt says to others, "Don't you dare hurt me again. I'm still mad about how I was hurt before. If you hurt me, you'll pay!" It is communicated in dozens of different ways, overtly and covertly, when people are in close proximity to each other. Although in the short term contempt can successfully prevent or reduce pain in relationships, in the long term it only serves to generate contempt from others in return. This is especially true in a parent-teen relationship, as in the case of David and Absalom.

We have one father in our church named Charlie, who received a lot of contempt from his dad while growing up. From as early as Charlie could remember, his dad called him "jerk." He recalled with tears how he didn't even learn until third grade that his real name was Charles and not "jerk." Charlie was wounded so deeply by his dad's cruelty as a child and teenager that by the time he married and started his own family he showed anger toward anyone who even looked at him funny.

When his children reached the age at which they began to express some contempt of their own, Charlie had great trouble disciplining them without letting his contempt show. When his wife saw this, she, of course, expressed alarm. Charlie interpreted her alarm as a personal attack and refused to do anymore of the disciplining of the kids. He took a hands-off approach in order to deny his wife any opportunity to hurt him again. By the time his two daughters became adolescents they, along with their mother, had little respect for him. They regarded him with contempt for his weakness and aloofness. When at last he couldn't stand it any longer, he ran away and left them for several months. It was the only way he knew how to express his contempt for how they treated him.

Eventually, Charlie came home and decided to get help to understand why he behaved as he did with his family. He is in the process of building a new kind of relationship with his wife and with his daughters, who are now college students. He had to start by acknowledging a painful truth about himself: he was a contemptuous husband and father.

To acknowledge that you're a contemptuous parent means to recognize that your style of relating to your kids has to some degree been angrily designed to keep them from inflicting more wounds and causing you more pain than your world has already dished out. The implications are clear. *There is something self-protective about the way you parent because there is something damaged about you as a person.* Once acknowledged, the contempt—like a scab that is peeled back—reveals a very tender, wounded part that lies beneath, a part parents find even more painful to probe. This is the second major reason parents are reluctant to do any extensive self-examination.

A Parent's Wounds

Once a parent allows herself to be exposed as a contemptuous parent, she opens the door to being exposed as a wounded parent as well. The fact that a parent almost inevitably bears some deep unhealed wounds is a reality that she communicates to her teen in dozens of subtle and not-so-subtle ways. Often she does this unintentionally because she has little conscious awareness of the wounds she carries from her past.

FIGURE 2
THE NONREFLECTIVE PARENT

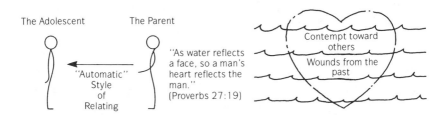

I counseled a young woman named Sally during her late high school and college years. She asked for counseling because, for some time, she'd been suffering from a number of anxiety-related symptoms: nightmares, insomnia, loss of appetite, hyperactivity, loss of concentration, panic attacks, hives, and acne—none of which the doctors could find an organic cause for.

Almost from the very beginning of our work together I became convinced that Sally's anxiety was directly connected to her relationship with her parents. They were separated and in contention over a divorce suit at the time. Sally felt caught in the middle. While growing up she had come to assume the role of rescuer and counselor for both her mom and dad. Since both behaved in such childish and irrational ways toward one another, Sally concluded early in life that her security depended upon protecting them from hurting each other. She spent long hours sitting and listening to them pour their hearts out, trying to persuade them of their love for each other. Once the separation occurred, she felt responsible to live half the time with each, being careful to maintain daily phone contact with the parent she wasn't living with at the time. Both tried to get Sally to side with them against the other, accusing her of betrayal and ingratitude if she refused.

There were obvious overtones of contempt in the way the parents demanded Sally's attention with such open disregard for her own health and desires. However, Sally had become so aware of how her parents had been wounded by others that she rationalized their contempt away as something that really wasn't their fault.

I found it interesting how her parents responded when I talked to them about Sally's anxiety problems. They both expressed grave concern because they saw her as such a "wounded" kid. They confessed their greatest fault to be that of letting Sally depend on them too much. They even excused that, however, because they felt so sorry for her. "She always seems so bothered with everything, the poor kid," her mother commented. Neither parent acknowledged being troubled personally, but each volunteered information about *the other's* "problems," upon which was fixed the blame for Sally's problems.

The more wounded a parent is, the greater the probability that he'll imagine the real sickness in the family to reside in someone else — the spouse or the children. It becomes his goal to get others in the family to "own" the sickness and rely on him for the cure. In the case of Sally, both her mom and dad were convinced that they knew what was best for her. In reality, both were wounded people whose interest in Sally was primarily self-serving in nature.

If it's true that all contemptuous parents are really wounded parents, the question arises, "Where do all these wounds come from?" After the death of Absalom, Joab used a very revealing sentence to rebuke David for mourning over Absalom in a way that humiliated his soldiers. It is a sentence that tells us something about the source of David's wounds. Joab said, "Now go out and encourage your men. I swear by the LORD that if you don't go out, not a man will be left with you by nightfall. *This will be worse for you than all the calamities that have come upon you from your youth till now*" (2 Samuel 19:7, emphasis mine). In essence, Joab was saying to David, "You think you're wounded now. Well, all the wounds you've received from your childhood until now will seem like nothing compared to the wounds you'll experience if your army deserts you!"

Although I doubt whether any added wounds really could have been more damaging to David than the wounds he'd already experienced, David heeded Joab's warning and hid his pain from his men. Perhaps this is a classic example of how David chose to deal with his wounds, especially later in his life. Joab's statement was revealing because he recognized the painful nature of David's past. It is important to remember that David's greatest blows or wounds always occurred in the context of personal relationships — relationships that were supposed to protect and nourish him, but tragically seldom did. These relational disappointments no doubt included his father's neglect because of his age and size (1 Samuel 16:7-12); his brother's mistrust (1 Samuel 17:28-30); his betrayal by Saul (1 Samuel 18:10-11); and his humiliation by Michal (2 Samuel 6:17-23). In the midst of such relational calamities it's easy to understand why David became drawn to Jonathan (1 Samuel 18:1). It was perhaps only with Jonathan that David ever felt truly loved (2 Samuel 1:25-26). And even this relationship was cut short after a very brief period. Each of these events in David's life left wounds on his heart. Wounds that invariably affected the way he led and parented. Wounds that prevented him from making himself vulnerable again to those he loved.

Like David, today's parents often carry wounds with them from their past relationships into their relationships with their kids. When and if parents begin to acknowledge their wounds from the past, they experience a great deal of embarrassment and shame. Their wounds represent an inability to get the people in their world to love them at critical times in the ways that mattered most. This inability, when realized, provokes intense thoughts of helplessness and shame: "What is wrong with me that I can't get the people I love to care for me in the deep ways I long for?"

Listen to David's despair over one of his greatest relational disappointments:

If an enemy were insulting me,
    I could endure it;
if a foe were raising himself against me,
    I could hide from him.
But it is you, a man like myself,
    my companion, my close friend,
with whom I once enjoyed sweet fellowship
    as we walked with the throng at the house of God.

                                     (Psalm 55:12-14)

David mentioned earlier in Psalm 55 (verses 6-8) that his first impulse was to try to escape the pain from this relationship by fleeing to the desert or withdrawing to a place of safety (getting away from any relationship that was hurting him). David used this relational style with his kids as long as he could. When at last Absalom's final rebellion made the pain too great and too pervasive to escape, David was forced to acknowledge that he was a wounded father. A father who was realizing his greatest fear—being seen as disgusting in the eyes of everyone who was important (and being helpless to do anything about it!). We return to Psalm 55 to get a feel for the intensity of David's anguish:

My thoughts trouble me and I am distraught
    at the voice of the enemy,
    at the stares of the wicked;
for they bring down suffering upon me
    and revile me in their anger.
My heart is in anguish within me;
    the terrors of death assail me.
Fear and trembling have beset me;
    horror has overwhelmed me.   (Psalm 55:2-5)

Often when parents encounter relationships that cause them some new disappointment, fresh salt is rubbed into wounds from the past. This was David's experience with Absalom. And this is often the experience of parents of a teen or young adult today. The almost inevitable disappointments parents face in relationships with their teen can plow up all kinds of unpleasant memories of other disappointments in relationships in the parents' past. Despite this, parents of teens still find ways to endure severe crises with their kids without ever acknowledging their own wounds. They usually accomplish this through an unwavering determination to keep their focus on their kids' problems and off their own.

In a parent's mind, wounds from the past reveal an even deeper truth about a person, a truth the parent is terrified others will discover about him. This becomes the third reason why parents avoid personal reflection.

A Parent's Failure

FIGURE 3
THE NONREFLECTIVE PARENT

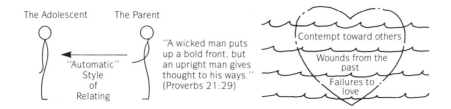

Both parents and their teens are victims of failed relationships because on some level every person has been failed by his parents — an inevitable consequence of living in a fallen world with fallen parents. The writer of Hebrews draws one important contrast between our heavenly Father and our human parents: "Our fathers disciplined us for a little while as they thought best; but God disciplines us for our good, that we may share in his holiness" (12:10). Our heavenly Father has righteous and loving goals in everything He does. Human parents do as they think best. Even at their best, we know parents often think with a misguided focus, with misdirected goals, and with misplaced dependency. The result is that their responses are often unlike God's (e.g., for the child's good, that he may be holy). When a response is guided by any other kind of intention (e.g., for the parents' good, that they may be unhassled), it is a failure of the parents to love.

At times every parent responds to his kids with intentions that are guided on some level by self-centeredness or self-protection. This truth (that as a parent he has failed to love his children in some significant ways) is often the hardest of all truths for a parent to face or admit. However, any parent who really comes to know himself at the core has to face the truth that he is such a person.

Many parents of teens place their hope in their own goodness. In the midst of whatever crisis that may arise with their sons or daughters, these parents cling to the idea that "real bad things don't happen to the children of people like us." They are actually depending on themselves, their own skills as parents, their own goodness as people, to prevent the calamities and heartaches of life. When parents have misplaced their dependency in this way, they must at all cost maintain the illusion of their own goodness in order to keep the foundation they have built their life on from crumbling.

Some parents reading this may find it easy to retort, "I know I'm not a perfect parent, and I've never held any pretense that I was. So tell me something else that's new." These parents must recognize the significant differences in ways parents can acknowledge their failure to love. They may acknowledge it at a rather casual level: "Yeah, I know I get grouchy sometimes and lose my temper with the kids. I really ought to be a little kinder." *When parents acknowledge failure at this level they feel very little pain.* They are really not aware of how their failure can be traced to something very damaged in themselves and something very damaged in their child. They still regard their sin as rather harmless. They therefore remain automatic parents who fail to substantially grow or change in their relational style because they see no serious need to change.

Other parents may acknowledge their failures in a chronic way. They can always be heard lamenting their failures and accepting the blame for everything their children do wrong. Even their kids get tired of hearing about it. Parents like these are experiencing pain, but pain different from that which comes from a core recognition of themselves as failed parents. It's more akin to a pain in the neck than a pain in the heart. Parents who chronically rehearse their failures are often asking people to come to their rescue and get them out of their pain. *The goal of chronic confessors is to get people to lower their expectations for them so the threat of being exposed as failed parents lessens.* By talking obsessively about their failures, they are able to get people to side with them and insist that "they really are not bad parents at all." In fact, everyone else looks like the culprit, while the chronic confessors come off looking like victims because their families have failed to appreciate or understand them.

A parent has not genuinely faced the truth that he is a failed parent until he acknowledges it at a core level. When I hear a parent talking about his failures, I look for three indicators that reveal how deeply he is acknowledging the truth about himself.

First, I look for *how much responsibility he accepts for the failures.* When a parent gets a glimpse of himself at a core level, he can make no excuses for himself. He cannot blame his insensitivity, preoccupation, or angry outbursts on someone else. He has to acknowledge that he has chosen his way of relating in order to protect himself from more pain. Having his wounds exposed does not provide him with a scapegoat; he can't say, "I can't be a good parent because of the way my dad treated me." Instead, having his wounds exposed gives him clear evidence of what his own motives for parenting are; he'll have to admit, "I'm choosing to be a distant parent because I don't want to be hurt again." The parent who knows what kind of person he is at the core accepts full responsibility for what he does as a parent. He doesn't kid himself that someone or something outside of himself controls his choices.

The second indicator I look for is *how aware a parent is of the impact his failures have on others.* When a parent gets an honest glimpse at what he's been doing as a parent he becomes painfully aware of its destructive impact on his kids. He begins to recognize how his relational style actually reinforces problem ways of thinking and relating in his kids. The pain the parent predominantly experiences is no longer the pain of disappointment over others' performances, but the pain of disappointment over his own performance. This parent recognizes that his failures at loving his kids have hurt them by strengthening their human tendency to depend on no one but themselves for the resources of life. This makes it even more difficult for them to believe they can depend on the love of a "heavenly Parent."

The third indicator I look for is *how much a parent expresses a desire to be a fundamentally different kind of parent.* When a parent gets a glimpse at who he really is in his heart, he longs for a change in himself. However, he knows he is powerless to accomplish this change on his own. At this point a desperate sense of need for God, on a level he has never experienced before, is born. *This parent recognizes that if he ever hopes to truly love his kids, he is absolutely dependent upon God to change something deep within him that he can't change by himself.* This results in some detectable movement in the parent toward deepening his relationship with Christ.

It is very possible that David chose to be a nonreflective parent in order to avoid facing the truth that he was a failed parent. There is some evidence that David acknowledged "errors in judgment" to Joab when he reversed his decisions to keep Absalom in exile or to keep Absalom barred from his presence (2 Samuel 14:21,33). However, there is no evidence that David ever considered how he might have failed Absalom until their relationship had deteriorated beyond remedy (2 Samuel 16:11, 18:33).

To what extent David ever acknowledged his failure as a parent at a core level we do not know. At times (as when he committed adultery and murder or disobeyed God by numbering his fighting men) David openly acknowledged his moral failures (2 Samuel 12:13, 24:10). Although he had an opportunity to face and deal with his moral failure as a parent to Absalom in the same way (2 Samuel 14:13-14), he evidently resisted this and continued relating to Absalom in a way that only encouraged him to pursue his self-destructive course of action.

Of course, every moral failure on the part of an adolescent does not necessarily point to a moral failure on the part of his parents. Every adolescent is a free moral agent who chooses what kind of person he wants to be (more will be said about this in the next chapter). Parents are not responsible for their adolescent's choices, since they really have no way of controlling the decisions their kid makes. However, parents are responsible for choosing what kind of parents they will be—how they respond to their adolescent's choices and what their underlying goals are as they respond.

God makes this very distinction in His rebuke of Eli, the priest, in 1 Samuel 3:12-14. Eli was held responsible, not for his sons' contemptible behavior, but for his own failure to respond in ways that would have discouraged their behavior. Likewise, David was not responsible for

Amnon's decision to rape Tamar or Absalom's decision to kill Amnon. But David was responsible for his own failure to respond in ways that discouraged his kids from continuing to go outside God's moral boundaries to get what they wanted. David's response only further exasperated his kids and encouraged them to violate God's moral boundaries again and again. This is what made David a failed parent.

THE CONSEQUENCES OF NONREFLECTIVE PARENTING

If a parent avoids reflection in order to avoid facing the truth that she's a contemptous, wounded, and failed parent, the question must be asked, "What are the consequences of a parent choosing to ignore the truth about her inward condition?"

Nonreflective parenting locks a parent into "automatic" relational styles. She tends to relate to her adolescent in unhealthy and immature ways by adopting one of three relational styles: (1) *dutiful,* (2) *dependent,* or (3) *detached.* The style this parent chooses depends on the interaction of her three primary relationships: her past relationships with her own parents and her current relationships with her children and with her spouse. Notice how this is illustrated in figure 4 on the following page.

Figure 4 portrays an imaginary scale that measures how much a parent is controlled by fear as she approaches her teens. *The more a parent is controlled by fear, the more threatened she is in her style of parenting.* The healthier or more mature a parent is, the less threatened she is as a parent. However, as she becomes more threatened, her style of relating as a parent becomes more disturbed and destructive. In its most threatened form, the relational style of a parent is characterized by almost total detachment from her teen. At this point, the parent becomes almost incapable of being impacted by anything her teen says or does.

Figure 4 also reveals the factors that determine how much a parent is controlled by her fears. Her sense of inadequacy as a parent grows out of the disappointment she has experienced or is experiencing in her relationships with her parents, marriage partner, and children. *The greater a parent's disappointment, the greater her sense of inadequacy, which fuels her fears and makes her a threatened parent.*

FIGURE 4
HOW PARENTS CHOOSE THEIR RELATIONAL STYLE

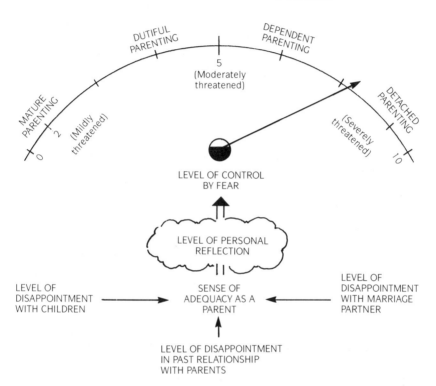

Figure 4 also depicts the impact a parent's personal reflection in light of the Bible has on a parent's style of parenting. When a parent chooses to be nonreflective, he forfeits any possibility of mediating the fear in his life. He becomes an immature parent tossed back and forth by every wave of disappointment that sweeps through his relationships. As long as the people in his family meet his desires, he is able to operate with some sense of adequacy and comes across as only mildly threatened. However, if the disappointment in his past or present family relationships has been great, without personal reflection and repentance he is unlikely to prevent the hurt he has experienced from dictating the way he parents. Only as he opens himself to substantial reflection on his relational disappointments from a biblical perspective can he begin to find the strength to parent in a non-threatened way in spite of his feelings of inadequacy.

When a parent chooses to avoid any deliberate reflection, he feels threatened in his role as parent because he dreads the possibility of being exposed as a failure. Therefore, he subconsciously chooses a style of parenting that is calculated to conceal the truth about himself.

Three Styles of Parenting

The *dutiful* parent believes her adequacy as a person depends on getting her son or daughter to avoid failure and achieve success in the eyes of others. To accomplish this, the parent overemphasizes the teen's outward behavior and tunes in on little of what the teen might be thinking or feeling (unless it starts to adversely affect the adolescent's performance). As a result, the teen experiences the parent as emotionally distant, because the parent is terrified to know about what is going on in the teen. Any exposure to her teen's depravity or disappointment only balloons her fears and makes her feel even more like a failure as a parent. Instead of dealing with her teen honestly and directly, the parent dutifully provides any service (the best education, the best private lessons, the best tools, the best advantages, the best privileges she can afford) that might increase the probability of her adolescent's success. The teen is left with a sense of obligation and pressure to succeed for the parent.

The *dependent* parent has a different plan as she approaches her adolescent son or daughter: She believes her adequacy as a parent depends on keeping her teen needing and appreciating her. To do this, she must keep the teen dependent by convincing him he's not competent to face life without the parent. The dependent parent is normally a more wounded parent (she has suffered more disappointment in her relationships) than the dutiful parent. Therefore, the dependent parent also views her child as wounded or fragile and goes to great lengths to keep anything from further wounding her teen. Thus, the adolescent sees himself as fragile as well and clings to the parent instead of developing the autonomy needed to be a healthy adult. As long as the parent feels needed by her teen, she feels more adequate as a person and the threat of being exposed as a failure lessens.

The *detached* parent approaches her son or daughter with still a different plan. She believes her adequacy as a person depends on avoiding any responsibility for what happens to her teens or for how her teens turn out. This parent is the most threatened of the three. She has experienced such profound pain and disappointment in her relationships that she's concluded that all intimacy must be avoided. Her family experiences her as detached and unmotivated when it comes to participating with them at almost any level. If they push her to get involved with them she responds with contempt, which she has built up through the years to keep people from getting close enough to hurt her again. She believes her detachment relieves her of all responsibility as a parent and any possibility of being exposed as a failure. Her kids are left with a sense of contempt for themselves for failing to be the kind of people their parent could love.

In the next chapter we'll explore even more about how a parent's relational style affects what kind of person her adolescent chooses to be. Clearly, the consequences of operating as a nonreflective parent are disastrous for both parent and teen. Personal reflection in light of Scripture becomes the parent's only avenue to break out of these kinds of destructive parenting styles.

THE CURE FOR NONREFLECTIVE PARENTING

It may seem obvious by now that the cure for nonreflective parenting is reflection. However, it should also be obvious that personal reflection is not an easy or natural thing for a parent to engage in. Personal reflection is a necessarily painful process for every parent. His natural mind-set resists the introspection necessary to expose who he really is. For this reason, a parent normally will not engage in deep personal reflection until three elements are present.

The first is *the presence of relational pain he cannot escape.* As long as a parent's relational style can keep life's pain and disappointment at minimal levels, he will remain nonreflective. In His genius, however, God has designed a way to make it difficult for adults to stay complacent and nonreflective about their lives. He plants time bombs in each of our families, set to go off just when it seems like we as parents have figured out how to make life stable and predictable. The time bombs are almost inevitably crises with our adolescent children. When our kids are teenagers, we have the greatest probability of facing the relational pain that renders all our normal ways of handling painful situations ineffective. There is clear evidence that this is one of the elements that finally drove David to reflect on his life with these words: "My heart is in anguish within me. . . . 'Oh, that I had the wings of a dove! I would fly away and be at rest'" (Psalm 55:4-6). David had finally encountered a kind of relational pain he could not ignore, deny, or fly away from.

A second element that must also be present before most parents will engage in reflection is *the presence of an encourager,* someone who guides and assists the parent in taking an inside look. The writer of Hebrews describes the job of an encourager this way: "See to it, brothers, that none of you has a sinful, unbelieving heart that turns away from the living God. But encourage one another daily, as long as it is called Today, so that none of you may be hardened by sin's deceitfulness" (Hebrews 3:12-13).

An encourager challenges the parent to shift his focus from the problems he's having with his teen to what is going on inside himself and then supports the parent while he's confronting these painful new realities. An encourager helps the parent identify his problem ways of thinking and relating, and then make the deep internal shifts necessary to parent from a pure heart.

This may have been the missing element in David's life. Although Joab tried to challenge David's thinking from time to time, whenever national security was at stake, no one seemed to care enough about David to confront him about what was in his heart as a parent. A lot of the blame for this can be placed on David himself, as it can on many parents of teens today. When parents choose to isolate themselves or cut themselves off from the kind of discipleship relationships where real encouragement can occur, they run the risk of becoming deceived or hardened to what is in their own hearts.

A third element crucial to any ongoing process of reflection in parents of teens is *a relationship with Jesus Christ.* Only in a personal relationship with Christ can a person find the strength to honestly face the painful truths about himself (Hebrews 4:14-16, 2 Peter 1:2-4).

If a parent has never entered into a personal relationship with Christ, he has nowhere to turn when his own contempt, wounds, and failures are exposed. When David's inadequacies and failures as a man were finally exposed in his relationship with his son, the only place he could turn to find comfort and hope was in his relationship with God, which he wrote about in Psalm 55:

> But I call to God,
>> and the LORD saves me.
> Evening, morning and noon
>> I cry out in distress,
>> and he hears my voice.
> He ransoms me unharmed
>> from the battle waged against me,
>> even though many oppose me.
> Cast your cares on the LORD
>> and he will sustain you;
>> he will never let the righteous fall.   (Psalm 55:16-18,22)

The inevitable result of personal reflection in light of Scripture is an erosion of a parent's confidence in his own ability to make life work for himself or for his children. Ultimately, a parent will not allow this to happen unless there is Someone else in whom he can place his confidence. God has designed parenting (especially the parenting of teens) so that it is impossible to do it effectively apart from shifting one's source of confidence from himself to Christ.

SUMMING IT UP

It is interesting to observe that when Jeremiah was commissioned by God to be his messenger and prophet he was given the responsibility both "to uproot and tear down, to destroy and overthrow," as well as "to build and to plant" (Jeremiah 1:10). The second task could not be attempted until the first was accomplished. A "clearing away of the old" must always occur before new growth or construction can begin.

Growing in your abilities to love as a parent must follow the same order. A "tearing down" or "stripping away" of those things that lock you into unhealthy patterns of parenting must occur. Although this is unpleasant and painful it is absolutely necessary.

The whole process begins with personal reflection—identifying the hidden realities in your own heart that get in the way of loving. Realities like the fear of being exposed as a failure, the fear of being hurt again by others, the fear of being vulnerable to your kids. Until these fears are recognized they will continue to control the type of parent you choose to be. But once you identify them, you can make the kind of choices that will enlarge your capacity to love your teen in the way that God intends.

NOTE   1. C.F. Keil and F. Delitzsch, eds., *Commentary on the Old Testament,* vol. 5, *Psalms* (Grand Rapids: William B. Eerdmans Publishing Company, 1973), page 156; and Albert Barnes, *Notes on the Old Testament,* Robert Trew ed., vol. 2, *Psalms* (Grand Rapids: Baker Book House, 1973), page 112.

FIVE

How an Adolescent Decides What Kind of Person He Wants to Be

One night after supper, I decided to take a risk and lead the family in a short Bible study. I began by reading Jesus' words in Matthew 7:24-27:

> "Therefore everyone who hears these words of mine and puts them into practice is like a wise man who built his house on the rock. The rain came down, the streams rose, and the winds blew and beat against that house; yet it did not fall, because it had its foundation on the rock. But everyone who hears these words of mine and does not put them into practice is like a foolish man who built his house on sand. The rain came down, the streams rose, and the winds blew and beat against that house, and it fell with a great crash."

I used this passage to get the kids thinking about the two different kinds of people in the world: foolish people and wise people.

Together we tried to list all the differences we could find in these verses between these two categories of people. One of our daughters observed that wise people build their lives on Jesus' ideas, while foolish people build their lives on their own ideas. Someone else observed that wise people are smart because they build their lives to withstand storms and trials, while foolish people build their lives on foundations that can give way when troubles come. We all concluded that living life as a fool would be pretty scary. You'd never know when a wave could come along and tear your whole life apart. Living as a wise person gives you much more confidence; you know that the foundation you've built on is secure.

As we talked, it seemed like one of those very rare moments when everyone in the family was on the same wave length. I was personally feeling great because I had everyone's attention.

I decided to wrap up our discussion with one final question, which I directed toward each member of our family: "Which of the two kinds of people do you want to be, and why?" One by one the members of our family enthusiastically stated their desires and reasons for wanting to be a wise person, until it was my adolescent daughter's turn. She didn't answer at first. "Christi," I asked, "which kind of person do you want to be? A wise person or a fool?" I'll never forget her response. Very soberly, she answered, "I don't know, Dad. I'll really have to give that one some thought!"

The Two Tasks of Adolescence

Probably no answer could have better exposed the real task that confronts adolescents than the one Christi gave that evening. Adolescents are confronted with the task of answering two crucial questions: *"What kind of person do I have to be to really be wanted and loved?"* and *"What kind of person do I have to be to make an impact that lasts?"* Every adolescent has to decide for himself whether he can accomplish these two things better as a wise person or as a fool. His decision will determine the kind of person he becomes.

Earlier in the Matthew 7 passage, Jesus taught about two kinds of gates: a narrow gate and a wide gate. Matthew records His words as follows:

> "Enter through the narrow gate. For wide is the gate and broad
> is the road that leads to destruction, and many enter through
> it. But small is the gate and narrow the road that leads to life,
> and only a few find it." (Matthew 7:13-14)

Jesus indicates that few people take the narrow gate that leads to life. The majority choose the wide gate that puts them on the road to destruction. In other words, very few choose Christ or His ideas as the foundation on which to build their lives. Most choose the sandy foundation of their own efforts or ideas. The writer of Proverbs actually defines a fool on this basis: "He who trusts in himself is a fool, but he who walks in wisdom is kept safe" (Proverbs 28:26).

Every person (including your adolescent son or daughter) has an active disposition to choose to be the kind of person who trusts in his own resources, rather than in Christ's, to make life work. This means that without significant intervention by Christ or someone He uses as one of His representatives, every person will in essence end up building his life on sand or traveling the broad road to destruction. This is why men, women, and children are portrayed by David in the Scriptures as foolish by nature:

The fool says in his heart,
    "There is no God."
They are corrupt, their deeds are vile;
    there is no one who does good.

The LORD looks down from heaven
    on the sons of men
to see if there are any who understand,
    any who seek God.
All have turned aside,
    they have together become corrupt;
there is no one who does good,
    not even one.   (Psalm 14:1-3)

Kids literally decide what kind of adults they are going to be during adolescence. They are doing this while under the control of a built-in tendency to believe that no God can be counted upon to give them what is vital for their existence. At least no God that can be counted upon to be anything but a hindrance. There is no doubt, then, about what kind of persons adolescents will choose to be if their tendency to factor God out of the picture is left unchallenged. They will choose to be fools. This accounts for the strong calls in Scripture for the kind of parental responses that will drive the foolishness out of a young person's heart. The writer of Proverbs records them as follows:

Discipline your son, for in that there is hope;
do not be a willing party to his death.   (Proverbs 19:18)

Folly is bound up in the heart of a child,
but the rod of discipline will drive it far from him.
(Proverbs 22:15)

The rod of correction imparts wisdom,
but a child left to himself disgraces his mother.
(Proverbs 29:15)

A relationship with parents is one of the primary forces that challenges or reinforces the foolish tendencies of a developing young person, especially in the early stages. The kind of relationships a child experiences with his parents greatly influences which strategies or styles of relating will become his pattern for life. In order for parents to be more active and deliberate in their influence over what kind of person their teen decides to be, they must first understand two things: (1) the stages through which a child develops the basic strategies he'll carry through life, and (2) how his relationship with his parents can influence the type of foolish strategy he ultimately chooses as an adolescent.

THE DEVELOPMENT OF ADOLESCENT FOOLISHNESS

Foolishness begins to develop in the human heart from birth. In infancy it is *aroused*. In childhood it is *learned*. In adolescence it is *incensed*. And in adulthood, if it is allowed to continue operating, it will become *rearranged*.[1]

Stage One: Aroused Foolishness
Foolishness is aroused in a child's heart before he is one year old. Even in infancy, foolish tendencies become aroused and ingrained in the

fabric of a baby's personality as he interacts with the people in his environment. The best parenting in the world cannot prevent this from happening.

To an infant, every desire seems crucial: the desire to suckle, the desire for a full stomach, the desire to be warm and dry. When these desires are not immediately fulfilled by the infant's primary caretakers, he experiences his first relational disappointment. This disappointment arouses within him a tendency to mistrust the abilities and intentions of his parents to give him what is vital for his existence. Though he doesn't yet have the capacity to understand his own thought processes, he develops his first real problem in thinking: "If I'm going to feel safe and secure I must do something to get my world to respond to me."

We read in Proverbs 13:12 that "Hope deferred makes the heart sick, but a longing fulfilled is a tree of life." Whenever the human heart experiences significant delays in having its longings fulfilled, it has a tendency to grow sick. In this way the disappointed heart of an infant also grows sick. The baby's predisposition toward foolishly trusting in only his own efforts to make life safe and secure is aroused (Proverbs 28:26). The more extensively the infant experiences delays in having his primary needs met, the stronger is his belief—based on his survival instincts—that life depends on trusting in no one's initiatives but his own.

The Apostle Peter admonishes his readers to stop satisfying their own desires by using foolish strategies like malice, deceit, hypocrisy, envy, and slander and to become like newborn infants (1 Peter 2:1-2). They should place their trust in a source of nourishment that will never disappoint them: "The one who trusts in [Christ] will never be put to shame" (2:6). This results in relational maturity, which requires trusting in Christ alone for the desires of the heart. *Problems in relating result whenever the heart keeps its trust in itself.* This is why even in infancy problem ways of relating can already be observed. The infant learns that by expressing his desires in the form of demanding cries, he can get his world to respond. Relationships have to be manipulated in order to be fulfilling, so the infant becomes a real student of the people around him. He watches and eventually learns the best ways to get them to give him what he wants when he wants it.

Stage Two: Learned Foolishness

From two years to adolescence, a child learns, practices, and becomes somewhat adept at doing what it takes to get the significant people in her world to satisfy her desires. In this stage a child is trained "in the way [she] should go" (in the sense of Proverbs 22:6) primarily through interaction with her parents. Although Old Testament scholars disagree as to the exact meaning of Proverbs 22:6, one basic principle seems clear: The training a person gets in the formative years of her life has profound impact on the kind of person she later chooses to be.

During the stage of learned foolishness, a child learns the basic foolish strategies she'll carry into her adult life. When a person emerges from infancy into early childhood she begins to learn some very important lessons about life in a fallen world. She learns that the deepest desires of her heart rarely get fulfilled if she fails to meet the expectations of others. The fact that, in most cases, she has to do something wrong to get attention leads her to silently ask, "Am I the kind of person who is really wanted and loved?" "Am I the kind of person who can do something others recognize as important?" When she is rewarded with affection or attention for meeting adult expectations, she concludes, "When I do _____, I am the kind of person who is loved and valued." This creates for her a temporary sense of security and predictability (soon to be undone by adolescence, however) that is rooted in her own abilities to meet the expectations of others.

All of this serves to strengthen the foolishness in her heart. Her problem ways of thinking deepen as her dependence on her own efforts grows more complete. And her problem ways of relating become rigid and compulsive as her relationships become the whole basis upon which she evaluates her worth as a person. *Only when she succeeds at earning the approval or attention of others can she consider herself the kind of person who is really wanted or valued.* A child at this stage is like the person who has built her house on the sand, but hasn't yet experienced a high tide or a storm. Little does she know that a great crash is awaiting her at stage three.

Stage Three: Incensed Foolishness

This stage begins when a child starts puberty and culminates when he's found a way to resolve the crises puberty triggers. During this stage a child's learned strategies for manipulating relationships meet with frustration and failure. Because of changes in others' expectations of him and changes in his perception of others, childhood strategies become inadequate to provide him with a sense of love and impact. And when what he's been conditioned during his childhood to trust in suddenly proves worthless, he feels *betrayed*. Betrayed by his world. Betrayed by himself. Even betrayed by God. He experiences great contempt for all three. He becomes an incensed fool!

Parents must not think they can prevent their sons or daughters from experiencing this stage. It is an inevitable consequence that confronts everyone who emerges from childhood having learned a way to make life pleasurable apart from entering into a vital relationship with Christ, which can only occur when he's been broken by recognizing the depth of his sin. In this sense, adolescence is a real gift from God. It can prevent the foolishness devised by a child from becoming the philosophy that guides him as an adult. *Adolescence is designed by God to literally stop kids in their tracks and make them wrestle with some serious questions before they proceed into adulthood.* There is no guarantee, however, that kids will be able to find wise answers to the questions adolescence evokes. The only guarantee is that the responsibilities of living in an adult world will seriously challenge them to question the foolish ideas they learned during childhood.

Proverbs 13:19 sheds light on the developing fool at this stage: "A longing fulfilled is sweet to the soul, but fools detest turning from evil." Whenever a fool discovers an effective way to fulfill his longings, he detests anyone or anything that tries to make him give it up (even though it is evil!). During adolescence kids often perceive that the adults in their world are conspiring together (perhaps even with God) to make them give up everything that has proved meaningful or useful in satisfying their longings (e.g., certain activities, certain privileges, certain freedoms, certain ways of treating others, etc.). Therefore, tremendous anger in teens can be generated and unleashed during this stage.

This theme is further amplified by Proverbs 19:3: "A man's own folly ruins his life, yet his heart rages against the LORD." An incensed fool looks for someone to blame after his own foolish plans have failed.

The adolescent often directs this anger toward God, which can account for some of the lack of interest in spiritual matters and the defection from churches that occur among kids at this stage. They are expressing blame toward God for the circumstances that keep them from finding satisfaction in this world. And on one level God *is* to blame. In His wisdom and mercy He has created a world in which fallen people have great difficulty finding life and fulfillment apart from Him.

During adolescence the incensed fool experiences increasing problems in his thought processes and relationships. He reaches the conclusion that fulfillment in life depends on him changing the kind of person he is and becoming some other kind of person (e.g., a thin person, an organized person, a funny person, etc.). He must be someone whom others will want, someone who has what it takes to get others to respond.

As the adolescent begins to make this his new goal, relationships can become much more threatening to him. There is the ever-present danger of being found out, or of being discovered for who he really is — something far less than the ideal. Therefore, the adolescent can become quite uncomfortable in close relationships, especially with those who might see through him. He may consider all adults "unsafe" for close relationships for a time. In his style of relating the adolescent may make it a practice to remain aloof and mysterious. Unless helped to see what he's actually doing, this can remain part of his style of relating for all of his adult life.

The stage of incensed foolishness can conclude very shortly, or it can continue for a very long time (even into the mid-to-late twenties). It culminates with the occurrence of one of two things: the *rearrangement* or the *repentance* of foolish strategies.

An adolescent rearranges his foolishness when he revises or adapts his strategies in a way that makes them start to work for him again. The crises puberty triggers (the threats to the adolescent's security, sense of impact, and sense of being loved) incense the teen because he now sees that his strategies to win these things have proven unsuccessful. If he can figure out a way to adapt his foolish strategies to his new adult environment, he'll be able to resolve the crises of adolescence through merely rearranging his foolishness. His anger will subside to some degree, and he will appear ready to face life as an adult. However, in his heart he'll remain independent of Christ, and dependent on himself.

In contrast, an adolescent repents of his foolishness when he makes a deliberate choice to forsake his foolish strategies. This means shifting his dependence to Christ alone and whatever He chooses to provide for his sense of love, impact, and security in his new adult environment. An adolescent stands little chance of choosing the pathway of repentance without someone helping him become aware of the actual consequences of his foolish strategies. While God can intervene directly in human lives, normally He chooses to work through human vessels to make this will known. If an adolescent is not fortunate enough to receive God's help through others, he will more than likely progress to the fourth stage in his development as a fool.

Stage Four: Rearranged Foolishness
In the fourth stage of foolishness, which begins in early adulthood, a person remains fixed until a major crisis occurs that renders her foolish strategies ineffective once again. At this point she often reverts to another period of "incensed foolishness." Many adults in their thirties or forties may experience this when their marriages disintegrate or when their teenagers rebel. Others may not experience such a crisis until they experience an "empty nest," a change of occupation (i.e., retirement), or the death of a spouse.

During stage four young adults remain committed to foolish strategies that in some significant ways resemble the style of relating they learned as children. Thus, the second half of Proverbs 22:6 rings true: "Train a child in the way he should go, *and when he is old he will not turn from it*" (emphasis mine). The fool remains a fool until he dies or repents. The crises of life are rarely sufficient in and of themselves to drive the foolishness out. Neither is corporal punishment, brute force, or a controlled environment. The writer of Proverbs 27:22 makes this very clear: "Though you grind a fool in a mortar, grinding him like grain with a pestle, you will not remove his folly from him." Even though external restraints or force may be adequate to temporarily control a person's foolish behavior, the foolish belief structure remains intact, "underground" or out of sight, in her heart—not to be expressed outwardly again until the restraints are removed. The writer of

Proverbs explains this with a colorful analogy: "As a dog returns to its vomit, so a fool repeats his folly" (Proverbs 26:11).

The best remedy for foolishness can be applied only in the context of honest, loving relationships. *Rarely will* adolescents or adults come to the point of forsaking their foolish strategies without allowing someone with maturity and wisdom to get close enough to show them what they are really doing to themselves and to others through their foolishness (Psalm 55:12-15, 141:5).

THE REMEDY FOR FOOLISHNESS

Solomon described how a remedy for foolishness can be applied when he wrote, "Blows and wounds cleanse away evil, and beatings purge the inmost being" (Proverbs 20:30). According to Solomon, combatting foolishness requires discipline that is applied by another and targeted at dislodging the foolishness within a person's heart. He even goes on in a later proverb to describe who can best apply such discipline: "Faithful are the wounds of a friend" (27:6, RSV).

Anyone who hopes to challenge the foolishness in the heart of another must do so in the context of a friendship. How to build such a friendship with an adolescent will be the theme of chapter 7. How such a relationship can be utilized to influence the kind of person an adolescent chooses to be is the theme of the second half of this chapter.

Before addressing that concern, however, I want to urge you as a parent not to leave this discussion of foolishness without first consider-ing the strategies or formulas for living you model around your own teens. The foolishness we observe in our kids' lives often mirrors the foolishness in our own. It would be futile to attempt to build a relationship with our kids that challenges their foolishness when our own foolishness goes unnoticed and unchallenged.

I am convinced my own foolish strategies are my worst enemy as a parent of a teenager. One foolish belief I learned as a child goes like this: *"I must keep other people convinced that I am competent in order to get them to respect or want me."* Whenever I allow that assumption to control me as I approach my daughters, I only reinforce a similar kind of foolish vein in them.

This foolish childhood strategy encountered a major roadblock as

I entered adolescence. The people in my world kept changing as my family transferred from state to state. As the perpetual new kid on the block, an average student, and a mediocre athlete, I was ill-equipped to impress anyone in junior high with my competence. Through tenth grade, life seemed to grow progressively lonelier for me. I was starting to become incensed over the cruel and uncaring treatment I was getting from the kids at each new school I attended. At the beginning of my junior year of high school, however, I got temporary relief from the effects of my wrong strategy.

During that summer, I earned my lifesaving certification and got a job as a lifeguard at a YMCA. Through lifeguarding, teaching swimming, and playing on a water polo team, I was able to make my wrong strategy prove successful. People at the "Y" began to respect me and value me for the competence I demonstrated at aquatics. At the end of my junior year of high school, I was asked to serve as the evening pool supervisor or head lifeguard. Other kids on the pool staff started to seek me out and invite me to parties. For a while it appeared as though this strategy would not need any revising. It seemed to work well enough even in an adult environment. But then the crash came.

At the beginning of my senior year of high school, a new aquatics director was hired at the "Y." He began to make life miserable for the whole pool staff. As one of his assistant supervisors I felt caught in the middle. Bob, the aquatics director, established a number of new and very rigid policies for the pool staff. It was my job to enforce these policies in the evenings when Bob wasn't around, and report any violations to him. In effect, I was put in a position in which to keep my job I had to serve as Bob's strong arm against the few friends I had in the world. At first I gave it a halfhearted attempt that made both Bob and the pool staff disgusted with me. Finally I resigned to escape a no-win situation. There was no way I could continue using my position at the "Y" to earn the respect and love I wanted.

This happened around the same time my parents moved and left me behind to finish my senior year. Losing my job at the "Y" was the final straw. It made me incensed and ashamed. I decided that I had to change the kind of person I was to make it in this world. That's when the things one of the men from the "Y" had been telling me about Christ started to make sense. I thought I really could get into this stuff about becoming a whole new person.

On one level, I believe I was sincere when I asked Christ to come into my life and make me a whole new person. But on another level, I think I saw it as a new way to get the respect and love I deeply desired from others. As a Christian, I suddenly found myself striving to be the most competent, effective worker in the church I possibly could be. Of course, that required choosing a vocation as either a missionary or a pastor. I believe I began my career as a youth pastor using my ministry to kids as merely a rearranged version of my old strategy (earning significance through competence). Although the arenas had shifted (from academics to aquatics to youth ministry), the purposes of my heart had not. *I was now a religious fool instead of a pagan fool.* And as such I was unable to offer the kids in my youth groups the kind of relationship that challenged their foolishness.

As a young adult my foolish strategies took their greatest toll on my relationship with my wife, Tina. My desire to be seen as significant in others' eyes drove me to become a workaholic in the youth ministry. The only way Tina could really feel close to me was by staying as involved in the youth activities as I was. However, at the birth of our first daughter this became impossible for her. As the responsibilities of motherhood restricted her level of involvement in my activities, my level of involvement in her life also dropped. I became a relationally detached husband to her. She became a very wounded wife.

It was only as Tina began to openly express contempt for the wounds I kept inflicting on her that I began to take a strong, hard look at my own life. Since that time our relationship has experienced several years of very hard, but very substantial, growth and healing. I have made progress at giving up the wrong strategies that placed my center of dependence on my own competence. However, this foolish strategy still hangs on more than I care to admit. In a weakened state but still alive, it rears its ugly head occasionally—especially when my teenager does something to make me feel incompetent.

That was the situation when I got the midsemester report about my daughter's failing language arts grade. It is in situations such as these that my demand to appear competent can too easily take precedence over my daughter's need to be understood or encouraged. When that occurs, my daughter receives an unspoken message that is loud and clear: "Christi, life depends upon being competent and always meeting the world's expectations!"

It is truly possible to offer our teens a relationship that increases, instead of decreases, their chances to become foolish adults. No approach can offer a guarantee of success at parenting. However, a biblical approach can offer the hope that your teen will not build his life on the foolish ideas he has detected in you or invented on his own. *The kind of relationship you offer your teen is the single most influential factor in shaping the kind of person he chooses to be.*

THE SHAPING OF ADOLESCENT FOOLISHNESS

If a parent cannot prevent foolishness from being aroused in his young child or from it later being incensed when the child becomes an adolescent, what kind of impact can a parent have? *A kid's foolish strategies are most vulnerable to a parent's influence when they break down and leave the teen in some level of despair.* This of course happens most prevalently to kids during adolescence. When a teen becomes frustrated and incensed at her inability to get her desires met on her own, she experiences a lot of despair. Her relationship with her parents at this stage will to a large degree determine how she handles her ineffective ways of thinking and relating as she moves into adulthood.

Parents have only two choices as to how they can impact their child during this stage. They can offer her a relationship that will encourage her to revise and strengthen her foolish ways of thinking and relating, or they can offer her one that will encourage her to forsake her foolish ways. The Apostle Peter offers a clue as to how parents can accomplish the latter:

> Therefore, rid yourselves of all malice and all deceit, hypocrisy, envy, and slander of every kind. Like newborn babies, crave pure spiritual milk, so that by it you may grow up in your salvation, *now that you have tasted that the Lord is good.*
>
> (1 Peter 2:1-3, emphasis mine)

According to Peter, it is an authentic taste of what the Lord is really like that motivates a person to stop manipulating her world to get love and impact on her own terms and depend instead upon the Lord for what will nourish her soul. *It should be the goal of parents, then, to offer their teens a genuine taste of God's loving-kindness.* Where else can kids get a sample of what God is really like if not in their relationships with those who are supposed to represent His interests and authority in their lives? Jesus urged people to look at their relationships with their earthly dads for a small glimpse of what their heavenly Father is like (Matthew 7:9-11). Parents, of course, are not capable even at their best of offering kids everything their Father in Heaven can. However, they are capable and responsible for offering to their children a small sample of what God wants to provide for them later on a much grander scale.

Two Major Contributors to a Teen's Repentance

There are two basic ingredients that a parent must demonstrate in her relationship with her teen to give him an authentic taste of what God is like: *unconditional involvement* and *uncompromising responsiveness.*

These are big words that communicate two big concepts to kids about the nature of their heavenly Father. A parent's unconditional involvement gives her kid a taste of *God's grace.* Uncompromising responsiveness gives him a taste of *God's justice or righteousness.* Without seeing the two modeled in the lives of those who teach them, kids can easily get a false idea of what God is like.

When an adolescent asks the question, "What kind of person do I have to be to get someone to want and love me?" unconditional involvement from another teaches him that he doesn't have to be anybody but himself to be loved and wanted. Unconditional involvement makes him aware of the kind of security that is available to him at any moment in a relationship with Christ. As a parent takes whatever initiative is possible to stay relationally near the child during problem times, the child gets a taste of the kind of grace God demonstrates to each one of us (parents and teens alike) in spite of all of our foolishness and sin (Romans 5:8). Even when we act like His enemies, God uses His Son, His Word, and even His people to communicate His desire to remain near (James 4:8). His grace provides everything we need to enter and enjoy relationship with Him at any time (2 Corinthians 5:18-20).

When an adolescent asks the question, "What kind of person do I have to be to accomplish something of lasting significance?" uncompromising responsiveness from another teaches him that everything he does has lasting impact because of who he is. Because God has created the person to rule with Him, his every action, word, and thought have great impact on both God and His creation. Uncompromising responsiveness can help him recognize the kind of impact his life and choices have from God's perspective. As a parent takes whatever initiative is necessary to develop her teen's awareness of the true impact his choices are having on God, others, and himself, the child can begin to understand and appreciate the significance his life really has in God's eyes. Fools have little understanding of their own ways, especially of the impact or consequences that result from them. They often attach too much significance to some actions (academic performance, athletic perfection, social popularity) and too little to others (slander, grumbling, cheating, or lying). And they often fail to attach any significance at all to the things God attaches the greatest significance to — the purposes of their own hearts. Parents have the responsibility to respond to their kids' purposes and actions in a way that encourages kids to attach the same significance and meaning to them that God does.

Two forces move a kid toward God. The kid's disillusionment with his wrong strategies to manipulate his world *push* him to a place where God's ways can become a desirable option. His parents can then *pull* him to God by exposing him to God's sufficiency to meet his deepest longings for love and impact. *Parents who offer their teen a relationship that gives him a taste of unconditional involvement and uncompromising responsiveness stimulate an appetite in that teen's heart for more.* When they direct the teen's attention to the relationship that God offers, they give the adolescent an automatic frame of reference. He has already tasted this kind of relationship and found it something that touched the deepest desires of his heart. When he tests other kinds of relationships and other ways of getting his desires satisfied, he will remember (much as the prodigal son did) the kind of genuine love that is waiting for him with God's Son and God's people. There is a high probability that he will return to that kind of relationship when his foolish strategies fail him. Parents have far less to fear about the kind of person their adolescent chooses to be or the kind of relationships he chooses to pursue when he has had an authentic taste of what God is like. God does very well in taste tests among those kids who have experienced an unconditional and uncompromising kind of love. Since these two ingredients are so essential to a teen's spiritual development, understanding how to demonstrate them to a teen is the focus of Part Three of this book.

The Four Styles of Parenting

Figure 5 depicts the four basic styles of parenting (there are many variations within each style). The matrix in the figure is formed by two axes. The vertical axis represents the level of responsiveness found in each style, while the horizontal axis represents the level of involvement in each. How parents incorporate or fail to incorporate these two ingredients into their relationship with their teen determines which of the four styles of parenting the teen receives.

Detached parenting. The lower left quadrant of the matrix represents the *detached* parent who measures low in both the amount of involvement he gives and the amount of responsiveness he shows. Although this parent's detachment from his kids leaves him too removed to demonstrate any consistent involvement or reponsiveness, his style of parenting still has profound impact on the teen's developing personality.

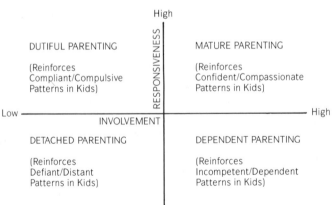

FIGURE 5
FOUR BASIC STYLES OF PARENTING

When an adolescent experiences a low/low (low in involvement and low in responsiveness) relationship with his folks, he is encouraged to develop a style of relating toward others (especially toward his parents and other authority figures) that is *defiant* and *distant*—defiant toward what others expect of him and distant toward them in relationships.

The reason kids choose this style of relating becomes logical once the basic foolish assumptions that low/low parenting reinforces are understood. When an adolescent experiences low or no involvement from his parents, he makes this assumption about himself: *"I must not be the kind of person anyone will ever want or love."* Combining his parents' low involvement with their lack of responsiveness, the adolescent makes a second assumption: *"When I try to be someone else, nobody even notices. I will never become someone who is significant to others."* This adolescent's goal becomes to get away from people altogether, especially those with expectations. The strategy is to avoid anything that would be a painful reminder of the kind of person he believes he is: hopeless and incorrigible.

Essentially, this teen says to himself, *"Life depends on escaping any situation in which an adult can get a glimpse of who I really am."* These situations would only give that adult another opportunity to reject, humiliate, or "give up" on him. The only way he can preserve a shred of self-esteem is by priding himself on his ability to elude or disrupt adult structures. In his mind all adult structures (e.g., family, school, church, etc.) exist to benefit adults and to exploit kids, something his primary experience with an adult structure (his own family) has frequently taught him.

In ignoring what their adolescent feels (low involvement) and does (low responsiveness), detached parents value only what they themselves feel and do. They view the adolescent as someone who is supposed to enhance their lives. And since an adolescent generally fails to do this, he is made to feel worthless and hopeless. It is no wonder a kid seeks to avoid or strike back at all adults since this has been his experience with the most important adults in his life.

I remember counseling an unmarried seventeen-year-old girl who had become pregnant. Lisa was struggling to put the pieces of her life back together but felt very uncomfortable accepting help from anybody, especially from authority figures.

Since any mention of her parents seemed to arouse a great deal of anger in her, I asked her to tell me about her experience growing up. She remembered feeling quite ignored and neglected by both her parents for most of her life. They worked a lot and were rarely home. Her primary caregiver was an elderly grandmother who tried her best to compensate for the lack of involvement and responsiveness in the home. As Lisa entered junior high school, her grandmother suffered a heart attack and died. This left her feeling very alone. By this time her parents had split up, and she lived alone with her mother, who was seldom home.

One day, out of anger, she ran away from home. After a few days, the police picked her up and brought her back. She remembered feeling terrified at what her mom was going to do to her. She said she'll never forget how her mom responded: she treated her daughter like a queen. She had Lisa's favorite meal waiting on the table for her when she arrived. She stayed home every night for a week just to spend time with Lisa. She bought her several new outfits. She never even brought up the running away incident or questioned her about it. Lisa said this treatment lasted for almost two weeks before things returned to business as usual.

A short time later, Lisa decided to run away again. She liked the involvement she'd received the last time. It seemed like a small price to pay in order to get what she wanted. However, the second time drew a much weaker response from her mother. Lisa learned that she had to do progressively more serious things to evoke any kind of response in her mother. Eventually, she started bringing her boyfriends home and asking them to spend the night just to get a response from her mother. Before long even that failed to get her mom's attention. Finally, Lisa decided to deliberately get pregnant. She thought a baby might really get her the attention she desired.

A detached parent like this mother typically responds by ignoring her adolescent's behavior or by rewarding her in an inappropriate manner. When disciplinary consequences are applied, they are applied very inconsistently. Involvement is given in spurts, and only when it is needed to avoid a crisis or to fulfill a perfunctory duty (e.g., a gift and a hug on the kid's birthday). In such an environment the adolescent prematurely declares independence from her parents and often deliberately chooses relationships and a way of life that will disgust the parents and smash any hopes or expectations they have left for their child. Without the resources that only a relationship with Christ can provide, the child *will carry a contemptuous and distant way of relating into nearly all of her relationships as she moves into adulthood.*

Dependent parenting. The lower right quadrant of the matrix in figure 5 represents *dependent* parents, who measure high in the kind of involvement they give and low in the amount of responsiveness they show. It is important to note, however, that the adolescent does not experience this high involvement as love. Just as God's grace would appear distorted if it was portrayed independent of His righteous character, high involvement is also distorted when it is given independent of uncompromising responsiveness.

When parents divorce grace from righteousness the adolescent eventually perceives them as so desperate for relationship that they're willing to compromise any standards. Although the adolescent feels wanted and needed by them, he will ultimately feel unloved. He sees his parents relating to him in a way that is designed to benefit themselves (keeping a relationship they need intact) rather than benefit him (showing him the path to life). Although the involvement is in a sense unconditional (the parents express the desire to be relationally near no matter what the teen says or does), it is given with strings attached (the teen is made to feel obligated to never withdraw relationship from the parents). *Dependent parents do everything they can to convince their adolescent that his existence is fused to their own. Any separation would destroy one or both of them.*

The adolescent who experiences a high/low (high in involvement and low in responsiveness) relationship with his parents is driven to develop a style of relating that communicates his *incompetence* and *dependence*: incompetence at doing the things necessary to make it on his own, dependence on others to do them for him.

When an adolescent's parents give him almost uninterrupted involvement in order to compensate for his own inability to act, think, and choose on his own, he draws a damaging conclusion about himself: Life depends upon keeping his relationship with his parents intact at all cost. When he consistently receives no response or a negative response from his parents whenever he acts, thinks, or chooses on his own, he draws a second damaging conclusion: He must be the kind of person who doesn't have what it takes to accomplish anything significant, and therefore his only chance depends on getting someone else to act, think, or choose for him. In this way his very existence becomes dependent on others, especially his parents.

Dependent parents are really insecure parents. They feel more secure when their son or daughter is acting too incompetent to handle life without them. Although these parents may complain about such incompetence, they are doing everything they can to fuel it.

The adolescent's goal then becomes avoiding responsibilities by using relationships. In order to accomplish this, *the adolescent chooses a style of relating that gets people to lower their expectations because he portrays himself as incompetent.* In this adolescent's twisted thinking, a person who admits he's incompetent is the kind of person others will still want and love. However, a person who tries to act competent and fails is the kind of person nobody would ever want or love. Therefore, the adolescent creates every excuse he can to be relieved of the responsibilities or expectations others have for him.

This type of teen is often the most difficult to work with in the counseling office. Staying in counseling and staying sick becomes a great way to get others to lower expectations and release him from responsibilities. These kids start to make progress in counseling only after they acknowledge what their parents have done to them. When this occurs, they become quite beside themselves with contempt and disgust for the way they have been used. *Dependent parents run the greatest risk of permanently losing relationship with their children.* Because these kids relied on their parents almost like some people rely on drugs, when they finally conquer the addiction they often choose to stay away from the parents in order to avoid re-addiction.

I remember working with one such guy named Bob. Bob had grown up in a home environment with a low/low (detached) dad and a high/low (dependent) mom. As is normal, Bob was most influenced in choosing the kind of person he was by the parent he spent the most time around—his mother. Bob's father was almost never around the house, and when he was he remained quiet and withdrawn. However, Bob's mother tried to compensate for the absent father by funneling all her energies into her son's life. The results were disastrous for Bob.

Bob's every decision and moment of time was dictated for him. As a high schooler, if he happened to make a decision on his own, he had to pay a high price in the hurt and terrified feelings it evoked in his mother. It would take days to calm her down and get things back to normal. Bob lived each day with two incredible pressures: coping with a world that made fewer and fewer exceptions and required more and more responsibilities; and coping with a mother who insisted on making all of his decisions and being included in all aspects of his life.

It wasn't until college that Bob started to successfully pull away from his mother, but not without great anguish and suffering. Not only did he have to deal with her dependency on him, but also his dependency on her. He had come to depend on her to handle all his finances, buy and launder all his clothes, do most of his homework, and solve all his interpersonal problems.

It is extremely difficult for an adolescent with an incompetent/ dependent style of relating to break free from an opposite-sexed parent, but it becomes doubly hard with a same-sexed parent. This is particularly true in mother-daughter relationships. Girls often experience tremendous guilt for making their autonomy a higher priority than their relationship with their mother. When they are forced to choose between the two, they experience incredible stress. Often they will choose to marry controlling husbands and let them battle it out with their mothers for their independence. This always backfires, however, because it leaves the daughters in incompetent/dependent relationships with their husbands.

Dutiful parenting. The upper left quadrant in figure 5 represents the *dutiful* parent who measures low in involvement and high in responsiveness. This kind of parenting tends to produce *compliant* and *compulsive* adolescents.

On the surface many parents, especially dutiful ones, consider this kind of teen a real joy to have around the house. He is compliant toward what is expected of him, and he is compulsive about being dependable and pleasant in his relationships. The low involvement from his parents has trained him to expect very little in the way of personal investment from others. The high responsiveness has led him to depend solely on his own actions and performance for personal nourishment. His basic assumption for living goes like this: *"I'm the kind of person who can get love and impact from others only by earning it."* His goal becomes to meet and if possible surpass the expectations of the important people in his life.

This type of adolescent thrives on adult expectations and structure. After being in an adult-structured environment all day, he chooses to put himself under more structure by overloading on extracurricular activities. The more structure and expectation he can get under, the better he feels. In his thinking, adult expectations carry with them the opportunity to win more approval and/or attention, the kinds of things he's starving for. Unstructured situations make him uneasy because the rules for earning approval are unclear. What he fears above all else is losing what little involvement or approval he has earned.

To avoid this he does two things. First, he compulsively seeks out or makes up rules for pleasing others and then keeps them at all cost. In the same way a defiant/distant kid becomes a compulsive rule-breaker, the compliant/compulsive kid becomes a compulsive rule-keeper.

Second, he puts pressure on himself to keep improving his performance, imagining that people's expectations for him always exceed his level of attainment. Therefore he can never rest in his accomplishments. He has learned from his parents that he is not the kind of person others naturally want to be involved with. He feels he must constantly convince others that he is worthy of their involvement. If someone offers him unconditional involvement, he does not regard it as real. In his heart he believes he is not the kind of person people would want or love apart from what he could do for them.

Sandy was a high school girl who bore all the marks of being a compliant/compulsive adolescent. She always went to great lengths to please everybody in her world. She was a 4.0 student who had never given her parents a reason to be alarmed. No reason, that is, until she cut one class during the final week of her junior year of high school.

Sandy's friends had invited her to skip her last period study hall in order to go for ice cream. Even though it was against the school rules, she decided to be uncharacteristically adventurous and leave early with her friends. After all, it was the last week of school and she did not have any homework to do.

A teacher saw the kids leaving the school grounds and reported it to the principal. The principal in turn called the parents of each kid. When Sandy arrived at home that day, her parents were angrily waiting for her. They quickly announced that she would be severely punished for breaking the school rules. Since her sixteenth birthday was just a couple of weeks away, she was told that she would have to wait another whole year to get her driver's license.

The response of Sandy's parents is typical of the way low/high parents often respond to their teen's failures to live up to expectations. Their responses are excessive in that they attach far too much significance and consequence to outward actions. They are also shallow in that they fail to take into account the inner purposes or longings of their teen. Even though these parents are highly responsive and seldom compromise their standards when they respond, their style of parenting makes their teen nonreflective and nondiscerning in the way she relates to authority.

When Sandy graduated from high school, she was expected to attend her parents' alma mater. In her compliant fashion she did as her parents wished. However, at the university something began to happen to Sandy that her parents hadn't counted on. The authority figures in the classrooms and dormitory had entirely different expectations than Sandy's parents did for how she was supposed to think and act. Overnight, it seemed to Sandy's parents that their daughter's behavior and values began to radically change. From their viewpoint, she started acting like an "unbeliever." She was saying and doing things that were not a part of her Christian upbringing.

Sandy's parents failed to recognize that she was merely responding to her environment the way they had trained her to do. She had learned from them that life depended on blindly meeting the expectations of those in authority. In her new university environment *she was simply following the same foolish strategy in a rearranged version.* She was choosing to be the kind of person her relationship with her parents had conditioned her to be: a rule-keeper. However, in this case the rules had changed. And her parents had neglected to teach her to be controlled by anything deeper, like convictions or righteous purposes.

Mature parenting. A fourth kind of parent can be found on the matrix in figure 5: the high/high, or *mature*, parent. Mature parenting creates an environment in which *confident* and *compassionate* adolescents can be developed, kids who will decide to live by depending on Christ.

SUMMING IT UP

Although operating as a mature parent of an adolescent (high in both unconditional involvement and uncompromised responsiveness) may come easier for some than for others, no one starts there naturally. Relational maturity (love) develops only as a parent comes up against problems with his kids that he doesn't handle very maturely, and focuses on changing the things inside himself that account for this.

The fact is, no parent really ever arrives as a no-fail high/high parent. It is a goal to shoot for, but a goal even a godly parent must get comfortable with frequently falling short of. Even the most mature parent will always be freshly aware of some problem in his thinking or in his relating that is getting in the way of loving his kids. Nevertheless it is essential that parents never stop pursuing the goal of maturity by combating the problems within themselves that keep them from offering unconditional involvement to their kids, or from responding to them in uncompromising ways.

The rest of this book is designed to help you do this very thing. Chapter six will identify the internal shifts every parent must make before he can be free to develop the skills needed to be a high/high parent. Chapters seven and eight describe the skills required for unconditional involvement with a teen. Chapters nine and ten describe the skills required for uncompromised responsiveness.

In the end, however, none of this help will be enough to make a mature parent of you overnight! That will be a slow process — a painful one at times, but also a joyful one. You will experience some of the deepest joy of your life when you see your own love for your teen deepen and your style of parenting mature.

NOTE   1. I have adapted the stages and many of the concepts about foolishness in this chapter from class and seminar lectures given by Dr. Larry Crabb.

SIX

What's a Parent to Do When He Doesn't Like Who His Kid Is Becoming?

Parenting an adolescent can be a terrifying experience. It is during adolescence that a parent begins to discover what kind of person his child really is. This can be both an exhilarating and an excruciating experience. Exhilarating because so many new parts of the child's personality are emerging, parts previously unknown that now can be explored, embraced, and enjoyed by a wise parent. Excruciating because some of these new parts give a parent his first penetrating glance at the real condition of his child's soul.

The foolish, selfish, and arrogant parts of the adolescent's personality reveal spiritual poverty and the seeds of ultimate disaster. When wise parents,and even not-so-wise parents, observe these, they can conclude that they don't like who their kid is becoming. They can become desperate about finding a way to change the patterns that are developing.

As I've observed my daughter Christi emerge into adolescence, I've experienced both the exhilaration and the pain. I can best describe the experience by comparing it to watching a rosebud open. When Christi was first given to my wife and me as a precious rosebud (as an infant), we had no idea what we would find inside as the petals opened. As she developed through childhood, we got a glimpse of the color of her personality as the closed petals separated briefly from time to time. However, our first full glimpses of what Christi was like at the core came as she began to express herself more freely as an adolescent. As she did, we become quite intrigued with this blossoming person. Could this really be the same person who had been growing in our home for the past twelve years?

As the flower has been opening, we've been peering inside with something much more than mild curiosity. At times we've been mesmerized by what we've observed: Christi's ability to think on her own, draw her own conclusions about life, and make her own decisions; Christi's longings, fears, hopes, and dreams; her perceptions of the past, of our family, and of her place in the world; her sensitivity, her sense of right and wrong, and her concerns for the welfare of others. She has truly brought a sense of fascination and wonder to our lives as her parents.

At other times, however, what we've seen within the folds of the blossom has transformed that sense of wonder into a sense of terror, unlike anything we have experienced before. We've been occasionally appalled by the focus of Christi's energies, her goals, the things she looks to and depends on for pleasure. We've been deeply disturbed by her frequent failures to love, her unwillingness to make sacrifices, her reluctance to face difficult situations, and especially her view of God and approach to things that concern Him. All of these have brought us to the realization that not all the petals bear a fragrant aroma; some of them are worm-eaten and diseased. We have a damaged flower on our hands.

This has led us to ask the same questions many parents of teens ask: "What are we to do when we don't like who our kid is becoming? How can we deal with the ugly realities that confront us as our teen's personality develops?"

Too often parents react to their adolescent's developing struggles and foolish patterns of behavior with the kind of focus that only serves to reduce or forfeit what positive influence they could be having. To shift this focus, parents must recognize why they can still have so much influence on their developing adolescent, how they can forfeit or misuse this influence, and how they can maximize it when they don't like the person their kid is becoming.

A PARENT'S INFLUENCE ON AN ADOLESCENT

Many believe teenagers are inevitably influenced more by their peers than by their parents. Sometimes, parents are urged to adopt this view so they can relax and accept the course of nature. They are told, "Your child is going to be who he wants to be and who his friends want him to be, no matter what you do. So why get all worked up about something you have no control over?"

There are two problems with this approach. First, it backfires. Telling parents they have little or no control over how their adolescent turns out only magnifies their fears and causes them to parent in a way that further reduces what positive influence they could have. Second, it is erroneous. Although peers sometimes do exercise more control over an adolescent's choice of dress, music, entertainment, etc., only when parents are extremely negligent do peers exercise more control over the teen's choice of beliefs and relational styles than they do. In the vast majority of cases *parents remain the single most important influence in the development of an adolescent's personality.*

I have found this to be true for at least four reasons.

Through Admiration

First, *every adolescent has a burning desire to be someone his parents admire.* This causes him to develop behavior patterns and personality characteristics that will accomplish one of two things: capture his parents' admiration, or avoid losing any of his parents' admiration.

The desire to be admired by his parents can be traced back to a deeper longing that every adolescent has; to be valued and wanted by others. Since no parent can ever do enough to satisfy these longings, no adolescent can ever get enough admiration. The adolescent tends to regard his parents' admiration as the missing ingredient on which life's fulfillment depends, which leads him to give his life to capturing or storing up as much of this ingredient as possible.

The most difficult adolescent to work with is the one who has concluded (usually only after being convinced by great effort from his parents) that he can never be the kind of person his parents will admire. His controlling goal in life becomes revenge—to hurt his parents and make them feel the same shame they've made him feel. He usually sees counseling only as another tool for accomplishing this.

It is important to note, however, how even the vengeful adolescent is still greatly influenced by his parents. He has chosen a defiant/distant style of relating as a response to what his parents have chosen to withhold from him. Because of a burning yet unfulfilled desire to be admired by them, he numbs his pain by pretending not to care about anything they think or say. Only by discrediting everything about them can he even moderately lessen the impact of their decision to withhold their admiration.

When an adolescent does receive admiration from his parents he tends to register some of his highest levels of concentration, motivation, and enthusiasm toward life. There is nothing like the admiring look of a parent for providing a teen with a temporary sense of exhilaration and aliveness. It can become more alluring and addicting than any drug, and it is one of the most powerful tools parents have in shaping a teen's developing personality and relating style.

Through Altering the Mental "Tapes"

A second reason why parents can exert so much influence on their teen has to do with a set of "tapes" every adolescent carries around in her head. These tapes influence her behavior and choices far more than any recording she might be exposed to on the radio or television; because these tapes are words, sentences, ideas, and assumptions recorded during the most painful and intimate moments of interaction she's had with the primary people in her life. During these relational encounters, numerous morals and lessons about life were branded into her memory.

Since the primary people in a child's life are her parents or parent-figures, her mental tapes reflect her parents' values and opinions about life. They play back to the teen the same basic notions that controlled her parents during the earlier stages of her life. *Unless the tapes are altered, these same notions will tend to control the adolescent as she emerges into adulthood.* Those most responsible for these early recordings usually have the most access to them during adolescence. By choosing to relate to an adolescent on the basis of whole new notions, parents can erase and record over any of the old tapes that are destructive.

Through High Levels of Interaction

A third reason parents can influence an adolescent is because their level of access and opportunity for interaction with their teen is high. No one else (peers, teachers, even favorite recording artists) has access to a kid like parents do. Parents can interact with a teen when he is sick, tired, disappointed, or heartbroken; when he is in a reflective mood at bedtime or in a talkative mood at mealtime; when he has time on his hands on weekends or vacations; when he has experienced something for the first time (his first date) or something for the last time (high school graduation); when he's suffered a major failure or celebrated a major success. In these instances and hundreds of others parents are exposed to an adolescent in ways like no one else is. *And exposure always breeds influence.* The question many parents must ask themselves is not "Why don't I have any influence over my teen?" but "Why do I take so little advantage of the exposure I do have with him?" The answer to the second question is very often the answer to the first.

Through Controlling Their Environment

A fourth reason parents can influence their teen is that *they still have some control over the most critical factors in their kid's environment.* Contrary to what many parents believe, most adolescents remain dependent on them, and therefore vulnerable to their influence, in most every important area of their lives. Think for a moment about what these areas of dependence might be for a student: transportation, clothing, extracurricular activities, use of free time, use of telephone, room and board, spending money, tuition, insurance, medical care. In the hands of wise parents any one of these items can be used to influence an adolescent's choices—choices about relationships, responsibilities, life!

Recently the parents of a college student complained to me about how little influence they had over the kind of lifestyle their son was choosing. He'd been coming home at all hours and neglecting his studies as well as his household responsibilities. Whenever his mom or dad had objected to his lifestyle, he blew up. On a couple of occasions he became so enraged he put his fist through walls in the home. The parents felt severely intimidated and concluded they had lost all control. They started to back off and let their son do whatever he wanted. Because that didn't seem the right thing to do, either, they decided as a last resort to seek counseling.

As we talked, they insisted they no longer had any influence over their son, even though he depended upon them for every one of the items listed previously. When I suggested that they withdraw the privilege of letting him use the car until his behavior changed, they nearly gasped in horror. The conflict such an act might cause seemed almost intolerable. *In an attempt to avoid conflict with their son, they had bargained away their ability to influence every major area of his life.* In reality, the opportunity for influence was still there when and if they chose to exercise it. However, as long as the goal of avoiding conflict with their son controlled them, they experienced little or no influence in his life.

Whenever parents have little awareness of or freedom to exercise their God-given influence in their teen's life, something is wrong inside them, not just inside their teen. *The kind of goals parents pursue in their relationships with their kids largely determines whether their influence will increase or decrease during adolescence.*

HOW A PARENT FORFEITS INFLUENCE

When a teen shows evidence of becoming a foolish person, the last thing parents want to do is forfeit any of the influence they could use to challenge the foolishness. However, parents often lose this crucial influence by falling into a style of relating I call the *consumer model* of parenting.

Listen to the words of Apostle Paul as he cautions his readers against operating by this model in their relationships.

> For you were called to freedom, brethren; only do not use your freedom as an opportunity for the flesh. . . . But if you bite and devour one another take heed that you are not *consumed* by one another. (Galatians 5:13,15; RSV, emphasis mine)

In Galatians 5, Paul identifies three characteristics of a consumer approach that can be recognized in parent-teen relationships. First, such an approach arises out of a misplaced dependency (5:16) on the part of the parent: "So I say, live by the Spirit, and you will not [be living to] gratify the desires of the sinful nature." Whenever a parent is not "living by the Spirit" or depending on the Spirit for what is crucial to his well-being, then the source on which he depends for life becomes his own flesh—his strength, his abilities, his efforts.

Second, when a parent's desires depend only on what his own "flesh" can provide for life (5:17), they become directed at the wrong things: "For the sinful nature desires what is contrary to the Spirit, and the Spirit what is contrary to the sinful nature. They are in conflict with each other, so that you do not do what you want."

The desires of the flesh-dependent parent, especially toward his children, are selfish or self-protective in nature. He begins to pursue goals (i.e., to control his kids, make them successful, keep them from hassling him, etc.,) that ultimately hurt them and make them less responsive to him. And while he is doing this, he loses his sense of freedom or fulfillment in being a parent. His style of parenting consumes his own energies and his kids' vitality and yet, even when he sees what he's doing, he's unable to substantially change his style of parenting. *As long as he's a consumer at heart, dependent on his own flesh to satisfy his desires, his relationships can be nothing more to him than a feeding ground*—a place where his own "flesh" must find a way to get people to satisfy his deepest desires.

Not only have "consumer" parents misplaced their dependency on their own "flesh" and misdirected their desires toward finding fulfillment in their relationships, but they also have *focused their energies on changing others,* especially those closest to them. Whenever a person adopts this focus, any behavior that gets others to respond favorably becomes justifiable. Paul continues his description of a "consumer" parent in Galatians 5:19-21:

> The acts of the sinful nature [the consumer parent] are obvious: sexual immorality, impurity and debauchery; idolatry and witchcraft; hatred, discord, jealousy, fits of rage, selfish ambition, dissensions, factions and envy; drunkenness, orgies, and the like. I warn you, as I did before, that those who live like this [as consumers in their relationships] will not inherit the kingdom of God.

Observe in figure 6 the impact parenting in the consumer model has on the parent-teen relationship. When a parent approaches his teen as a consumer, his goal is to get his teen to satisfy (or help satisfy) his deepest desires (i.e., to feel wanted and to impact others). The parent depends on his own "flesh" (i.e., his parenting skills or his goodness as a person) to pull this off, and all he needs, in his thinking, is a little help from others, especially those in his family.

As a parent approaches his teen with this kind of focus, he inevitably finds the teen inadequate to provide all the help his flesh requires. His disappointment balloons and his teen's inadequacies become magnified in his eyes. His awareness of his kid's shortcomings and flaws becomes so sharpened that he can focus on nothing but correcting or changing them. He ends up using his relationship with his teen to manipulate the improvements he wants.

FIGURE 6
THE CONSUMER MODEL OF PARENTING

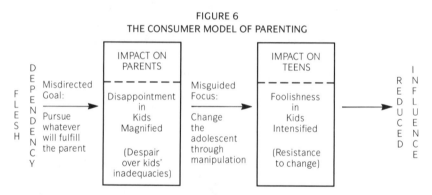

A teen usually reacts to this style of parenting by becoming driven to escape the pressure he feels in his parents' presence. A teen learns that any kind of open relationship with them is subject to manipulation and exploitation. *Whatever foolish style of relating he's adopted to protect himself in relationships only intensifies around his parents.* The compliant/compulsive kid makes up more rules for himself with the hope of being less disappointing to Mom and Dad. The defiant/distant kid breaks more rules in an attempt to make his parents so disappointed with him that they'll give up on him and leave him alone. The incompetent/dependent kid acts sicker and more helpless in order to convince his parents that their disappointment is unfair and their expectations are unreasonable. The result in every instance is an increasing distance between the parents and the adolescent, and a decreasing influence for the parents in combatting their adolescent's foolishness.

As a parent's disappointment grows and his influence decreases, he often begins to lose interest in the relationship altogether, or he avoids it because it now represents a threat to his own sense of fulfillment. A consumer's motto regarding disappointing relationships always goes like this: *"Nothing is to be gained by staying in a painful relationship if it doesn't benefit me."*

Rather than pulling out right away, however, most parents will first try to revise whatever style of consumer parenting they have been using (e.g., detached, dependent, dutiful) in hopes of finding a more effective way to make their relationship with their kids more fulfilling. However, no matter how much these parents might change their style of relating or try new "parenting techniques" their kids will still see them as "consumers" until a deeper, more fundamental change occurs. Such a change requires stepping into a whole different model of parenting.

Mitch experienced this kind of change in his relationship with his kids. As a brilliant surgeon, he had learned the value of consulting with other specialists when he came up against a case that defied routine procedures. When he consulted with me, the case needing review was his own family. Mitch had run out of ideas about how to get his three teenage children to respond to him positively. He was hoping I could suggest a new parenting technique that would work.

Mitch was typical of the kind of parent I had been seeing week after week in my counseling office and parenting classes: educated, bright, well-read, an avid attender of many family seminars. Outwardly a committed Christian who saw the need for a healthy family life, Mitch was also a walking handbook of principles and formulas for raising children. But also—very privately—he was frustrated, afraid, and unfulfilled, because in his estimation, none of it was working. Though his colleagues and patients held him in high esteem, he came home each day to face only disdain and disrespect from his children. He had tried everything to change them and the circumstances that caused them to be like they were, but to no avail. He was close, in his own words, "to admitting defeat and letting the patients die."

Mitch had discovered what every parent who tries to change his kids on the basis of his own "flesh" or parenting abilities discovers: namely, *that no amount of effort or skill at parenting can, in and of itself, turn kids around.* As long as the purposes in a parent's heart remain flesh-dependent (i.e., "I will find a way to make my life work without depending totally on the Spirit of God"), his impact on his kids will only strengthen their foolishness.

After several months of work on his own life, Mitch came to a startling revelation about himself. "You know," he said. "I'm starting to understand at least part of the reason why God gave me the teenagers He did. They're tough kids, but God knew I needed tough kids to bring me to the end of myself. Before they became adolescents, I thought I had it made. In regular surgeon-style, I had everything sewn up, so much so that I didn't need God in a practical way. When my kids started to bleed, in a manner of speaking, I went to work to sew them up too. But nothing I did worked after they reached thirteen. It was the first time my mind and skills weren't enough.

"I still have no idea how my kids will turn out, but I've begun to trust the Lord for the strength and wisdom to parent them in a whole new way—a way I never knew was possible. Something had to completely shift inside of me before I could start to love them just the way they are. I think they sense something has changed in me. And I really think that's had more impact on them than anything I could have ever said or done."

The shift Mitch experienced involved a basic change in the model of parenting he was using. As soon as he shifted models, he began to have a whole new kind of influence in his kids' lives.

HOW A PARENT WINS INFLUENCE

The kind of model Mitch shifted to is outlined in the fifth and sixth chapters of Galatians. The Apostle Paul describes a second approach to relationships, one I call the *ministry model* of parenting (5:13-14):

> You, my brothers, were called to be free [not to be enslaved to the will and rules of others in order to find life]. But do not use your freedom to indulge the sinful nature [to use others for the

purpose of self-fulfillment]; rather, serve one another in love [use your freedom to pursue others' well-being, not your own]. The entire law is summed up in a single command: "Love your neighbor as yourself."

In order for a parent to operate in the ministry model, she must shift the source of her dependency, the direction of her desires, and the focus of her energies (5:22-26):

But the fruit of the Spirit [the fruit of a Spirit-dependent approach to relationships] is love, joy, peace, patience, kindness, goodness, faithfulness, gentleness and self-control. Against such things there is no law. Those who belong to Christ Jesus have crucified the sinful nature with its passions and desires [have entrusted their desires to God, rather than trying to fulfill them on their own]. Since we live by the Spirit, let us keep in step with the Spirit [focus our energies on the same things in relationships that God focuses on]. Let us not become conceited, provoking and envying each other [start thinking we can make it on our own again and shift back to the consumer model].

When a parent makes these fundamental shifts toward the ministry model, her relationship with her teen will be profoundly affected. Notice that in figure 7 (see the following page) a shift in dependency and goals still results in a magnification of the disappointment the parent experiences. However, the main source of her disappointment shifts from her kids' inadequacies to her own. The more she moves toward them with goals of self-sacrifice and love rather than with goals of self-protection and fulfillment, the more she discovers flaws within herself that make her inadequate to love very well. As a result, her focus shifts completely. *Rather than devoting her energies to trying to change her kids' conduct, she concentrates on changing her own character.* Although her awareness and concern over her kids' character and conduct continue to grow, she understands that, apart from the Spirit of God doing a work in her own heart, she can have no constructive influence in their lives.

FIGURE 7
THE MINISTRY MODEL OF PARENTING

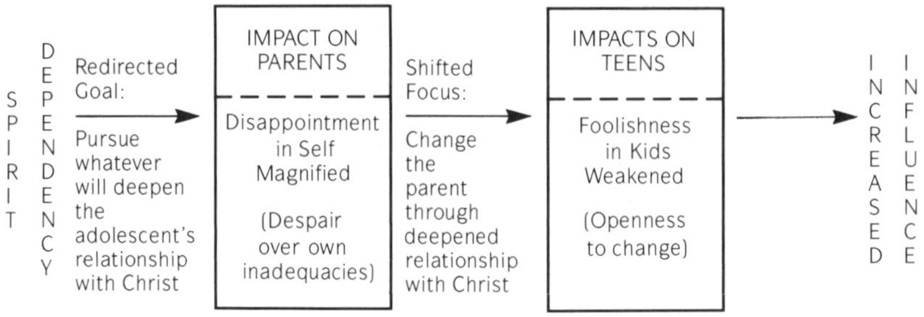

SPIRIT DEPENDENCY → Redirected Goal: Pursue whatever will deepen the adolescent's relationship with Christ →

IMPACT ON PARENTS
Disappointment in Self Magnified
(Despair over own inadequacies)

Shifted Focus: Change the parent through deepened relationship with Christ →

IMPACTS ON TEENS
Foolishness in Kids Weakened
(Openness to change)

→ INCREASED INFLUENCE

When an adolescent sees evidence in his parent of brokenness and genuine sadness over the parent's own inadequacies, the teen often begins to soften and to reveal his own problems. Relationship with his parent, and the dependent relationship with Christ he sees his parent now enjoying, become attractive to him. He begins to sense a new strength in his parent because of the motto that guides one who operates in the ministry model: *"Any amount of pain in a relationship is worth enduring if it will benefit another's relationship with Christ."*

A ministry-driven parent comes to occupy a position of greater influence in her adolescent's life. Even though there is still no guarantee a teen will give up all his foolish ways, the probability increases that he'll be attracted to a life of dependency on Christ, since it is now being modeled for him by his parents.

Shirley was a single mother who experienced these very changes in her relationship with her seventeen-year-old daughter. When I first met Shirley, she was operating as a dutiful mother whose husband had left her for another woman just two years before. For years she had allowed her husband to abuse her and her kids verbally and emotionally because she feared he would abandon them, or even go insane if she said anything. The marriage had long ago stopped being fulfilling to her, but out of her belief that being single would be even less fulfilling, she did nothing to challenge her husband's foolish ways. By allowing him to operate blatantly as a consumer in the family without resistance, she was herself operating as a consumer in a more subtle way. As she depended on her own ability to preserve her marriage and determined to protect herself from further loss, she allowed her family to be slowly "consumed" by her husband's abusive ways.

When the inevitable finally happened, and he left her in spite of all her efforts, Shirley figured all she had left was her one unmarried daughter, Janet. However, out of anger and disgust for Shirley's inability to handle her dad better, Janet soon started imitating her dad's abusive ways toward her. Once again, Shirley permitted the abuse because she feared her daughter might decide to leave her too. Dutifully, she waited on her daughter hand and foot, while also withholding any intimate expressions of affection in order to protect herself from the impact of Janet's cutting remarks. Meanwhile, Shirley was slowly losing any positive influence she might have had on the kind of person her daughter was becoming. In many ways Janet was turning into the same kind of foolish person her dad was.

To help parents like Shirley to be motivated to change involves helping them recognize two things: (1) the style of parenting they've adopted to deal with the disappointing relationships in their family, and (2) the real impact this style of parenting is having on everyone involved. Once a parent like Shirley gets an honest glimpse at these two facts, an initial shift in focus usually takes place. The parent no longer wants to pour her energies into trying to make her consumer style of parenting work. Instead, she is ready to focus on doing whatever it takes to parent in a new style. However, such a shift requires the parent to shift her source of dependency and the direction of her goals in relationships.

Once these deeper shifts occurred in Shirley's life, her daughter began to experience a whole different kind of mom. In the ministry model, Shirley found the strength to parent in two ways that had eluded her previously. First, she began to move toward her daughter to express the kind of emotional warmth and affection she'd never been able to express to anyone before. Second, she began to resist her daughter and ex-husband's abusive remarks by terminating conversations until their tone and attitude changed. She even found the strength to withdraw some privileges from Janet (without withdrawing her involvement) until her daughter showed her more respect.

At first Janet didn't like the changes she saw in her mother. The first time Shirley refused to rub Janet's feet or draw her bath water for her, Janet became livid. However, when she saw that her anger could no longer intimidate her mother, she began to respect her. Losing the use of her car for a week just because of one remark didn't seem fair to her either, but in time Janet even came to respect her mom for making that decision.

The real test for Shirley came when Janet announced her plans to go to Florida for spring break with some older teens. Shirley genuinely thought that allowing her daughter to go under the conditions described was not in Janet's best interests. When Shirley told her she couldn't go, Janet packed up and moved in with her dad. Through a feat that required incredible dependence on Christ, Shirley stood her ground and faced the possibility that terrified her the most: *total abandonment!*

For the first time, Shirley deliberately put herself in a situation in which she had only Christ to sustain her and give her the sense of love and security she desired as a woman. Because she chose a ministry path with her daughter, she had no choice but to shift her dependence from her family to Christ, something she'd been avoiding most of her life. *Shirley was banking on the fact that her relationship with Christ alone would provide the strength and joy to live, even if everyone else abandoned her.* When she put this kind of dependence in Christ, she was not disappointed. She found His help and presence real in a way she never would have had she not shifted to the ministry model.

In a matter of weeks, Janet asked for Shirley's forgiveness and the privilege to move back home. Although Janet's father permitted her to do anything she wanted, it was in her mother's presence that she really felt what she longed for the most: unconditional involvement and uncompromising responsiveness.

By parenting in the ministry model and making the hard internal shifts it required, Shirley came to love her daughter in a way that won a deep and lasting influence in her life. Today Janet is starting to show real signs of becoming a different kind of person than her dad, signs that indicate changes in her heart that started as a response to changes in her mother's heart.

There is no guarantee that teens will always respond to changes in their parents' hearts like Janet did. However, parents who make the kinds of shifts Shirley did are guaranteed to find the same strength and joy from Christ as she did to sustain them no matter what kind of people their kids choose to be.

HOW A PARENT SHIFTS MODELS

For anyone who desires to follow after Christ, especially in the way they relate to others, Jesus indicates that a major shift in the human heart is not only possible, but necessary. Figure 8 illustrates the shift He calls for in Luke 9:24.

FIGURE 8

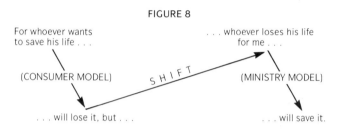

How can such a shift be made? Jesus' words in Luke 9:23 are probably the most concise declaration of what any deep shift from the consumer model to the ministry model must involve. He said, "If anyone would come after me, he must deny himself and take up his cross daily and follow me."

According to this statement, there are two essential elements involved in "losing one's life for Christ's sake," the same two Christ demonstrated when He chose to endure crucifixion for the sake of those He loved. Christ's death was His profound expression of *self-denial* and *self-sacrifice,* the same elements a parent must express if he is to be relationally mature (highly involved with and responsive toward his kids).

It is interesting to note that the Apostle Peter's instructions to both wives and husbands about relational maturity were introduced by the phrase, "in the same way." Peter wrote, "Wives, *in the same way* be submissive to your husbands" (1 Peter 3:1) and "Husbands, *in the same way* be considerate as you live with your wives" (1 Peter 3:7, emphasis mine).

"In the same way" as what? Peter's reference comes in the preceding chapter:

To this you were called, because Christ suffered for you, leaving you an example, that you should follow in his steps. "He

committed no sin, and no deceit was found in his mouth."
When they hurled their insults at him, he did not retaliate;
when he suffered, he made no threats. Instead, he entrusted
himself to him who judges justly.   (1 Peter 2:21-23)

"In the same way" that Christ responded to those who crucified Him. This is the pattern Peter gives for men and women to follow when responding to those who disappoint, hurt, or betray them. *When parents are disappointed in their teens' foolishness, the only mature response is the one of self-denial and self-sacrifice that Christ demonstrated toward His executioners.*

Genuine self-denial and self-sacrifice are impossible for anyone who doesn't rely on Christ for his core security and significance. A person cannot be free to make another's well-being his top priority until he has entrusted his own well-being to Another. Through self-denial and self-sacrifice, a person entrusts to God all that is crucial to his own well-being, just as Christ did (1 Peter 2:23). This frees him to enter even the most painful relationships as Christ did (1 Peter 2:22)— with the goals of a servant rather than those of a consumer.

Self-Denial

If the elements of Christlike self-denial and self-sacrifice are so crucial to effective parenting, then it's important to understand what they look like. Self-denial for a parent does not mean denying any of the painful realities about himself or his family. In fact, *for a parent to "deny himself," he must first acknowledge what he has been denied by those closest to him.* He must recognize how others, in their foolishness and selfishness have often denied him the love and impact he deeply desires.

A parent practices biblical self-denial when he decides to allow these desires to go unfulfilled by others—a decision he can make only by choosing at the same time to trust Christ to meet his desires in the way and time He chooses. *Self-denial, therefore, is essentially a decision to approach others only with goals that reflect one's belief that Christ is sufficient to meet the deepest desires of the heart.* This decision involves both a mental shift and a behavioral change. Not only must the parent consciously relinquish any demand to have his desires met by others (especially his own children), but he must also stop pressuring them to come through for him.

Self-Sacrifice

Self-sacrifice requires a second decision that builds on the decision to deny oneself. Whereas self-denial is a decision to entrust the fulfillment of one's own desires to Christ (by no longer attempting to get them met by others), *self-sacrifice is the decision to take whatever personal risks are necessary to help another enter into a trust relationship with Christ.* Such risk-taking once again requires trusting Christ in the midst of any danger or pain that may arise. The act of "taking up one's cross daily," then, is something that can occur only in relationships. It is a decision to continually pursue whatever will promote deeper relationship with Christ in others, no matter what the personal cost may be.

The five concentric circles in figure 9 represent different levels of relational pain a parent may experience as she risks loving her teen sacrificially.

FIGURE 9
LEVELS OF PARENTAL PAIN

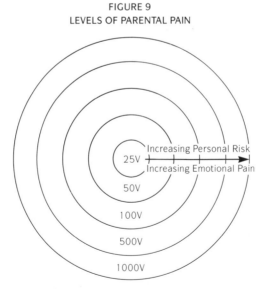

Imagine that relational pain can be measured in volts, like electrical shock, and notice that the very inner circle represents the smallest risk, only 25 volts. As a parent takes greater risks, she moves into the outer circles that threaten from 50 to 1000 volts of pain.

More often than not, by the time a person is the parent of a teenager, she has mastered a style of relating that exposes her to no more than the lowest levels of relational pain (25 or 50 volts). Because healthy parenting of an adolescent requires a willingness to endure a great deal of disappointment and conflict in order to promote what is best for her child, a parent who is committed to avoiding any high-voltage risks will never be free to love in self-sacrificing ways. Instead, she'll depend on her own guarded style of relating to protect herself and approach her kids as a consumer. Her goal will be to keep them from giving her any high-voltage relational shocks.

The Apostle Paul often exposed himself to the highest voltage of pain in order to promote the welfare of others. In his second letter to the Corinthians, he taught that self-reliance (or flesh-dependent living) can only be relinquished through taking risks that would destroy us if Christ were not there to protect us:

> We do not want you to be uninformed, brothers, about the hardships we suffered in the province of Asia. We were under great pressure, far beyond our ability to endure, so that we despaired even of life. Indeed, in our hearts we felt the sentence of death. But this happened that we might not rely on ourselves but on God, who raises the dead. He has delivered us from such a deadly peril, and he will deliver us. On him we have set our hope that he will continue to deliver us.
>
> (2 Corinthians 1:8-10)

Paul seemed to be banking on two promises from God as he lived his life boldly. Every parent must bank on the same two promises if she's going to take the high voltage, self-sacrificial risks that parenting a teen requires. First, she must believe that God has built her to take up to a thousand volts of pain without losing what is vital for her strength and joy as a person. Second, she must trust that God will never allow more than a thousand volts to come into her life at one time.

A parent who believes in these promises and acts on them, relates to her teen with a high degree of confidence and self-sacrifice. A parent who doesn't, relates to her teen with a high degree of fearfulness and self-protectiveness. The way a parent chooses to relate to her teen determines the level of influence she will have in his life. *The greater the level of voltage she risks for her teen's benefit, the greater the level of influence she will have as a parent.*

The parent who practices self-denial and self-sacrifice is on the road to changing from the inside out. Only the parent who travels this road will know how to respond effectively when her teen starts to travel down the wrong road. And the way she responds will be a powerful influence toward holiness in her child's life.

SUMMING IT UP

Warning! If you are operating in the consumer model, do not trust your own instincts when you go to respond to your teen. The probability will be too great that what seems like the right thing to do will be motivated by fear and misdirected goals. Chances are, too, that your responses will not be helpful to your teen. Parents who have not begun to shift their model of parenting are at a decided disadvantage. They are not free to regulate their responses on the basis of what will promote the ultimate well-being of their child. Their own interests too often take precedence and dictate responses that do not take into account the needs of their adolescent.

A parent who is operating in the ministry model can start to trust his own instincts. His dependency on Christ and goals of ministry allow him to think about and move toward his adolescent in fundamentally new ways—loving and self-sacrificing ways. He can stop asking the question, "What *should* I do with my teen?" and begin asking the question, "What do I *want* to do with my teen?" What he comes to want for his teen starts to parallel what God wants for him. Imagine the confidence and freedom parenting in the ministry model affords.

PART THREE

SKILL
*What a Parent of an
Adolescent Must Do*

SEVEN

Developing the Kind of Relationship with an Adolescent That Can Weather Conflict

Sitting before me was a very intelligent and sincere father of a seventeen-year-old girl. The question he posed seemed very reasonable to him: Would I speak to the parents of his daughter's boyfriend, without letting on that he had talked to me, about their decision not to let their son date his daughter anymore?

"If you're so concerned about their decision," I asked, "why don't you talk to them yourself?"

"Oh, I could never do that," the father replied. "That might only make things worse for my daughter and her boyfriend."

Still not getting it, I inquired, "How could it make things worse? They're not even allowed to see each other now."

"Yes, but now they can at least sneak out and see each other secretly. If I talked to his parents directly, they might get wise and start keeping closer tabs on their son."

With a hint of shock in my voice, I asked, "Are you comfortable with them sneaking out like that?"

"Oh, no. That's why I was hoping you would talk to his parents. If they could only see what they were doing, maybe they'd change their minds and not force Lisa and Robert to be dishonest. I don't think it's a healthy situation for them to be seeing each other that way, do you?"

For the first time, I sensed a little impatience or anger in his voice. Obviously, he saw no logical reason why I wouldn't want to help his daughter and her boyfriend out of this dilemma.

"There is another alternative, another way to get Lisa and Robert out of this unhealthy situation," I said. "If you'd be interested . . ."

"Of course I would!" the father cut in. "I'd be interested in doing anything that would help my daughter."

"Well, here's my suggestion. You talk to Lisa and Robert. Tell them you're uncomfortable with them seeing each other under these circumstances, and offer to go with Robert to talk to his parents about the situation. Maybe after you hear things from his parents' perspective, and they from yours, a mutual agreement could be reached. Meanwhile, ask Lisa and Robert to suspend all of their dating activities."

When I made this suggestion, I knew the father was perfectly capable of coming up with such a plan on his own. He didn't need my help because he was missing the intellectual ability to make a wise decision. He needed my help because he had a blind spot. For some reason, something inside him was keeping him from seeing all the alternatives clearly. I suspected my suggestion would strike a chord of terror in him. His response confirmed my suspicions.

"That is out of the question!" he said. "It would never work. The risks are too great."

"Can you help me understand what the risks are?" I said, hoping he would accept an invitation to talk about the terror.

"Kevin, you just don't understand what my daughter would do if she was forced to give up this boyfriend. Especially if she thought it was my fault."

"What do you think she'd do?" I said.

"She'd probably never talk to me again." As he spoke that sentence, I could hear the deep fear and hurt in his voice.

"You're really afraid of losing her, aren't you?"

"I feel like I'm this close." His eyes filled with tears as he held up his fingers, showing me how close he felt he was to losing her. "I think she'd hate me if I did anything to break up her and Robert. She's capable of going stone-cold on me for weeks on end even if I cross her a little bit. For something like this, she may never speak to me again."

It was obvious that this father was allowing himself to be emotionally blackmailed by his own daughter. In the face of conflict, she had learned that by withdrawing relationship from her father she could get him to back off and let her have her own way. He had come to the conclusion that a good relationship with his daughter depended on avoiding all conflict with her, even if it meant letting an unhealthy situation continue.

There is nothing like conflict between a parent and a teen for exposing the true nature and condition of their relationship. When their relationship is shallow or underdeveloped, conflict results in hardening and hostility toward each other. But when a deep relationship has been pursued and cultivated, conflict can result in mutual growth and understanding.

RESPONDING TO CONFLICT

Many parents discover that the kind of relationship they have with their teen is not sufficient to weather the conflict that often must be faced during adolescence. When conflict arises, a parent can respond in one of three ways. He can, as Lisa's dad did, *regard the conflict as the real threat to his relationship with his teen.* By doing this, he makes avoiding conflict with his teen his top priority, which results in the kind of conditional involvement and compromised responsiveness that fuel a relationship's deterioration. On the surface, enough relational harmony can be maintained to at least temporarily quiet the parent's fears, but at work underneath is a destructive dependency on maintaining relational harmony for his own well-being.

A second response a parent can choose is to *use the conflict to maintain distance in the relationship.* The parent regards the conflict as an ally that gives him the excuse and means to keep his teen at bay. Whenever he senses potential for the relationship to improve or deepen, he creates conflict. Of course, this also creates an environment low in parental involvement and responsiveness — the kind of environment that keeps the intimacy, which threatens the parent, from growing.

A third way a parent can use conflict is *to identify and address the weaknesses it exposes in his character and in his teen's.* This parent always makes deepening his relationship with his teen a priority, although not his highest priority. He doesn't depend on his relationship

SKILL: WHAT A PARENT MUST DO

with his teen or on conflict to promote his own well-being. Instead, he views them both as means for promoting a deeper, richer relationship with Christ in his teen, which is the parent's highest priority. As a result, when conflict occurs, he uses it as an opportunity to become more deeply involved with his teen and more responsive to the needs, both in himself and in his teen, that the conflict exposes. He doesn't enjoy conflict, but he doesn't fear it either. Instead, he welcomes it as a learning experience. He knows that, handled properly, conflict can be used to strengthen his relationship with his teen and cultivate maturity in both of them.

Each of these three uses of conflict can be plotted on a scale of relational maturity (see figure 10). Notice that the way conflict is handled, not the conflict itself, moves a parent to one extreme of relational immaturity or the other.

FIGURE 10

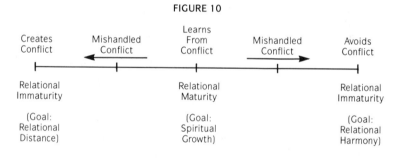

If parents are to use conflict with their teen to promote spiritual growth, they need to know what healthy conflict is, how to build a relationship that can withstand it, and how to build a bridge to a resistant adolescent. The result will be a style of parenting that is characterized by unconditional involvement and uncompromised responsiveness.

HANDLING CONFLICT WITH TEENS

There is probably no better example in Scripture of handling conflict than Nehemiah. Although the book of Nehemiah isn't about parenting *per se,* Nehemiah faced a challenge very similar to the one parents of teens face today—helping a disillusioned group of people find a new way to live when everything they'd trusted in had failed them.

In Nehemiah 5, we get a glimpse of the kind of relationship Nehemiah had built with the people he was called to "parent." Conflict broke out among Nehemiah's charges, and they were abusing and mistreating each other (Nehemiah 5:1-5). Some decided to bring their complaints to Nehemiah. His first response was the same one parents today often have toward conflict in their families: "When I heard their outcry and these charges, I was very angry" (Nehemiah 5:6).

Remember that Nehemiah really had his hands full. He had given up a very prestigious position as a cupbearer to the king of Persia and had taken great risks to travel hundreds of miles to help these people. As he led the project to rebuild the walls of their city and deliver them from further disgrace and ridicule at the hands of their enemies, he was making a lot of personal sacrifices. He surely would have appreciated a little cooperation and gratitude from those he labored for, but that was not to be. Instead, many of them came to him complaining about abuse and mistreatment at the hands of their own "brothers," or countrymen. Perhaps their complaint was even directed at Nehemiah himself and the way he was running things.

In the midst of this conflict, we see a very healthy "parent" in operation, a parent who stops himself before he nonreflectively reacts and, instead, responds to conflict in a way that deepens relationships and maturity among his followers. Nehemiah demonstrates several characteristics of healthy conflict management. First, he encourages emotional vulnerability when those in his "family" are hurt and angry. Next, he allows the pain and troubling events that surface in their complaints to impact him. Third, he takes initiative in the midst of the conflict to immediately relieve whatever parts of their suffering he can. Fourth, he takes initiative in the wake of the conflict to relate to them in a way that takes into account the needs and wounds the conflict exposed. Finally, he gets the fuel to face conflict from Christ rather than from those under his charge.

Encouraging Vulnerability

We read in verse 6 how Nehemiah listened to the people's "outcry" even though it made him angry or uncomfortable at first. It is never easy for a leader to permit others to be honest about their feelings, especially when he has a lot invested in them. When they are honest and open about how they feel, the leader will almost always feel attacked. Their complaints feed the sense of inadequacy and failure with which every leader or parent struggles. This is why it is all too easy for parents of teens to allow themselves to react automatically with contempt when their sons or daughters express hurt and anger. To do so, however, discourages emotional vulnerability and teaches the adolescent that Mom and Dad value comfort over truth, their own well-being over others'.

Nehemiah encouraged vulnerability in the midst of conflict. By nondefensively listening to what others had to say when they were angry, he allowed the conflict to bring to the surface what was really troubling those he loved. This put him in a position in which he could become more involved and respond more appropriately to them.

I remember one mother and father who asked my help to get at what was troubling their adolescent son. I spent several hours over several months getting to know Chad and listening to what was really bothering him. He showed signs of severe depression, and although he spoke openly to me about most of the things that angered and hurt him, he wouldn't let me schedule a meeting for him to share any of these things with his parents.

As I tried to determine why he was reluctant to talk openly with his parents, I began to discover a great fear he had about being emotionally vulnerable with anyone, especially with his mother. He recalled that, as he grew up, the unwritten rule in his home was "Never get Mom upset." The only times he ever experienced angry words or looks from his dad were when he broke that rule. Somehow he got the message that people were fragile and that conflict, hurt, or angry feelings would permanently hurt or destroy them. As a result, Chad learned to hold everything in. Now, as an adolescent, when everything and everybody in life seemed to be hurting him and making him angry, he felt helpless to do anything about it. To say anything would mean to break the rule and hurt others, something that was never permissible according to what he'd learned from his parents. His only recourse seemed to be to keep it all in and give up on anything ever being different. This decision was what was making him sick.

When I tried to share some of these things with his parents, they got very angry at me. "Do you mean," the mother asked indignantly, "that he thinks we would get upset at him if he told us how he was feeling?!" "Yes," I replied. "I suppose he fears getting the same kind of response I am getting right now."

These parents claimed they wanted to hear what was troubling their son, but not if hearing it made them feel uncomfortable or ashamed. Adolescents often get these kinds of double messages from their parents. On one hand, they are told they can tell their parents anything. On the other hand, they experience something akin to persecution if they say anything that sounds the least bit critical. Such double messages might succeed in keeping conflict to a minimum, as it did in this family, but in the long term it prevents the relationship and the maturity level of the family members from deepening.

Allowing Impact
Nehemiah took time to find out all the troubling details of the people's complaints. Not only did he listen, but he "pondered them in [his] mind" (Nehemiah 5:7) and let their full meaning really impact him. The implications of what really troubles people are usually great for the leader, because he often discovers that he contributed to the problem, or at least failed to do everything he could to protect his people from what caused their distress.

Conflict in the parent-teen relationship can give parents the same opportunity Nehemiah had—to not only hear about what troubles their kids, but to feel it with them and to understand what role they as parents might have had in causing it.

I have been with a good number of parents when they hear their kids describe details of painful events they've kept to themselves for years. I remember being with one father when his teenage daughter told him for the first time about being molested by a neighborhood boy years earlier. In so many ways, the daughter wanted her father to feel her pain and humiliation with her. She even wanted him to take some of the blame for failing to protect her from such things as a little girl. Instead, his response went like this, "Well, these things happen, you know. I suppose you know we're going to have to tell your mother. Don't worry about her. I know how we can tell her so she won't get too upset. You know she might be mad that you didn't tell her before."

Afterward, as I talked alone with the daughter, I asked her how she felt now that she had told her dad. "Worse than before," she said. "Why's that?" I asked. "Because he acted like it was no big deal. Like it wasn't even important that that guy made me hurt so bad and feel so dirty." She told me that when she told her youth leader at church he cried with her and hugged her. What a sad contrast to her dad's response. When she told him, he handled it matter-of-factly and turned his attention to how they could prevent a scene with her mother.

A traumatic event can cause adolescents intense pain at two different times: when it occurs, and when they tell their parents about it. When Nehemiah's people told him the details of their pain, he felt it with them. He didn't add to it or drive it back underground. He controlled the anger he felt and allowed their pain to move him to appropriate action.

It is in the midst of conflict that some of an adolescent's most important wounds, hurts, and disappointments surface. A parent who is ready, not only to allow these to come out, but also to let them deeply move him, is using conflict in one of the most beneficial ways possible.

Relieving Suffering

As soon as conflict erupts and people have an opportunity to air their complaints and hurt feelings, their eyes turn to the leader to see what kind of action he will take. When he initiates no action—or attempts only to relieve himself of the immediate discomfort caused by the conflict—he discourages his people. They will respond either by creating more conflict in hopes of evoking a more satisfactory response, or they'll distance themselves even further in the relationship, convinced nothing they say or do will ever move their leader.

Adolescents, like the people Nehemiah led, are capable of enduring a lot of disappointment and hardship in their worlds. In fact, for an adolescent whose environment is populated largely by other disappointed and unstable adolescents, relational betrayal and disillusionment are inevitable. There is nothing a parent can do to prevent this. The problem comes, however, when kids are exposed to as great or greater doses of relational tension inside the home as they are outside. This, parents can do a lot to prevent.

When family conflict involves an adolescent, it can alert the parents to where unnecessary and excessive relational tensions exist for the teen within the family. When parents take initiative to relieve these tensions as soon as they become aware of them, much of the adolescent's energy can be redirected toward the more important tasks of understanding how to live in a world that is hostile and unpredictable. This was the very thing Nehemiah's initiatives accomplished for the folks he led.

Listen to the actions Nehemiah took after he'd allowed the people's plight to penetrate his awareness:

> I pondered them in my mind and then accused the nobles and officials. I told them, "You are exacting usury from your own countrymen!" So I called together a large meeting to deal with them. . . . They kept quiet, because they could find nothing to say. So I continued, "What you are doing is not right. Shouldn't you walk in the fear of our God . . . ? I and my brothers and my men are also lending the people money and grain. But let the exacting of usury stop! Give back to them immediately their fields, vineyards, olive groves and houses, and also the usury you are charging them. . . ." "We will give it back," they said. "And we will not demand anything more from them. We will do as you say." (Nehemiah 5:7-12)

Nehemiah was highly responsive to the immediate needs of his people and proved they could depend on him to relieve whatever stress in their lives he could.

It is incredible how often parents fail to take initiative in conflicts with their teens. Such was the case with one couple who came to me asking what they should do with their fourteen-year-old daughter who kept picking fights with her mother. The problem had become so severe that the mother would lock herself in her own bedroom from the time Gina came home from school until the girl's father arrived home from work about two hours later. The mother figured this was the only way she could avoid a violent argument with her daughter every afternoon.

As I probed for more details about the situation, I learned that the arguments always seemed to involve Gina's relationship to her younger brother or older sister. Either she was disrupting something one of them was trying to do, or she was verbally attacking her mother for doing something for one of her siblings that she hadn't done for her. When I pointed out this common theme to the parents, they didn't act surprised. They said they had noticed it, but they had no idea what to do about it. I suspect they had no idea what to do about it because their goal had not been to get to the root of what was bothering their daughter (which conflict always offers the opportunity to do). Instead, their goal had been to restore equilibrium in the house in order to stave off a second nervous breakdown for the mother. But they had no idea how to accomplish this, since everything they'd tried only made matters worse.

Any initiative the mother and father would take following a violent outburst with Gina was solely designed to relieve their suffering (e.g., a punishment to make Gina think twice about causing more trouble or a bribe to get her to quit claiming she wasn't getting something her brother and sister were getting). Any initiative designed to really address the girl's core complaint had been ignored.

I asked the parents, "Looking beneath all your daughter's actions and words, she seems to be crying out with one core concern: 'I am not loved by you two, especially Mom, like my brother and sister are.' Could there be any truth to what she's expressing?"

As I posed this question, I noticed they sheepishly looked at each other. The father was first to respond: "There probably is. You see, Kevin, from the very beginning Gina has been a very difficult child to raise. When she was very young, she had some learning difficulties and some problems with hyperactivity. My wife has always been the kind of person who needs to have everything ordered and predictable. But with Gina around, unlike our other two kids, it was impossible for my wife to keep things ordered and predictable. In fact, we're pretty sure stress from raising Gina caused my wife's first breakdown. That's why she tries to spend as little time around Gina as possible."

The more I discovered about the situation, the more I could understand what Gina was trying to say through her actions. Her parents were failing her in two ways. First, they were failing to let her be emotionally vulnerable about her core complaint. Every time she tried to tell them how she felt, they treated it as an "unpleasantness" that was just part of her personality. They ignored her, changed the subject, or sent her away. They were unknowingly putting her in a position in which she had to grow more and more violent to get her message across.

Second, they were failing to take any initiative that addressed her core complaint or relieved the pain she was feeling. The fact was, she was *not* being loved equally or treated fairly. It could have been a great relief for Gina just to hear her parents acknowledge this. "Yes, Honey, there is a problem. How you feel is something we understand and care deeply about. Mom has some problems of her own that are making it hard for you. We're going to do something about them. In the meantime, let's talk about what kinds of things are making it difficult for you here at home, and what we can do about them."

Dealing with conflict by deepening relationship in this way is not something that comes naturally to parents operating in the consumer model. They approach conflict with the question, *"What should I do in the light of the distress and discomfort I feel?"* Parents in the ministry model approach conflict from an entirely different angle. They ask, *"What do I want to do for my child in the light of the distress and discomfort she feels?"*

Altering Relational Style
Just as Nehemiah learned through conflict what troubled his people, he also learned what it would take to be a fundamentally different kind of "parent" to them.

> Moreover, . . . when I was appointed to be their governor . . . neither I nor my brothers ate the food allotted to the governor. But the earlier governors—those preceding me—placed a heavy burden on the people. . . . Their assistants also lorded it over the people. But out of reverence for God I did not act like that. Instead, I devoted myself to the work on this wall. . . . I never demanded the food allotted to the governor, because the demands were heavy on these people. (Nehemiah 5:14-16,18)

Nehemiah realized how those he loved had been wounded in previous relationships, and he resolved before God to relate to them in a fundamentally different way. Conflict then became a great opportunity for him to gain the knowledge he needed to lead his people "according to their need," on the basis of what would promote their health and welfare (Ephesians 4:29).

One day in a heated discussion with my daughter about why I wasn't permitting her to do something with one of her friends, she blurted out how lonely and friendless she felt. Some of it she blamed on me for not being friendly to her friends when she brought them to the house. What I heard about how she and her friends perceived me really pained me. Of course, my first response was to get defensive and in effect punish my daughter for her emotional vulnerability. But, I caught myself before I went too far in that direction. As painful as it was, I decided I wanted to learn from Christi. I wanted to learn how I could be a friend to her friends, how I could be a fundamentally different kind of person in relating to teenagers.

As I listened to Christi, I began to hear a lot of pain about how she and her friends had often been treated by adults (i.e., teachers, parents, etc.). She talked about Kathy, one adult friend of our family who treated her like "a real person," and how that made her feel important and alive.

I knew I wasn't entirely responsible for her feeling alone and insignificant, but I knew I was partly responsible. I made a resolution in my heart not to be like her "earlier governors," approaching her with the same selfish demands. I made it a goal to relate to her in a way that communicated a deeper level of acceptance to her and her friends. I chose to be less hurried around them, focused my attention on listening to them more, and looked for opportunities to affirm anything positive I could see in their lives. This was quite a contrast to the "busy pastor" they encountered in the halls at church.

When leaders or parents decide to use conflicts in this way, they become drained. That's why it's important to understand one last characteristic of healthy conflict management, which is seen in Nehemiah's life.

Drawing on Spiritual Resources

Parents and teachers are often left feeling unappreciated and drained in the wake of conflict, even when they have handled the conflict constructively. Notice how Nehemiah found the fuel to go on, following the events in Nehemiah 5: "Remember me with favor, O my God, for all I have done for these people" (5:19).

Nehemiah could have never found enough "favor" in the eyes of those he led to keep going. The impact even good leadership has on people is not enough to satisfy the longings of a leader or parent's heart. In the end, Nehemiah had to find his fuel for living from his relationship with God, and from the impact he knew his self-denial and self-sacrifice had on Him.

We see the same example set by Christ in the Garden of Gethsemane on the eve of His crucifixion (Matthew 26:36-45). Christ asked those closest to Him for just a little support as He reflected upon and prepared Himself for the greatest act of self-denial and self-sacrifice the world would ever know. But His disciples fell asleep, leaving Him to bear His anguish alone.

It certainly isn't wrong for a dad or a mom or a Christian leader to ask for some secondary support from those closest to them. Christ certainly did. But He didn't depend on them for the primary support or strength to "take up His cross" and sacrifice Himself for those He loved. When they failed Him, He didn't turn His simple request for support into demands. He didn't turn back and take a less difficult or less painful path, and He didn't go it alone as a martyr, either. He turned to His Father, as Nehemiah did, to find the strength to lay down His life for an unappreciative but hurting people.

Parents of teens won't be able to face conflict in their family and use it to cultivate maturity and deeper relationships unless they, too, regularly find strength from God to endure loneliness and pain. Living with teens and dealing honestly with conflicts as they arise result in both. Perhaps this is why so many parents opt to let their relationships with their kids deteriorate once they reach adolescence. Part of the price of healthy relationships is the anguish of enduring conflict, something parents cannot face for very long without humbling themselves and asking God for the strength they lack. When parents humble themselves in this way, they are strengthened by the hope and assurance that nothing (not even conflict or the threat of losing those they love most) can rob them of what they need to ultimately experience all they long for from God (1 Peter 1:3-6).

BUILDING RELATIONSHIPS WITH TEENS

Just how can parents build relationships with their teens that can weather conflict?

I believe that strong relationships are always developed through increasing levels of involvement. Careful study of Nehemiah's ministry to the disappointed people in Jerusalem reveals gradual deliberate steps by which he slowly got involved and developed his relationships with them. Parents who build strong and lasting relationships with their kids get involved with them on the same levels Nehemiah did with his people. They begin with involvement on an intellectual level and progress to the deeper levels: material, empathetic, dynamic, and prolonged.

In figure 11 I've diagrammed these levels in the order I believe they must occur. Parents who try to get involved with their teens often attempt to jump to the advanced levels without developing the simpler ones first. Their kids often recoil because they're not comfortable with being involved at more intense levels until time has been taken to cultivate mutual involvement at more superficial levels. Parents who try to push into their teens' lives too deeply too fast will only be frustrated.

I believe many parents fail to deepen their level of involvement with their kids because of the increased risk of pain each successive level offers. Each concentric circle in figure 11 represents a different level of involvement parents can cultivate with adolescents. The earlier levels aren't as threatening to parents because the involvement is less personal and requires less intimacy. The later levels, however, carry the threat of "high-voltage" pain for parents because they require increasing vulnerability and intimacy. Kids sense this too and therefore resist involvement at the later levels until they're certain their parents don't have hostile or selfish purposes.

Notice also in the diagram how each successive level of involvement requires an increasing output of energy from the parents. Involvement with teens is draining. And it will never seem like a wise or desirable way for parents to focus their energies as long as their goal is to find self-fulfillment. The more energy parents pour into their teen, the more energy they can see is still needed. Parents who are highly involved with their teen can go for years without experiencing any noticeable appreciation or return on their investment. Maintaining long-term intensive involvement is possible only when the parents are pursuing ministry goals that do not demand visible behavior changes in the adolescent.

FIGURE 11
LEVELS OF PARENT-TEEN INVOLVEMENT

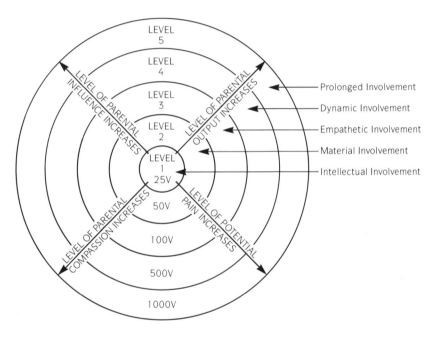

The two other consequences of increasing involvement in an adolescent's life are positive and rewarding. As a parent's level of involvement increases, so do his levels of compassion and influence. When he starts to lose patience and compassion toward his adolescent, deeper involvement is the only antidote. Compassion for an adolescent can be developed only through a deeper awareness of his unmet desires and failed plans. And this kind of awareness can only be cultivated through personal involvement with the teen. Notice how involvement with people made Jesus aware of their needs and filled Him with compassion toward them. Matthew writes,

Jesus went through all the towns and villages, teaching in their synagogues, preaching the good news of the kingdom and healing every disease and sickness. When he saw the crowds, he had compassion on them, because they were harassed and helpless, like sheep without a shepherd.   (Matthew 9:35-36)

The more a parent is filled with compassion for his teen, the more he wants to get involved with him. Involvement fuels compassion, and compassion fuels greater involvement. And as a parent's involvement increases, so does his influence. Kids tend to watch, follow, and imitate the people who are most involved in their lives.

Let's take a closer look at each level of involvement a parent can pursue.

Level One: Intellectual Involvement

A parent becomes intellectually involved when he develops an awareness and appreciation of his teen's circumstances, particularly the troubling ones. Observe how Nehemiah cultivates this level of involvement with his Jewish brothers:

Hanani, one of my brothers, came from Judah with some other men, and I questioned them about the Jewish remnant that survived the exile. . . . When I heard these things [the painful circumstances they were in], I sat down and wept. For some days I mourned and fasted and prayed before the God of heaven.   (Nehemiah 1:2,4)

Notice several characteristics of intellectual involvement. First, it can be achieved without living in the exact same circumstances as the other person. Nehemiah became intellectually involved with his brothers even though they resided hundreds of miles away in quite different circumstances. In the same way, believers in one nation can be intellectually involved with mission workers in another nation. And parents can be intellectually involved with their teens, even though they spend most of their waking hours in a school building, enmeshed in a culture quite foreign to anything the parents are experiencing.

Notice also Nehemiah's greatest tool in becoming intellectually involved with the people he would later lead: a burning curiosity to know what they were experiencing. This drove Nehemiah to seek out the troubling details of their lives. *A curiosity about what their kids are experiencing at school, in their relationships, and in their families is the best tool parents have in starting to get involved with their kids.* If their kids will not volunteer information about themselves at first, parents may have to start by reading, or asking others, for information about teenagers.

The wholesome curiosity I'm referring to is something quite different from morbid preoccupation, however. When a parent slips into the consumer model, his curiosity to know his teen better can easily be transformed into an obsessive need to know everything the teen is thinking and doing. The goal of this kind of parent actually is not to know his teen better, but to protect himself from any surprises or potential embarrassments the teen may cause. He is incapable of asking open, caring questions of his son or daughter and, instead, resorts to interrogating, intimidating, and intruding on his teen's privacy in order to get his information. The end result is decreased awareness and involvement because the adolescent finds it necessary to back away and hide most of what he's going through in order to keep his parent calmed.

Another tool Nehemiah used to be intellectually involved with others was prayer. Prayer that identifies with the troubling circumstances of another and brings them before God should never be underestimated. There is something unique about how a parent who is involved in praying for his kids relates to them, especially in his level of compassion. The Apostle Paul seldom stopped at just praying for those he was involved with. He often told people exactly what and how he was praying for them, which deepened his intellectual involvement with them even more.

One last feature of intellectual involvement has to do with its impact on parents. Even though it is only the starting place toward deeply meaningful involvement, it is a level that can evoke powerful reactions. Nehemiah was visibly and forcefully impacted by what he learned of his Jewish brothers' circumstances.

I believe it is virtually impossible for parents of an adolescent to become intellectually involved in their child's world without being forcefully moved, as Nehemiah was, to weep, pray, and then get more involved. What an adolescent has to face and endure on almost a daily basis is incredible. Many parents don't take the time to get curious about what life looks like through their adolescent's eyes. In failing to do so, they miss the only doorway there is to deep and meaningful involvement in their teen's life.

Level Two: Material Involvement
When a parent pursues the level of material involvement with her adolescent, she takes tangible steps to help her teen experience dignity and love in the midst of whatever painful circumstances the teen is in. It took Nehemiah four or five months after he became intellectually involved with the troubled people back in Jerusalem before he could find a way to become materially involved with them. Nehemiah 2:1-5 records how he sought an opportunity for material involvement through returning to lead them in rebuilding their broken city walls.

> I took the wine and gave it to the king. I had not been sad in his presence before; so the king asked me, "Why does your face look so sad when you are not ill? This can be nothing but sadness of heart." I was very much afraid, but I said to the king, ... "Why should my face not look sad when the city where my fathers are buried lies in ruins, and its gates have been destroyed by fire?" The king said to me, "What is it you want?" Then I prayed to the God of heaven, and I answered the king, "If it pleases the king ... , let him send me to the city ... so that I can rebuild it."

Nehemiah's example shows that material involvement is not just random acts of kindness done to help others feel better. Rather, it is purposeful acts of kindness done for others to communicate to them how they are still loved and valued by God. This is why it's impossible for someone to become involved with another on this level without first becoming intellectually involved. It is only after developing an awareness of what others are experiencing that a person has some idea of where and how God's love and presence can be expressed to them in a meaningful way. Nehemiah came to Jerusalem as God's representative to deliberately "promote the welfare of the Israelites" (2:10), not just to help them feel better.

Many parents of teens may mistakenly think they have reached this level of involvement when they provide for their kids basic material needs or give them whatever they ask for. However, such provisons that are given routinely or as a matter of duty often fail to communicate real involvement.

Take, for example, the mother who came home to find her sixteen-year-old daughter sitting in a depressed heap on the couch. "What's wrong?" she asked. Her daughter replied, "I'm the only girl in the whole school who doesn't have a date to homecoming this weekend." "Oh, is that it?" the mom countered. "I know what will make you feel better. Come on, get your coat on. We're going shopping."

I suspect the mother's actions did little to promote her daughter's awareness of still being loved and valued by God despite her snobbish behavior that prevented her from having a date. Perhaps she'll even view her mother's attempt to cheer her up with a pretty new dress as confirmation of all the lies she has been believing about herself. "What kind of person am I that people have to feel sorry for me before they want to do something special for me?"

If the mother had become curious about how this event was affecting her daughter, she might have gotten more information before she responded. In fact, she might have found out her daughter had turned down three guys who had invited her to homecoming in hopes of being asked by one of the cuter boys in school. And she might have found out that as her daughter was slumping on the couch, she was feeling real despair over her own foolishness. She was thinking how cruel and unfair she had been to the other three boys, and how she was just getting what she deserved for being so snobbish.

With this kind of knowledge the mother could have made a material gesture that would have communicated God's perspective to her daughter. She could have said, "You know, honey, I'm really proud of the way you're taking an honest look at yourself through all of this. I know it's hard, and I don't think many people would be willing to do it. By the way, I would really like to spend the weekend with you. I love you even when you act like a snob. I want to spend time with you. How about staying home with me? We'll find something to do together.

We can also talk about rebuilding your dating life."

There are probably a dozen legitimate ways the mother could have responded to become materially involved with her daughter. As long as the mother's goal was to help her daughter in some tangible way to feel the positive impact her life could still have, she would have promoted her sense of dignity. And if her goal was to help her daughter become aware of the love that was still available to her, she would have promoted her sense of being a person worthy of love.

A parent who is looking for ways to become materially involved with her adolescent must exercise great patience for two reasons. One, she may have to remain intellectually involved for several months before she sees an opportunity to touch her teen deeply with an act of kindness. Two, it usually takes time for kids to open themselves for material involvement with their parents. A teen might turn down several invitations from his parents to do something meaningful with them before he accepts one. In the meantime, parents need to continue studying the situation as Nehemiah did (Nehemiah 2:11-18), looking for the right time and circumstances to offer material involvement.

Level Three: Empathetic Involvement

In the third level of involvement, the parent comes to understand the very personal forces (unmet desires and foolish plans) that motivate his teen to be who he is, and he responds to his teen with gentleness and empathy. This level of insight and involvement is rarely available to a parent until his teen feels accepted and safe enough in his presence to let down his defenses and give his parent a real glimpse of himself. That's why a parent must often remain materially involved with his adolescent for months before the door to even deeper involvement will open.

For example, if a dad will commit himself to spending long hours helping his son rebuild an engine in the garage, his son may eventually let him in to share the deeper realities of his life. As the father sacrifices his time in a tangible way to help his son feel confident and loved, his son may begin to hunger for his dad to know him more deeply. Part of what the son hungers for is help in areas of his life that confuse him far more than the disassembled engine does. However, laying his own broken parts before his dad is far more threatening to him than laying out the broken parts of the engine. As his father interacts with him over the broken engine, the son will be watching to see if it's safe to interact with his dad over the broken parts of his life as well. The people of Jerusalem finally came to the conclusion that it was safe to bare their hearts to Nehemiah after watching him deal with them for several months while they rebuilt the city together. Nehemiah earned the right to move to this deeper level of involvement with them by first cultivating involvement at the less intense levels. In Nehemiah 8:1-12, we see the first real opening of the Israelites' hearts, not only to Nehemiah and his men, but also to the Lord. As the people exposed their pain and sin, Nehemiah responded with the kind of gentleness and empathy that prepared the way for an even deeper level of involvement.

Level Four: Dynamic Involvement

When a parent enters the level of dynamic involvement with her teen, she can help him to make the inner shifts necessary to change the kind of person he is becoming (one bent on foolish strategies to find life apart from Christ). This level of involvement is rarely available to a parent who has not first done the demanding and tedious work of cultivating intellectual, material, and empathetic involvement with her teen.

How to cultivate involvement at the empathetic and dynamic levels will be the focus of the whole next chapter. Parents, it seems, have the least experience and expertise at getting involved with their kids at these levels. Some parents can get so good at understanding their kids' circumstances and helping them cope that they forget these levels of involvement are only means to a more important end: seeing their kids' lives transformed from the inside out.

It is to Nehemiah's credit that as a governor, architect, and engineer, he never lost sight of his most important role: pastoring his charges to a dynamic life change. Nehemiah 9 records one of the greatest revivals among God's people in all of the Bible. The core dynamic that drove these people to live their lives independent of God shifted. As a result of Nehemiah's involvement in their lives, they experienced a new dependence on God and radically changed the way they lived their lives.

Although parents must never expect that this kind of dynamic life change will come naturally or easily in their teens' lives, they must never fail to strive for it. When parents start to get involved in their kids' lives, even at the initial levels, they begin a process in which God can ultimately use their lives to transform their kids' lives. The most important rule is to never go back. Never retreat from involvement but always patiently look for opportunities to deepen it.

Level Five: Prolonged Involvement

The deepest level of involvement is really nothing more than a parent's commitment to stay involved with his teen at each of the first four levels until the teen reaches a point of maturity where he can do the same for others. We learn from Nehemiah's example that this can and will involve years of investment. Many years after he first heard of his fellow Jews' plight, Nehemiah was still dynamically involved, challenging the foolish and sinful ways of the same group of people (Nehemiah 13).

Some of the richest relationships I have are with adults I've been involved with since their high school years. When I look at the current lives and ministries of just a handful of these kids and see what kind of impact prolonged involvement can have in a life, I get excited about the privilege I have as a youthworker and as the dad of a teenager. The more involved I get in kids' lives, the greater my partnership is with God in helping them change in deep and lasting ways.

GETTING INVOLVED WITH A RESISTANT ADOLESCENT

When parents have failed to develop deepening levels of involvement with their child before he reaches adolescence, they will no doubt experience his resistance to their involvement after he becomes a teenager.

Parents who find themselves in this situation must realize that even an unwilling adolescent cannot totally block his parents' involvement at all levels. The more parents deliberately and gradually try to develop the levels in order, the more likely they'll be to find a crack in their teen's armor.

When a parent does encounter resistance, he must be careful to respect his teen's decisions. Although it's appropriate for the parent to express regret, he must never express anger or despair. To do so would be to demand something from his teen and depend on him in an unhealthy way. Accepting the teen's decision not to talk or spend time together is showing respect for him. The parent, however, must never stop asking for or offering involvement. When a parent's overtures for involvement spring from a desire to minister, it will be very difficult for a teen to keep up his resistance for long.

A parent should always use his adolescent's reluctance and discomfort at being involved with him as a mirror to look at his own relational style and parenting model. The teen may be reacting to impure motives in the parent that he himself is not even aware of. When a parent senses resistance in his teen, it is imperative that in a friendly way he call it to his teen's attention and bring it up for discussion. Many times his teen will explain what makes involvement difficult for him.

Ultimately, parents must remember what their adolescent longs for more than anything else: a relationship that will not fail him. When they offer him unconditional involvement at even the most superficial levels, it's very likely he'll eventually soften toward them and want more.

SUMMING IT UP

Unconditional involvement means involving yourself in your teen's life no matter what the climate or conditions are at the time. Often the climate will seem unfavorable or downright unpleasant. And involvement may often require enduring conflict. But when you choose to stay unconditionally involved with your teen, even when the going gets tough, he ultimately will come to feel deeply valued and loved.

Involvement with a teen, unlike a child, must be offered mostly on his terms, that is, mostly on his "turf." A parent must show interest in the things his teen is doing, thinking, and feeling. He must enter his teen's world and become a part of it, discuss with him the things that trouble and preoccupy him, communicating a desire to be with him as he experiences and decides how to live in his world.

This kind of involvement with a teen often requires parents to enter a world that is in many ways strange and unfamiliar to them, uncomfortable and perplexing to say the least. But unconditional involvement always requires parents to take this kind of initiative. Conditional involvement requires just the opposite. It forces the teen to come into the parents' world to find the involvement he longs for—and few adolescents are willing to do this for very long.

Maintaining and deepening your relationship with your teen, then, depends primarily on you and your initiatives to offer unconditional involvement, no matter what the cost.

EIGHT

Making Sense of an Adolescent's Behavior

Parents can't offer their adolescent unconditional involvement unless they first know who their son or daughter is on the inside. Most adolescents assume that no one, especially their parents, would want to be deeply involved with them if they knew what they really were like. Often an adolescent can't believe that others' involvement with him is unconditional until they get an inside look at him and still want to stay involved.

Because kids generally are afraid to directly expose themselves to others, parents normally get their best glimpse at who their adolescent is by becoming a student of his behavior. It is the adolescent's own words and actions that give parents a window into his heart. Therefore it's often only as parents learn to read beneath their adolescent's actions and words that they'll be able to understand their teen on a deep level and communicate unconditional love.

Roger was a high school student who had experienced very little involvement from his family as he grew up. He had chosen a style of relating while still very young that made it difficult for anyone in his family to really know him or get involved with him. At the age of six, Roger was molested by a baby-sitter and he kept it a secret from the family. Since it had occurred on several occasions and he had done nothing to stop it, he felt very ashamed about it. He blamed himself and believed that if anyone in his family found out he would lose their respect and love. To prevent this from happening, he chose to relate to his family as a quiet, good little boy who never gave them any cause to guess that "he was the kind of person who would permit his baby-sitter to do those awful things to him." Although quiet little boys who never do anything wrong do avoid most forms of negative attention, they miss out on most forms of positive attention as well. This was Roger's experience. Because he was quiet, he often felt ignored and left out of conversations and activities with his parents and five older siblings. This only reinforced his belief that deep inside he was the kind of person no one really wanted to be involved with.

Roger's family failed to see through his style of relating to all the fears and foolish assumptions that lay underneath. Roger's parents assumed his shyness was just an ordinary part of his personality. In fact, they kind of enjoyed the peace and quiet he contributed to the household, so they never challenged his shyness or encouraged him to express himself more openly. As Roger became an adolescent, his shyness no longer served him very well as a shield to ward off negative attention. In fact, it caused him severe social complications. He was unable to build good peer relationships, and his parents became increasingly critical of his shyness because it left them out of the life of the only child they had left at home. As Roger's shyness failed to win him the involvement with others he longed for, he felt more inadequate as a person, which only made him more shy. This gave his parents a second opportunity not only to recognize that all was not well with Roger, but to tune into Roger's fears. However, they failed to inquire about the causes of Roger's increasing shyness and allowed it to continue without challenging his underlying assumptions that he was a "disgusting" person whom no one could love.

Finally, Roger's isolation grew so great that he ventured outside his usual way of relating and let one of his youth leaders at church know that he wanted help. His youth leader sent him to me and we began spending time together each week finding out who the real Roger was. Eventually, Roger allowed me to involve his parents in the counseling, and for the first time the whole family started to make sense of Roger's shyness. As they did, they were able to genuinely offer Roger unconditional involvement for the first time. With a full knowledge of Roger's deepest and darkest secrets about the past, his parents could finally challenge Roger's assumptions about himself by demonstrating that getting an inside glimpse of him only increased their desire to be close to him.

FIVE SKILLS FOR UNDERSTANDING ADOLESCENTS

The purpose of this chapter is to equip parents to make the offer of unconditional involvement to their own teens. The book of Proverbs describes five basic skills that are essential to parents operating in the ministry model. These skills enable parents to discern "the need of the moment" in their teen and choose a response that will truly minister to that need.

Skill One: Redirecting a Parent's Goals Toward His Adolescent

> An unfriendly man pursues selfish ends;
>   he defies all sound judgment.
> A fool finds no pleasure in understanding
>   but delights in airing his own opinions.   (Proverbs 18:1-2)

Solomon identifies a perpetual danger every parent faces in his relationship with his teen—that of allowing "selfish" or foolish goals to distract him from ministering to his child as God intends. According to Proverbs 18:1, parents who allow the wrong goals to control them as they approach their teen will suffer two consequences. One, they will be perceived by their teen as "unfriendly." Two, they won't be able to make "sound judgments" about themselves or their child.

Parents who want to understand their teen and get more involved with him must learn how to recognize their foolish goals and shift them to goals of ministry.

Recognizing foolish goals. For a parent to recognize her foolish goals, she must first understand their nature and then be able to recognize when they are controlling her. *The main characteristic of a foolish goal is that it is easily thwarted.* What makes it foolish is its aim toward fulfilling a crucial desire that is outside the parent's ability to fulfill apart from God.

The foolish goal of a detached parent is to find fulfillment in life by escaping as much responsibility as possible for who her adolescent becomes. No matter how hard she tries to make this plan work, however, one of two things will always frustrate it. Either she will fail to drown out the nagging voice of her own conscience that instinctively holds her responsible for how her teen develops, or she will find life rather meaningless and empty because the route to a meaningful existence always requires intensifying relational commitments rather than escaping them.

The foolish goal of a relationally dependent parent is to find life by assuming all responsibility for who her adolescent becomes. This parent's plan will be blocked because she'll fail to exert enough control over her adolescent to make the child provide the sense of fulfillment she longs for.

The dutiful parent's foolish goal is to find life by trying to take responsibility for her kid's good qualities, while placing responsibility for the bad qualities on the kid's own shoulders. This goal, too, will eventually be foiled when the parent sees her teen's good qualities disappearing and the bad ones multiplying as the kid tries desperately to maintain a sense of identity and personal impact.

When a parent's goals are foolish, they are easily blocked by uncooperative adolescents. And blocked goals give the parent one of her best opportunities to recognize when she is still operating in the consumer model.

God has given each of us a "warning system" to alert us when we are pursuing a foolish goal. This system consists of a series of *signal emotions*[1] that reliably indicate the nature of the goal we are pursuing at any given moment. For example, the Apostle Paul admonished his readers to recognize their anger as a signal to alert them to potentially sinful attitudes and actions (Ephesians 4:26).

Signal emotions come in three categories, each of which signifies something different about the foolish goals a person is pursuing. The first category includes emotions that stem from anger, such as irritation, frustration, and contempt. When a person experiences one of these, it's often a sign that some foolish goal he is pursuing has been blocked. Something he considers crucial to his fulfillment is being withheld. *In a parent-teen relationship, a parent's anger toward his adolescent almost always signals the fact that the teen is blocking his parent's foolish goal.* No wonder James declares that "Man's anger does not bring about the righteous life that God desires" (James 1:20). When a parent approaches his adolescent with goals that often leave the parent frustrated, it is certain he's not pursuing the kinds of goals that will cultivate righteousness in his family.

Parents must make a careful distinction between goals and desires for their children. Although it is my desire that my daughter maintain at least a B average in school, keep her room neat, and pick up after herself, these things should never be my goals as a parent. If they are, I will be frustrated and angry if my daughter (who has total control of making these things happen) blocks them by not performing well.

Instead, I should express these things as desires, both to Christi and to God, and make it my goal to lovingly control my responses toward Christi when she fails to meet them. My goal should be to respond to her in a way that communicates unconditional involvement no matter how she responds to my requests. But I also want to be uncompromisingly responsive if she decides to ignore them (e.g., withdrawing privileges until my requests are honored).

To achieve such goals I need only control myself, not her, thus relieving the frustration I would experience if I tried to control her. At the same time, she will learn that she is the one responsible for controlling her impulses, not me. By making it my goal to consistently provide painful consequences for my daughter's disobedient or destructive choices, I provide the best environment for teaching her the necessity of self-control.

A second category of signal emotions a parent might experience stems from fear: anxiety, worry, pressure, and many forms of stress. These emotions usually signal a foolish goal whose attainment seems uncertain. Fear is usually an indication that a person has put her trust in someone or something for her fulfillment but is unsure that person or thing will deliver. *When a parent experiences some kind of fear around her adolescent, it indicates her reliance on a foolish plan to which the teen poses a threat.* The exception to this, of course, would be when a real threat of physical violence or harm exists. In this case, fear would be healthy and should lead a parent to seek physical protection for herself and her family (i.e., the police).

The third category of signal emotions stems from guilt. Shame, embarrassment, and self-pity are common examples. When a person experiences one of these without violating God's moral boundaries, it actually may be a signal that he's failed to reach one of his foolish goals. Since attaining a foolish goal carries with it a promise of life, failure to reach it can produce shame and despair in a person who has foolishly come to believe that finding fulfillment depends on his own efforts. A parent may experience guilt or shame when he feels like he's failed to be an ideal parent or when his kid has failed to be an ideal son or daughter.

When a parent's emotions signal that some goal she's pursuing is in jeopardy, she may respond by changing her goal, or by increasing her efforts to reach the same goal. Many parents automatically choose the second option simply because they're not aware of the goals they're pursuing. They know that certain events or circumstances evoke anger, fear, or guilt in them, but they don't take time to reflect on the underlying goals they have that might account for such reactions. Instead, they assume that anything they can do to get rid of their negative emotion must be the right thing, and they find relief simply by trying out a new way to reach the same goals.

Wise parents understand that negative emotions can tell them something very important about themselves. If a plan of theirs for finding fulfillment is being thwarted by their adolescent, they recognize their foolishness in trying to control what they can never control. *They allow their emotions to alert them to their need for some fundamental changes in what they are pursuing.*

Even pursuits that seem to parents to be in their adolescent's best interest can be based on foolish goals. For example, although it should be every parent's desire to see his child become a godly person, it must never become part of a parent's strategy for finding life. If it does, it shifts his center of dependence away from Christ and onto his child or on his abilities to raise his child a certain way. *A parent can maintain a deep desire to see his kid turn out well without making his own life and fulfillment dependent on whether it happens or not.* Wise parents make it their goal to stay in the ministry model no matter what kind of person their adolescent becomes. They understand that *life does not depend on the results of their parenting, but in whom they trust as they parent.*

Shifting misplaced dependencies. Once a parent has recognized her foolish goals, it is important that she acknowledge them as sins against God. God's forgiveness is always available to those who confess their sins and seek God's help to change (1 John 1:9). For a parent to confess her sin, however, she must first understand where the sinful goals are coming from. *Beneath every foolish goal or choice are unmet desires that a parent is seeking to fulfill through someone or something other than God.* Once a parent can trace her foolish goals to deep unmet desires that never have been and never will be fulfilled by anyone but God, she is in a position to deeply repent. Notice what the prophet Hosea indicates is involved in real repentance. He writes,

Return, O Israel, to the LORD your God.
　　Your sins have been your downfall!
Take words with you
　　and return to the LORD. [A shift in focus.]
Say to him:
　　"Forgive all our sins
　　and receive us graciously,
　　that we may offer the fruit of our lips. [A shift in goals.]
Assyria cannot save us;
　　we will not mount war-horses.
We will never again say 'Our gods'
　　to what our own hands have made,
　　for in you the fatherless find compassion. [A shift in center
　　　　of dependence.]"　　　　　　　　　　　(Hosea 14:1-3)

Hosea identifies repentance as a shift in what a person is ultimately depending on for life, in where she is seeking satisfaction for her deepest desires for "compassion" or unfailing love. This person stops using her own foolish plans or "what [her] own hands have made" to gain "compassion" for herself. Instead, she brings her deepest need to God and entrusts it to Him for satisfaction. This kind of repentance is never a one-time act for a reflective parent. She must repeatedly shift her center of dependence as she makes the effort to respond to her adolescent in the ministry model.

Choosing a new goal. After a parent has shifted her dependence from herself to God, she is free to pursue entirely different goals as she relates to her teen—goals that will free her to function as a biblical parent. Not only will her actions minister to her teen, but the attitudes of her heart will also.

Notice in figure 12 the two criteria for determining whether or not a parent's initiatives and responses are biblical. The first criterion is God's moral boundaries for actions, the second, His moral boundaries for purposes (i.e., goals). A parent who is truly "biblical" will fall within God's boundaries for parenting (as described in the Bible) in both her actions and her purposes.

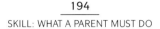

FIGURE 12
THE CRITERIA FOR BIBLICAL PARENTING

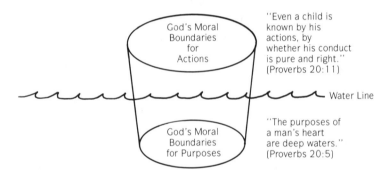

When a parent's actions toward her kids begin to fall outside God's moral boundaries, she can be certain her purposes have become unbiblical as well. It is not possible for a parent to become unbiblical in her actions while remaining biblical in her purposes.

The opposite, however, is possible. *Parents may appear biblical in their actions while remaining unbiblical in their purposes.* Many parents are lulled into believing they are "biblical parents" merely because their actions look okay, when in fact they can be sowing destructive consequences in their kids' lives because of the selfish and foolish goals that fuel their actions.

Norm and Shelly seemed to everyone to be model parents, as well as model Christians. Therefore it really threw them and everyone who

knew them for a loop when their teenage daughter had to be hospi-
talized with an eating disorder. No one could imagine how this ideal
Christian couple could have a daughter who stubbornly insisted on
starving herself.

Based on the first criterion alone (God's boundaries for actions),
no one could find anything "unbiblical" in what Norm and Shelly were
doing as parents. Their household rules and standards seemed very
reasonable. Their responses as parents seemed very appropriate. And
yet their daughter was literally killing herself.

As I worked with the family and learned more about Norm and
Shelly's style of parenting, I became convinced that in some very subtle
ways they were violating one of God's boundaries for parental conduct.
On a very real level, they were "exasperating" their daughter; that is,
they were making it virtually impossible for her to experience any
sense of esteem or love without going outside God's moral boundaries
(i.e., punishing her body).

Throughout her life, Jill's schedule had been filled either with
activities her parents chose for her, or ones she chose because she
knew her parents wanted her to. Whenever she had expressed her own
preferences, her parents either discouraged them openly through
forbidding words, or subtly through ignoring her requests.

To make matters worse, Jill was never encouraged to take much
personal satisfaction from the activities and accomplishments she did
do for her parents, even though she was able to do most of them very
well because of the variety of natural talents she had. Norm and Shelly
often took credit for her good performances, citing all the opportunities, training, and inspiration they'd provided for her along the way.

By the time she was in high school, Jill felt exasperated. Her deep
desires to be loved for who she was and respected for what she could do
on her own were untouched by her parents. They'd taught her that in
order to be loved and esteemed she had to be what they wanted her to
be. But after spending most of her elementary and junior high years
working at being exactly that, she decided that it really wasn't getting
her what she most deeply desired.

Finally in desperation she looked for something she could do to
get people to love and respect her for herself. Much to her parents'
surprise, and even against their wishes, she chose to go out for her

school's gymnastics team. Neglecting many of the activities her parents preferred her to be doing, she gave everything she had to becoming the best gymnast she could. In a short time, she captured her coach's, her teammates', and a large part of her school's admiration for her talents. After Jill's name appeared in the local sports page, even Norm and Shelly began to change their minds and become honestly excited about their daughter's gymnastic abilities.

It seemed Jill had finally found a strategy that worked. However, this strategy had a flaw, as does every foolish strategy. To stay on top as a gymnast, Jill had to stay trim — no small feat for a growing adolescent girl — and to maintain her "trimness," she began to severely reduce her caloric intake through reduced eating.

At first this seemed to help her gymnastic performances, so she became committed to undereating as a way of life. Later, when the weight loss began to affect her strength and hurt her performances, she concluded that she must still be too heavy and only doubled her commitment to lose more weight. Eventually, when she became too weak to participate in athletics, the superior self-control her thinness represented to her replaced the gymnastics as her primary strategy for winning the love and respect of others. This strategy, she decided, was worth pursuing, even if it meant dropping out of everything else. She came to literally prefer death to facing life without the prospect of the love and respect she believed only her thinness could win for her.

Helping Norm and Shelly see their role in their daughter's problems became one of my greatest challenges in helping Jill. I knew I couldn't help them make sense of her behavior until they saw the impact their style of parenting had had on her. And since their style of parenting was so subtle in the way it violated God's outward standards for parental conduct, I knew I had to first expose how it violated His inward standards for parental purposes.

As we explored how their commitment to be the parents of "superior" children arose from painful experiences they'd each had during adolescence and early adulthood, it became obvious that the goals behind their matter-of-fact, business-like, and perfectionistic behaviors toward their daughter were self-protective in nature. The purpose of their parenting style was to a large degree to keep the kind of painful experiences they'd endured earlier from repeating themselves. As their eyes were opened to how they had violated God's moral boundaries in their purposes toward Jill, they suddenly could see clearly how they were violating those boundaries in their actions as well. As they consciously chose a new goal of ministry toward their daughter, their actions began to change too.

The changes in Norm and Shelly didn't immediately result in changes in Jill. However, their new goal of giving her unconditional involvement began to confuse her. This gave me an opening to begin challenging her foolish notions about love and respect depending always and only on winning people's admiration through perfection and performance.

Once parents have developed the skill of redirecting their own purposes, as Norm and Shelly did, they are in a position to start making sense of their adolescent's often baffling behavior. They'll be able to pick up clues about their teen's inner workings that they never saw before.

Skill Two: Listening Beneath an Adolescent's Words

> The words of a man's mouth are deep waters,
>   but the fountain of wisdom is a bubbling brook . . . .
> A fool's lips bring him strife,
>   and his mouth invites a beating.
> A fool's mouth is his undoing,
>   and his lips are a snare to his soul.   (Proverbs 18:4,6-7)

A person's words often carry oceans of meaning and betray what is really going on inside him. If a fool is allowed to speak, he will eventually "snare his own soul" or give some reason why he deserves "a beating." It is through careful listening to what an adolescent says that parents can discover the foolish purposes or plans in his heart.

Rarely will adolescents have the ability or courage to explicitly tell others what they're really thinking or feeling. And, even if they decided to throw caution to the wind, most teens haven't practiced using conceptual communication skills enough to readily attach words to their deepest thoughts and feelings. Parents won't get a lot of information in "plain English" from their adolescents, but their understanding of them can grow significantly if they'll listen for the messages hidden beneath their teens' words.

Not all of an adolescent's words carry implicit messages, of course. As an adolescent guy arrives home from school and tells his mother he's starving and wants a sandwich, she would be unwise to say, "What do you *really* want?" What he really wants is what he has explicitly asked for: a sandwich. When a parent tries to find an implicit message in this kind of exchange with her teen, she comes across as a psychological vulture—enough to turn any kid off.

However, as the adolescent guy arrives home from school and answers his mom's question "How was your day?" with the statement "Meaningless as always," she would be wise to suspect a hidden message beneath his words. They ring of despair or cynicism.

If parents want to genuinely minister to their adolescent, it is vital that they don't miss these kinds of messages. There are two ways parents can sharpen their skill of listening beneath their teen's words. One, they can learn the kinds of words that usually carry implicit messages. And two, they can reflect on how their teen's words affect them and allow them to penetrate.

Recognizing implicit messages. Certain kinds of words kids use are almost always pregnant with implicit meaning. For example, words that are colorful or graphic generally have a lot more to say about how the teen is thinking about himself or his world than words that are more mundane or routine.

Notice how the words in the following sentences carry implicit messages:

Seventeen-year-old son: I can't believe it, Mom. Can't you ever *get off my back*? I just want to go out and have some fun for a change.

Sixteen-year-old daughter: I don't know why you don't like him. At least *he treats me like a real person.*

Fourteen-year-old son: I don't want to go anywhere with you tonight. I'd rather *drink poison* first.

Thirteen-year-old daughter: What should I do when my dad says *dirty* things to me? It makes me feel like *jumping out a window* whenever he comes close.

Fifteen-year-old son: Don't wake me up in the morning. *I don't know if I ever want to wake up again.*

Seventeen-year-old daughter: Sometimes I just wish I could change who I am. I'm tired of being *stepped on* by everybody.

Eighteen-year-old son: Dad, I'm tired of you treating me like *a piece of trash.* Let's see how you like it for a change.

It's obvious how graphic words can tip a parent off to his teen's inner feelings. Words expressed in angry, frightened, or shameful tones are also usually loaded with hidden messages. So are words that kids use over and over again without even realizing it. Notice what three words repeated by a high school girl reveal about an unfulfilled desire in her life:

> I just don't have any *good relationship* with anyone right now. I thought I had a *good relationship* with Sal, you know, one where I could *share* anything, but now I really wonder how good it was. Marty is a friend, but not a real good one. We can't really *share* very openly together. And my dad, well, he just doesn't know how to *share* anything with anyone. With my mom, well, she does all the sharing, and you have to do all the listening. I've just about given up hope at ever having a *good relationship.* I once thought that maybe I could have *good relationships* if I was just more outgoing, and confident, but. . . .

Allowing personal impact. If your own kid had said the statements you read above, how would you have felt? How would the statements have affected you? Would you have let them impact you?

The scale in figure 13 measures how much impact a parent allows his adolescent's words to have on him. When a parent's goal is to stay comfortable around his teen (operating, of course, by the consumer model), he must never allow his teen's words to move the needle out of the low range on the scale. He must find ways to keep, not only the implicit messages (good or bad) of his kid's words from getting to him, but often the explicit ones as well. To protect himself, the parent incorportes one of four strategies into his style of relating.

First, a parent may choose to *not listen to any of his kid's words at all.* In this case he totally tunes his teen out, ignoring whatever the teen says. He accomplishes this by staying unavailable or preoccupied.

Second, a parent may *subject everything his teen says to selective* perception, choosing to acknowledge only what makes it possible for him to keep the needle from moving outside the low range. He can't even allow his teen's words to register outside the low range on the positive side of the scale, for to make himself vulnerable to the positive impact of his kid's words also makes him vulnerable to their negative impact.

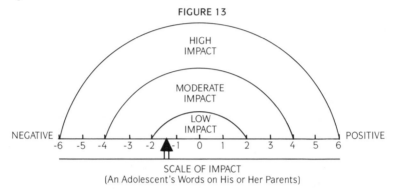

FIGURE 13

SCALE OF IMPACT
(An Adolescent's Words on His or Her Parents)

A third strategy a parent might use to protect himself is to *deliberately misinterpret his kid's words*, which again leaves the adolescent feeling powerless. No matter how he might try to influence his parents with his words, he feels frustrated because they never have the impact he intends.

A fourth strategy is *to attach overriding significance* to any word the kid uses that even hints at moving the needle. In effect, the parent trains his teen to not even dare say anything that might ruffle him. The adolescent learns from violent experiences with his parent that to move the needle at all means to virtually send it off the scale altogether. Therefore he learns to limit his words to the bare minimum and to weigh each one carefully in order to avoid arousing any kind of reaction at all in his parent.

It should be the goal of healthy, mature parents to become "accurate listeners," to grant to each of their adolescent's words the exact impact he intended (either consciously or unconsciously) when he spoke them. To allow their adolescent's words to impact them, however, does not mean they allow the adolescent to control them. *A healthy parent allows her adolescent to impact her emotionally, but not volitionally.* She lets her kid's words anger, frighten, and even shame her, but she doesn't let her emotions control her outward reactions. Only her own carefully chosen goals control how she acts toward her teen.

In order for a parent to allow her kid's words to have their intended impact, she must be willing to do a lot of self-reflection, asking herself such questions as: "How do these words make me feel?" "What is it about these words that makes me feel so uncomfortable?" "What is my kid trying to get me to feel or do by choosing to use these words?" "What is he really trying to say to me?" "What message do his words carry that he might be afraid to say to me directly?" Reflecting in this way prepares a parent to use a third skill in making sense of her adolescent's behavior.

Skill Three: Opening Doors to an Adolescent's Purposes

> He who answers before listening—
>   that is his folly and his shame. . . .
> The heart of the discerning acquires knowledge;
>   the ears of the wise seek it out. . . .
> The first to present his case seems right,
>   till another comes forward and questions him.
> (Proverbs 18:13,15,17)

Solomon extols the virtue of listening before responding. However, in verse 15 he is careful to draw a distinction between two kinds of listening: passive and active. A person uses his "ears" to "seek out knowledge." He takes an active role in the listening process. Verse 17 indicates that the best way to listen actively is to ask the kinds of questions that get to the truth in another person's heart. Parents who use the skill of listening beneath their adolescent's words for implicit messages are prepared to take the next step of asking their teen the kind of questions that will invite her to make her implicit messages explicit. When parents use penetrating questions to do this, they encourage their teen to talk about the desires and purposes of her heart, things an adolescent will rarely reflect on without being skillfully questioned by an adult.

Some questions parents ask close rather than open doors to deeper sharing from their teen. Questions that open doors have three basic characteristics: they are *nondefensive, open-ended,* and *biblically perceptive.*

Asking nondefensive questions. According to Proverbs 18:15, a wise person asks questions to acquire knowledge or understanding, to get at the truth no matter what the cost. Too often, however, a parent's goal is quite different. *She actually wants to keep the truth from coming out,* or at least keep herself comfortable as she's asking the questions.

A parent can't get to know the deepest parts of her teen if she takes a defensive stance. Her questions will carry an implicit message warning her teen not to answer in a way that might increase the parent's pain or discomfort. The teen is pressured to cushion or compromise the truth in the way he responds. Below are some examples of defensive questions parents might ask, along with the hidden messages they carry.

> "What do you mean you think our rules are strict and unfair?" (Implicit message: "Don't you dare accuse me of treating you unfairly. That thought is unacceptable to me.")
>
> "Why do you always make unkind remarks about me? What did I do to deserve them?" (Implicit message: "Nothing you think about me can justify your hurting me, so don't even try. I demand that you not say anything unkind.")
>
> "Who do you think you are, anyway, acting like you have a right to do anything you want no matter who it hurts?" (Implicit message: "You don't have the right to be the kind of person you are. So it'd better stop.")
>
> "When did I ever say or do something to make you think I don't love you?" (Implicit message: "It's not my fault you feel unloved. It's not fair to make me feel guilty.")

Notice how defensive questions are very often introduced with a word like *who, what, when,* or *why.* By nature these words challenge a person to defend his position, to justify what he thinks or feels rather than explain, illustrate, or expand on it. Such questions slam doors to deeper sharing between a parent and a teen. Sooner or later the teen concludes that he can never adequately justify having thoughts or feelings that hurt or agitate his parents. Therefore, he learns to either keep all his feelings to himself, or to deny he ever feels anything that would make his parents feel uncomfortable.

Asking open-ended questions. Open-ended questions encourage a teen to talk freely about the source of her concerns or the purpose of her actions. They don't seek clipped, concise answers, nor do they manipulate the teen to give the exact answer the parent is looking for. Below are several examples of questions that are phrased in both high-structured and low-structured ways. Notice how *low-structured (open-ended) questions promote further communication,* while highly structured questions tend to limit it.

> High-structured: "Are you mad at me?"
> Low-structured: "Tell me how you're really feeling about me."

> High-structured: "Are you trying to get me to give in to you?"
> Low-structured: "I'm not sure what you want me to do. Can you help me understand?"

> High-structured: "You're afraid of looking foolish in front of your friends, aren't you?"
> Low-structured: "You're hesitating for some reason. I wonder what's holding you back."

> High-structured: "I don't understand why you can't. Aren't you being a little selfish?"
> Low-structured: "I don't understand your 'no.' Can you explain to me what's behind it?"

> High-structured: "Don't you want what's best for everyone?"
> Low-structured: "Tell me about what you really want."

When a parent's goal is to get one specific piece of information from her teen, then a high-structured question is very appropriate (e.g., "Where are you going on your date, and what time will you be home?"). It would be absurd for her to ask, "I wonder whether you'll be coming home tonight after your date?" However, when the parent's goal is to probe the recesses of her child's heart, she must use low-structured questions (e.g., I'm curious about how you're feeling these days about the boy you're dating. Do you mind talking? I'd love to know where you're at.").

Asking biblically perceptive questions. To get to the heart of what his teen is all about, a parent must ask perceptive questions, questions that are guided by a biblical understanding of what makes people tick. A parent with this understanding knows his adolescent feels disappointment. Deep within, the teen despairs over the fact that his desires for unfailing love have never been fulfilled by anyone in his world.

A perceptive parent also knows that his adolescent is thinking foolishly about how to deal with his unfulfilled desires. He is struggling over what to do with the plans or strategies he used to try to get these desires met.

Parents who view their teen with this understanding have a distinct advantage. By looking at their teen through biblical "eyeglasses," they can see the deeper realities in his life and pose questions that get him talking about his unmet desires and foolish plans (see figure 14). Once he begins to talk openly about these things, his parents can start teaching him about the nature of both (i.e., what the teen really desires can only be fulfilled by Christ; what the teen is trying to accomplish can never succeed because it is against Christ). Until the nature of his desires and plans has been openly discussed, parents will have a hard time making Christ seem relevant to his life.

FIGURE 14
A PARENT'S BIBLICAL EYEGLASSES

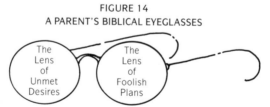

Below are several examples of the kinds of questions parents wearing biblical eyeglasses might ask.

Questions designed to get teens talking about their desires:
•"What do you hope to get out of school this year?"
•"What kinds of things make school a scary or difficult place for you?"

•"If you could wave a magic wand and change anything about your friends or your parents, what would you change?"

Questions designed to get teens talking about their plans:
•"If you could accomplish anything you wanted this year at school, what would it be?"
•"What kinds of things are making you the most mad and frustrated these days?"
•"If you could wave a magic wand and change anything about yourself, what would you change?"

Questions like these can be great tools for parents who know what they're looking for and who aren't afraid of involving themselves deeply in their kid's life. Parents who approach their teen with a biblical understanding of people know what they will find inside him. They know what kinds of questions to ask to direct his attention and conversation toward these things. And they know the kinds of answers to anticipate when their teen finally starts to talk from his heart.

However, words are just one form of a teen's behavior that parents can study. His actions are another. Interpreting these requires another skill.

Skill Four: Tracing Behavior to Unmet Desires and Foolish Plans

The Lord does not let the righteous go hungry,
    but he thwarts the craving of the wicked. . . .
What the wicked dreads will overtake him;
    what the righteous desire will be granted. . . .
Do not those who plot evil go astray?
    But those who plan what is good find love and faithfulness.
(Proverbs 10:3,24; 14:22)

As people who are moving into the stage of incensed foolishness, adolescents are on a collision course. The writer of Proverbs asserts that sooner or later every person who is twisted in his thinking (i.e., wicked) will experience two things: (1) his desires will be left unfulfilled; and (2) his foolish plans for self-fulfillment and self-protection will fail and backfire. Parents can be certain that both will occur to their children sometime during their adolescence or early adulthood. Those who want to make sense of their adolescents' behavior must be able to understand what it communicates about their unmet desires and foolish plans.

Figure 15 shows how the four basic forms of adolescent behavior each developed in response to increasing disappointment in the teen's life. An adolescent's first form of behavior is the relational style he learned and carried over from his childhood. This remains his normal style of relating as long as it continues to win him security, love, and impact. By midadolescence, however, the new crises and disappointments triggered by puberty usually render the teen's strategies ineffective. When this occurs, his first response is to exaggerate or intensify his relational style in an effort to make what worked in childhood keep working despite all the new obstacles adolescence has put in his way.

FIGURE 15

THE FORMS OF ADOLESCENT BEHAVIOR

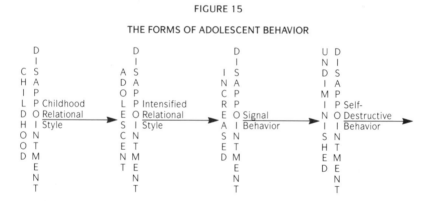

When an adolescent intensifies his childhood style of relating, his basic foolish plan for life remains intact. He has not yet reached the level of despair in which he is willing to rearrange or revise the very foundations of his life. He still operates much as he did as a child, yet with increasing energy, activity, and stress. The compliantly good kid moves toward being a compulsively good kid. He intensifies his goal of being good to being the best! The defiantly mischievous kid moves toward being defiantly malicious. His goal of being bad is intensified to being the worst! The incompetently dependent kid moves toward being more incompetent and more dependent. He intensifies his goal of getting a lot of the attention from the adults in his world to getting all of their attention.

If, after intensifying his style of relating, an adolescent continues to experience increasing disappointment in his life, he will move to a whole new form of behavior called *signal behavior*. As the disappointment in his life becomes almost unbearable, he will send an "SOS" through uncharacteristic behaviors that are designed to shock or get the attention of the people around him. Underneath his behavior is often a message to his parents: *"Help me, Mom, help me, Dad. I'm in so much pain I don't know what to do."*

Signal behavior for a compliant/compulsive teen often involves breaking rules laid down by an authority figure. A defiant/distant teen may signal others through some uncharacteristic gesture toward improving a relationship with an authority figure. And the incompetent/dependent teen may take a stand of independence or defiance toward a person in authority.

Parents typically become quite confused or threatened by their adolescent's signal behaviors and therefore respond inappropriately by overreacting and pulling away from him, or by ignoring his behavior altogether and treating it as "just another phase" of adolescence.

Unless a parent acknowledges the message underneath his teen's signal behavior and takes some action to lessen the disappointment in his teen's life, one of two things will happen. If the signal behavior offers the teen a more effective way to manipulate his world and make it less disappointing, he will adopt it as his new foolish way of relating. The compliant kid may convert to a defiant kid, the defiant kid to a compliant kid, and the incompetent kid to either defiance or compliance.

If, however, the signal behavior fails to lessen the teen's disappointment, he will see no other recourse than to pursue self-destructive behaviors. *Rarely will a teen resort to this form of behavior unless he has first sent out some very clear signal behaviors to his world.* Self-destructive behaviors in teens may include outright suicide attempts, reckless behavior, and/or physically abusive behaviors (e.g., drug abuse, eating disorders, etc.).

As an adolescent moves from a childhood style of relating to sending out signal behaviors to pursuing self-destructive behaviors, a parent can have a clear idea of what is going on inside him. The teen loses more and more hope that his desires will ever be fulfilled (Proverbs 13:12), and he becomes more and more incensed over his continually failing foolish plans (Proverbs 19:3). As a parent becomes aware of this, it is imperative that he exercise one last skill of ministry, one that will give hope to his disappointed adolescent and will, more than any other skill, communicate unconditional involvement.

Skill Five: Putting into Words an Adolescent's Thoughts and Feelings

> The tongue of the wise commends knowledge,
>   but the mouth of the fool gushes folly. . . .
> The tongue that brings healing is a tree of life,
>   but a deceitful tongue crushes the spirit. . . .
> The tongue has the power of life and death,
>   and those who love it will eat its fruit.
>
> (Proverbs 15:2,4; 18:21)

Parents who want to understand and minister to their adolescent must learn how to speak "life words" to him—words that capture and articulate what he is thinking and feeling.

Such words accomplish three things. First, they help the teen make sense of his own behavior. When a parent summarizes for his teen what he sees going on in his life, he gives the teen some life-giving knowledge. "You know, Greg, it seems to me that you're starving to know somebody really values you just for who you are. Much of what you do seems pointed toward getting that one deep desire satisfied. But, it doesn't seem to be working very well for you. I think that's why you must be feeling so empty lately."

Words like these, expressed tentatively and compassionately, communicate to teens that there really are logical reasons for what they think and feel. Many kids suffer for years under the secret belief that they must be crazy. These words assure them that they really are sane. The problem they're having is a problem we're all having: trying to find dignity and love in a fallen world.

Second, life words give parents an opportunity to have their teen confirm or dismiss the conclusions they are drawing about his behavior. When parents have taken the time to listen beneath his words, ask him door-opening questions, and trace his behaviors to unmet desires and foolish plans, their conclusions will most likely be accurate. In order to know for sure, however, they need to get their teen's reaction. If the teen responds as if their hunches have missed the mark completely, the parents may need to return to the drawing board and reflect further about their kid.

Finally, parents can use life words to communicate unconditional involvement to their teen. When parents reveal that they really are aware of the troubled parts of his soul, they give him a message of hope: "I see who you really are and you are the kind of person I want to be more involved with. Seeing all your broken parts just makes me love you more."

When parents develop the capacity to enter into their adolescent's life with an awareness of what is happening inside him, they become "alive" to him and can stimulate his appetite for deeper relationship with Christ. These parents stand in stark contrast to "dead" parents who enter their relationships with an awareness of nothing but how their own interests are faring. Their interaction with their teen only squelches his desire for a deeper relationship with Christ.

When parents really get to know their kid, they discover a person in despair—one whose foolish plans have failed to win him the love and impact he deeply desires. How to respond to an adolescent's despair is the topic of the next chapter.

SUMMING IT UP

As I have been describing "unconditional involvement" to you in the last two chapters, does it sound like something you want someone to offer *you*? If I have described it accurately, it should be something you hunger for yourself. Can you remember others offering you this kind of relationship?

In working with parents of teens over the years I have come to suspect that so many of them are not good at offering unconditional involvement to their kids because they have rarely been offered unconditional involvement themselves.

Really, it should be no surprise that few have tasted unconditional involvement in their relationships. Solomon implied that such would be the case when he asked the question, ". . . a faithful man who can find?" (Proverbs 20:6). The quality of every person's love is affected to some degree by a sinful nature that continues to plague him until death.

The quality of a person's love, of the involvement he offers to others, can progressively improve as long as he lives, but not to any great degree unless he tastes unconditional involvement himself. The ultimate relationship in which a parent can come to fully experience and understand the nature of unconditional involvement is with Christ. The skills described in this chapter really can be mastered only by parents who have tasted and enjoyed the kind of involvement that only He can give.

NOTE   1. For more about signal emotions, see pages 126-136 in *Effective Biblical Counseling* by Lawrence J. Crabb (Zondervan, 1977) and pages 171-189 in *Understanding People*, also by Lawrence J. Crabb (Zondervan, 1987).

NINE

Responding to the Desires of an Adolescent's Heart

My wife and I were in the kitchen when we first heard the news over the radio: The teachers in our local school system were finally returning to their classrooms following a two-week strike. Excitedly, we hurried into the family room to share the good news with our daughters. We thought they'd be excited too since they'd been complaining about missing their friends and facing the prospect that the school year might extend into their summer vacation. We thought our oldest daughter, Christi, would be especially thrilled since the first half of her seventh-grade year had been such a positive experience. Her reaction, however, was not what we had anticipated. Disappointment covered her face and tears began to well up in her eyes. When we asked her what was wrong, she stunned us with her answer. "I hate school. I never want to go back to that place. I don't have any friends there, and everybody treats me mean."

Christi's feelings about school were a revelation to us. We'd never heard her despair about anything before. As we tried to get her to talk more about her feelings, we learned that many of her relationships at school had been disappointing to her in ways we never knew about. During the strike, she'd had time to think about all the ways she'd been hurt, and now the thought of going back into these relationships and facing more disappointment seemed overwhelming. The more Tina and I talked to her about her pain, the worse she felt. When she realized we wouldn't go along with her idea of staying out of school for the rest of the week, she angrily withdrew and locked herself in her room.

Tina and I felt deflated. Despite the fact that we had both made professions out of coaching parents to cope with their troubled teens, neither of us felt very confident in dealing with our own daughter while she was in this much despair. It was obvious to us that Christi was experiencing, at an intense level, the consequences of living in a world that failed to meet her deepest desires. It was also obvious that she saw us as failing her by refusing to provide for her an escape from the people and circumstances that threatened to add to her pain. Tina and I knew that our response to her and the unmet desires she was experiencing at the time were very critical. Some of her most important lessons about life, herself, and even God would be learned in the context of events like this.

When kids experience betrayal and disillusionment in their relationships, some very real internal crises occur. Their sense of safety, their sense of worth or impact as a person, and even their sense of feeling loved and wanted — all these can be threatened. In the midst of these crises, some basic foolish assumptions all kids have about their unmet desires begin to emerge. How parents respond to these crises will determine to a large degree whether these foolish assumptions are strengthened or challenged. At no other time is it more important for parents to respond biblically to their teens than when they are tasting the despair of unmet desires. To do this, parents must first understand how teens respond to their own despair.

HOW AN ADOLESCENT RESPONDS TO PERSONAL DESPAIR

To understand how an adolescent responds when the events of life deny him what he deeply wants, we must first understand what assumptions he draws when this occurs. Since every teen has foolish intentions to make life work apart from God, *his basic assumptions about the events of life are always designed to maintain his illusion of self-sufficiency.* This enables him to avoid facing two painful realities: the unpredictable and hostile nature of his world and the helpless and dependent nature of himself. No adolescent wants to accept the fact that the world will never be the kind of place that can deeply satisfy him, or that he will never be the kind of person who can find satisfaction in it on his own.

When the events of life deny an adolescent a sense of safety, significance, or security for any significant period of time, one of the first assumptions he jumps to is that something must be wrong with him. His reasoning goes something like this:

> It seems like most of the people around me are doing okay. The world really must be the kind of place that treats you okay if you are okay yourself. Since I'm not getting what I really want from the world, there must be something really wrong or deficient about me. The key to life then lies in finding a way to get the world to give me what I want even though I'm the wrong kind of person. In order to do this I must figure out a way to get the world to see me differently.

The adolescent experiences a gap between what he thinks he's "required" to be before others in his world will want to satisfy his desires, and what he believes he's "perceived" to be in their eyes at the present time. Life (the fulfillment of his deepest desires) then becomes dependent on his own ability to close this gap.

Normally, as a child enters adolescence and experiences new expectations for how he's supposed to think, relate, and look, this gap begins to widen. He develops an image of himself as deficient mentally, relationally, physically, and/or sexually. Failures in one or all of these areas are branded into his memory and contribute to his perception of himself as a person who is unlovable and worthless. He's sure others will find out what kind of person he really is and despise him if he lets them really get to know him. This image he has of himself becomes the motivation to focus his efforts on changing how others perceive him. He reasons that the smaller the gap, the less harsh and disappointing his world will be.

In addition to the assumptions the adolescent draws about his world and himself, he also draws some basic assumptions about the future. He assumes the future will be unbearable unless he can find a way to keep the gap relatively narrow. He may suffer from depression and loss of motivation if his efforts to close the gap meet with little success. "What's the use?" he figures. "I'll never be able to be the kind of person others require me to be. I've tried, but I can't change who I am."

When an adolescent reaches this conclusion, he experiences a great deal of contempt along with his despair. Although he wants to direct his contempt toward the world for denying him what he deeply desires, his foolish assumptions require him to direct most of it toward himself. After all, how can he blame the world for not giving him what he wanted? The world is a generous place to anyone who is the right kind of person. There are "happy people" all around him to prove that. The only one left to blame and despise is himself.

An adolescent goes on to make some basic assumptions about God. He assumes God wouldn't want a relationship with him either until the gap is closed. And, of course, God has much higher expectations for him than anyone else does and therefore must see him as being even more deficient than others do. A relationship with God seems very unreachable, and perhaps even very undesirable to him. He may even prefer to believe that God doesn't exist at all. By eliminating God, some of the adolescent's requirements are also eliminated, making what is expected somewhat easier for him to attain.

This may be why so many adolescents develop an aversion toward church and religion. Any exposure to teachings about God or the Bible only widens the gap and makes them feel more deficient as people. And when life depends on closing the gap, as it does in an adolescent's thinking, then moving closer to God seems like moving closer to death.

Too often the teens who find church attractive are the compliant/compulsive kids who possess the iron will to keep all the rules that are given to them in the name of God. These kids can use a system of Christian rules pretty effectively as a strategy for closing the gap. This is a tragic irony since the very thing that is supposed to be generating sole dependence on Christ is really strengthening a kid's dependence on himself. *As long as a kid can find a way to present himself as "the kind of person the world and God can be proud of," he will experience little need for a personal relationship with a God whose desire it is to do for him what he still believes he can do for himself: correct his own deficiencies* and satisfy the longings of his soul.

When Christianity or a system of Christian standards or rules is presented to kids as a strategy for closing the gap (or for capturing the respect and love of others in their world), then it ceases to be anything truly Christian at all. Instead, it teaches them how they can get their deepest desires met apart from entrusting those desires to Christ.

In Psalm 62 David spoke of himself as a man with a gap. He had an image of himself as a person who was weak, the target of many people's contempt. Most of the world was certainly denying him the desires of his heart. David wrote,

> How long will you assualt a man?
>> Would all of you throw him down—
>> this leaning wall, this tottering fence?
> They fully intend to topple him
>> from his lofty place;
>> they take delight in lies.
> With their mouths they bless,
>> but in their hearts they curse. (Psalm 62:3-4)

Imagine the counsel a young man facing the same kind of despair today might receive from his parents or friends. Imagine the counsel you would give your teen. How would it compare with the counsel David gave his own soul in Psalm 62? David discovered a way of responding to his despair that did not require correcting personal deficiencies or changing the way the world looked at him. David writes of it in the middle verses of the psalm:

> Find rest, O my soul, in God alone;
>> my hope comes from him.
> He alone is my rock and my salvation;
>> he is my fortress, I will not be shaken.
> My salvation and my honor depend on God;
>> he is my mighty rock, my refuge.
> Trust in him at all times, O people;
>> pour out your hearts to him, for God is our refuge.
>> (Psalm 62:5-8)

The basic foolish assumptions kids make, however, do not allow them to respond to the despair of unmet desires in this way. Instead, they increase their efforts to close the gap in order to get the world to see them differently. And every kid seems to come up with her own way of trying to accomplish this.

The Compliant/Compulsive Teen's Strategy

The compliant kid, who believes fulfillment depends on meeting the expectations of others, tries to close the gap by improving how she is perceived. She becomes obsessed with correcting deficiencies others call to her attention. A passing comment like "You must be a lazy person" is enough to blow the gap wide open and drive the teen to extraordinary measures in order to keep anyone from being able to say that about her again. Even the slightest criticism can devastate her for weeks and launch her on a new campaign for self-improvement.

I remember working with one high school girl named Pam who was literally living to earn her father's approval. Since she longed to feel accepted by him, she did everything she could to prevent him from giving her a disapproving glance or word. She believed acceptance as a person depended on making herself into the kind of person no one, especially her dad, could ever criticize. Only once did she remember telling her father about an unmet desire. He'd promised he'd spend the weekend of her sixteenth birthday doing a couple of special things with her, but a few weeks before he forgot his promise and scheduled a business trip for that weekend. When Pam told him how disappointed she was, he got angry and accused her of being selfish and ungrateful for everything he had done for her. He committed the typical error dutiful parents make: *He misinterpreted his teen's unmet desire as an unreasonable demand.*

Pam's father's words hit her like a ton of bricks, and she decided she'd never divulge her desires to anyone again. She decided to accept whatever people offered her and always pretend to be grateful. Her strategy had some devastating consequences in all her relationships. Based on her behavior, her parents thought she was the "happiest" girl in the world. Other kids enjoyed her company because she never required or asked anything from them. They often took advantage of her "good nature" since she never objected to any way they treated her or anything they asked her to do. Everybody at school thought Pam was just great and came to her whenever they needed anything. Meanwhile, Pam was feeling all alone and totally unloved for who she really was. She was convinced that if people really knew what she was feeling they wouldn't accept her. Although she succeeded in narrowing the gap most of the time through her people-pleasing strategy, the world was still not giving her the real acceptance or love she longed for.

When teens are encouraged to respond to their disappointment and despair by concentrating on self-improvement (whether it be of their personality, talents, or aptitudes), they set themselves up for even greater disillusionment later. They come to expect a "pay-off" from their world if and when they get close to being what the world wants them to be. Inevitably, however, even the most successful efforts at self-improvement will fail to win the deep kinds of admiration and affection from the world that teens are really searching for.

The Incompetent/Dependent Teen's Strategy

The incompetent/dependent teen has an altogether different approach for dealing with the gap. He assumes it can be closed, not by improving himself so the world will perceive him as competent, but by presenting himself in such a way that the world will see him as incompetent and require less of him. He usually finds a way to display to others how he is really too inferior or incompetent to be expected to measure up to what otherwise might be required. He tries to persuade others to give him the attention, respect, or affection he wants without requiring as much from him as they do from other people. He is convinced that unless he can play on people's sympathies, he has no hope of having his deepest desires fulfilled.

Sammy was a high school student who used just such a strategy. Early in his life, Sammy came to two conclusions that shaped his response to the pain of unmet desires. First, he concluded that no matter how hard he tried, he could never earn the same kind of respect and attention others got. In academics, athletics, household responsibilities, and even in games his family played together, Sammy never did as well as his two older step-brothers. Naturally, this made him feel inferior, and he feared he would lose what little parental attention he currently received. His biological dad rarely had time for him. His step-dad seemed more taken with his own sons. And his mother's energies and attention, which were solely his before she remarried, now had to be shared with three other people. By the time he became a adolescent, Sammy believed he lacked the talents and abilities to earn the respect he wanted from his world. This hurt so much that he tried to escape by avoiding anything in which he'd be compared unfavorably with his step-brothers. He refused to do the same household chores they did. He refused to participate in sports they were good at. He even refused to try at school subjects they excelled in. Before long, he was avoiding all of his responsibilities, which, naturally became a great source of concern to his parents. Thus, Sammy came to a second major conclusion about dealing with the pain in his heart: He could at least get some of the attention he longed for by convincing others he was an inferior kind of person.

His step-dad saw Sammy's avoidance patterns as nothing more than laziness and irresponsibility. Since his own sons never avoided their responsibilities, he had very little patience with Sammy. He didn't believe the disappointments Sammy had experienced in the past should excuse him from responsible behavior now. He dealt with Sammy through stern lectures and severe penalties (e.g., loss of television and phone privileges for a grading period, grounding for a month, etc.).

Sammy's step-dad erred in viewing Sammy's problem through only one lens of his "parenting glasses" (the lens of foolish strategies), while Sammy's mother erred in viewing it only through the other lens (the lens of unmet desires). Because she felt guilty that Sammy had been deprived of a normal childhood relationship with his father, she thought Sammy shouldn't be expected to perform as well as the other kids should. So she began to come to Sammy's defense and make excuses for his behavior. She mistakenly attributed his behavior problems solely to his unfulfilled desire for attention and involvement from his dad. His step-dad mistakenly attributed them solely to Sammy's foolish scheme for getting what he wanted without having to take any responsibility for his life. The mother wanted to lessen expectations and increase involvement, while the step-dad wanted to increase expectations and withdraw involvement until Sammy's behavior changed. Neither of the responses helped Sammy because they failed to take into account his unfulfilled desires and foolish plans.

Finally after several confrontations, Sammy's mother convinced her husband to back off and let her handle Sammy her way. She began to shower her son with attention and special privileges, which strengthened Sammy's strategy for getting what he wanted by portraying himself as "a victim of neglect." As Sammy moved through high school, however, his style of relating to others as an incompetent and pathetic kid began to backfire. His peers found his style of relating unappealing, and his teachers proved less than willing to give him the breaks earlier teachers did. Sammy's traditionally below-average grades became failing grades. As he found the school environment more and more hostile to him, he depended even more on his mother for his sense of self-esteem. He felt ashamed about this dependence, however, and began to resent his mother for encouraging it. He felt trapped. Although he hated how dependent he'd become, the prospect of facing life on his own terrified him. *He was convinced he could never get others in his world to respect him without getting them to lower what they expected or required of him.* And the older he got, the more it seemed the only place this strategy worked was in his relationship with his mother.

This kind of strategy inevitably presents adolescents from developing the emotional and social independence and skills they need for a healthy sense of self-esteem. When kids like Sammy are permitted to respond to the disappointment and despair that they feel by avoiding responsibility and potential failure, they develop an unhealthy dependence on others that later will become their greatest block to finding any authentic sense of significance as people.

The Defiant/Distant Teen's Strategy

A defiant adolescent does not try to close the gap by improving how people perceive him or by convincing people to require less of him. Instead, he drives anyone who might see his gap out of his life. His strategy is to create a new world for himself, one populated only with people who require little of him and perceive him as deficient in nothing that matters. He can allow no one to be near him who acts morally superior or critical toward him, which usually requires him to distance himself from all authority figures (parents, teachers, etc.), adults, and peers who are high achievers. *He believes that the pain of his unmet desires can be relieved only by escaping or destroying any relationship that exposes him as deficient.*

One high school girl I worked with was a typical "hard kid." Whenever a teacher or an adult leader from her church tried to talk to Jean, even to express a kind word, she would look away and pretend she hadn't heard it. She knew that sooner or later, when people failed to get a reaction from her, they would give up on her and leave her alone. Her parents had become exasperated with her unresponsiveness and no longer made much effort to communicate with her or motivate her to do what they wanted. They'd decided it would teach her a good lesson if they just gave her the same kind of cold shoulder she gave them. As a result they chose to ignore most of what Jean said and did, which they believed, would eventually bring her to her senses. They failed to recognize that underneath Jean's behaviors were both unmet longings and foolish plans that their response would only magnify.

Jean had grown up feeling a lot of despair around her parents. She could hardly remember a time when she felt warmly accepted by them. They were bright, well-educated, and professionally successful, which made them not only busy, but also unable to empathize with Jean when she started experiencing learning difficulties in elementary school.

Jean's parents had showered her with attention and affection when she was an infant and toddler. She was their "little princess," the future heiress of all her parents' labors, status, and success. However, their style of relating to her took a quick turn after her intellectual limitations became apparent. They turned over a great deal more of her care and training to an elderly aunt who lived with the family. They rarely allowed her schoolwork or difficulties to be mentioned or discussed. They began to take a matter-of-fact approach in dealing with her, expressing few expectations or affirmations and offering little involvement. By detaching themselves in this way, Jean's parents found some relief from the disappointment and shame they felt about their daughter.

Jean keenly sensed her parents' rejection and naturally assumed it was because something was wrong with her. She spent years doing anything she could think of to try to win her parents' affection back. But they remained resigned to the idea that Jean would never be the kind of person the family could be proud of.

As Jean entered adolescence, she began to express outwardly the resentment she felt at being cast by her parents into a "blacksheep" role—a role she felt she could never escape. There was no relief from the gap she felt whenever she was in their presence. When she tried to express her hurt and anger, it confirmed to them everything they'd already chosen to believe about her. "Will this girl ever cease to find new ways to disappoint and shame us!?" They detached themselves even more, which convinced Jean that her only chance to feel whole as a person depended on building a whole new life for herself—a life that totally omitted her parents and anyone who saw her the way they did.

Jean's strategy for getting out of pain meant replacing her family relationships with peer relationships. It was only around peers that she could get a taste of the acceptance and love she desired. But in time Jean discovered that everyone with whom she built a relationship eventually became like her parents in one way or another. They became disappointed with her, grew cold toward her, and at times even ignored her. *The only way she could stay out of pain was to stay out of prolonged relationships.* Her strategy sentenced her to a lonely and hopeless existence, one in which she was constantly searching for a group of people to be the nurturing family she had lost.

Inevitably adolescents will respond to their despair in foolish and destructive ways unless someone gets involved with them and shows them a biblical way. One of the most critical responsibilities parents face may be responding to the despair in their teen's heart in a way that will help him or her discover the biblical route to fulfillment.

PREPARING A PARENT TO RESPOND TO HIS TEEN'S DESPAIR

When Christi angrily withdrew to her room after we told her she'd have to return to school the next day, I had to decide how to respond as her parent. I considered the option of ignoring the incident. Maybe Christi was just going through a "phase." Or maybe she was just tired and irritable because she'd been cooped up at home since the teachers' strike started. Maybe it would be best just to forget the incident and let her have her space for the rest of the evening.

However, something inside me sensed I would miss a critical

opportunity if I ignored Christi's pain in this way. To do so would be to trivialize her experience with her friends and to treat the betrayal she felt as something that should be no big deal.

But it was a big deal, a painful reality of life she'll be experiencing with regularity for the rest of her life. If I ignored it, even this one time, I risked teaching her that life depends on being calloused and not letting people get to her. If she adopted this as her way of surviving in a disappointing world, she would have to deny how others really make her feel. Not only would she become numb to the bad things people do to her, but also to the good things. She would have little or no capacity to enjoy or interact with people deeply, or to feel pain or joy with them. Although it was tempting, I decided not to dismiss what Christi was experiencing as "something she'll get over if I just let her handle it herself."

Another tempting response was to give Christi a fatherly "pep talk." I could sit her down and teach her to deal with her despair by telling her that things really weren't as bad as they seemed. That people really didn't dislike her. That she really wasn't the kind of person other people would intentionally hurt or betray. That the world really wasn't the awful kind of place she perceived it to be. That the gap she felt really didn't exist. But I knew the underlying message Christi would pick up would only set her up for more problems later.

A parent who gives her teen this kind of pep talk subtly teaches him that life depends on seeing himself and his world only and always in a positive light, that living with a negative image of himself and/or his world precludes any kind of happiness or joy. That finding joy depends on convincing himself that both he and his world are basically good, even though his heart tells him otherwise.

A message like this only reinforces two foolish assumptions in a teen: *that he really is sufficient in and of himself to make life work in the midst of his circumstances, and that God is not.* As long as an adolescent is encouraged to deny the seriousness and hopelessness of his circumstances, he can successfully maintain the illusion that he really can handle things without God. And, if he were to acknowledge the seriousness and hopelessness of his circumstances, life would be unbearable—not even God could provide what it would take to endure the pain.

When adolescents learn to deal with their despair in this way, they enter adulthood quite unprepared to deal honestly with the complexities and tragedies of real life. As adults they fail to acknowledge the seriousness of problems until they get so big they can no longer be glossed over. By then, however, there will be irreversible consequences and undeniable despair. Despair they were never equipped to cope with or find relief from. Despair that could drive them to take some disastrous and desperate actions.

As I reflected on Christi's pain and my likely response to it, I considered approaching her with some kind of plan for self-improvement. "After all," I reasoned, "if Christi could just be a little more outgoing, a little more talented, a little more athletic, or at least a little more scholarly, perhaps the kids and teachers at school would treat her with higher regard." My idea was nothing more than the proposition that Christi could make the people in her life less disappointing if she could only improve their perception of her.

On the surface the idea of self-improvement can sound very "Christian." Scripture certainly advocates changing and growing as a person. But when a kid is taught to respond to feelings of worthlessness and rejection by losing weight, raising grades, improving athletic performance, changing clothing styles, mastering some new social skill, etc., she comes to build her life on an erroneous principle: *The quality of my life depends on the quality of other people's perceptions of me.*" When kids operate by this principle, they come to depend on their own self-improvement efforts, rather than on a relationship with Christ, for satisfying the desires of their hearts. And they live with a nagging pressure to improve themselves so others will treat them well.

Any encouragement toward self-improvement or gift-development that kids are given to help them make their lives less painful teaches them to use their personal assets and abilities for the wrong purposes. It's certainly not wrong for parents to challenge their children to develop whatever gifts God has given them. Not to do so would be a grave error. However, kids should never be challenged to do this for the purpose of making the world a more fulfilling place for themselves. *The purpose of gift-development and self-improvement should always be to better equip themselves to love and serve others in the name of Christ.*

When kids are taught to turn to self-improvement strategies whenever they feel despair, they become the kind of people that can never rest and feel comfortable about themselves. Because they live in a hostile and unpredictable world, despair will always be present with them to some degree and they will always feel pressure to improve something about themselves. When no amount of self-improvement finally makes the world an amiable place, they will blame themselves for the way others treat them.

Another option I came up with as I reflected on how to help my daughter was to give her a lesson on self-assertion and commanding the respect she deserved from her friends. I thought she could take a couple of them aside and let them know how they were making her feel, and make it clear to them how she expected better treatment in the future. There certainly couldn't be any merit in encouraging my daughter to passively stand by while her friends mistreated her.

Just as I had about decided to go upstairs and urge Christi to confront her friends, another thought struck me. Although expressing her desires and feelings to them seemed appropriate and almost necessary to do at the time, I feared I was about to counsel her to do this for the wrong reasons. If I told her to confront them in order to ease her own pain and to get them to better satisfy her longings for unfailing love, I would be reinforcing the idea that the purpose of friendships is self-fulfillment. I would just be teaching her how to be a more effective consumer.

If kids are to have healthy friendships they must learn how to be honest about their desires and to confront disrespect or abuse by others. However, teens should be encouraged to do this only to deepen their relationships and promote mutual growth, not to get their needs met by each other. Kids who use self-assertion and self-expression to get people to treat them better become more inclined and equipped to rely on their relationships as their primary source of fuel for living rather than on Christ.

I'm almost too embarrassed to admit that I also seriously considered teaching my daughter "self-indulgence" as a way to cope with her pain. As I ruled out self-delusion, self-improvement, and self-assertion as good responses, I thought to myself, "Why not just go upstairs and tell her to get her coat on because we're going out?" I could take her to the electronics store and let her pick out that new stereo she'd been wanting. Why not just get her mind off what was troubling her by helping her indulge herself with whatever material pleasures were available?

I didn't have to reflect on this approach for very long, however, until its long-term implications brought me to my senses. The lesson Christi would learn could set her up for any number of addictions. As she discovered that temporary relief from despair could be found through immersing herself in material pleasures, she might choose this as her routine way of handling disappointment. It would become addictive if she chose to depend on it, instead of on a relationship with Christ, to make life in a fallen world bearable.

By encouraging kids to indulge themselves with whatever activity will drown out their troubled feelings, parents are actually contributing to the development of addictive personalities in their children. Addictions to such things as spending, eating, exercising, television-viewing, or compulsive sexual practices just to name a few, can easily develop.

As I attempted to respond to my daughter's despair, I wondered how I could help her find comfort without strengthening her foolish tendencies. I am convinced it is impossible for parents to even begin to accomplish this task until they have a handle on two things. First, they must understand the biblical route for satisfying the deepest desires of a teen's heart. Second, they must model this route for their teen.

Understanding How God Satisfies Teens' Desires

When parents encourage their teen to find relief from despair by doing something that is designed to change or deny her circumstances, they are only reinforcing her belief that Christ is not sufficient to meet her deepest desires in every situation. *The biblical route for satisfying the deepest desires a teen has does not require her to change or deny anything.* The psalmists frequently described what the biblical route requires:

> Taste and see that the LORD is good;
>> blessed is the man who takes refuge in him.
> Fear the LORD, you his saints,
>> for those who fear him lack nothing.   (Psalm 34:8-9)

As a father has compassion on his children,
  so the LORD has compassion on those who fear him;
But from everlasting to everlasting
  the LORD's love is with those who fear him,
  and his righteousness with their children's children.

(Psalm 103:13,17)

The LORD is near to all who call on him,
  to all who call on him in truth.
He fulfills the desires of those who fear him;
  he hears their cry and saves them.   (Psalm 145:18-19)

When a teen feels despair over her unfulfilled desires, the Bible calls her to do the most unnatural thing she could possibly do: *Fear the Lord.* This is the only condition she must meet to experience rest from her unsuccessful strategies for finding stability, esteem, and love. The writer of Proverbs says, "The fear of the LORD leads to life: Then one rests content, untouched by trouble" (Proverbs 19:23).

To fear the Lord, a teen must live her life in a way that reflects her belief that God can and will do what He says He will do. During times of despair, a teen must respond in a way that reflects her trust in God alone to satisfy her deepest desires in the time and way He chooses.

When a teen has genuinely chosen to entrust her deepest longings to God in this way, her parents will notice two characteristics about her behavior. First, *she'll display a sense of rest—not pressure or panic—around others.* As she waits on the Lord to provide the stability, impact, or love that seems to be missing in her life, she won't be working to get these things from people in her world. She'll be able to relax and feel comfortable with any gap she feels around them.

For each of the three types of teens I talked about earlier in this chapter, resting would mean something different. For Pam, the compliant/compulsive kid, resting would mean being with other people without working for their approval, ceasing to second-guess what they want from her, and instead, making it her goal to be herself with them.

For Sammy, the incompetent/dependent kid, resting would mean being with other people without trying to convince them that he's inferior. It would mean allowing them to place expectations on him and come to their own opinions about how competent he is.

For defiant/distant kids like Jean, resting would mean being with people without working to push them away before they had an opportunity to push her away. It would mean ceasing to run from people who may hurt or disappoint her.

Second, the behavior of a teen who fears God will be characterized by *a willingness to face situations that scare him and threaten to take away his sense of stability, impact, or love.* As he trusts in God's ability to protect and provide what is vital to his existence, he demonstrates a willingness to take high-voltage risks for the benefits of others. It will be obvious that he is operating in the ministry model.

Again, "risk-taking" means something different for every kid, depending on what threatens him and how he's learned to protect himself from it. What threatens compliant kids like Pam is the prospect of incurring the disapproval of others. She protects herself from this threat by being the type of person whomever she's with at the time wants her to be. For her, living in the ministry model means doing whatever is necessary to promote the welfare of others, even when it's something they might disapprove of. Kids like Pam take a big step toward maturity when they are able to do this with their own parents.

What dependent kids like Sammy are most afraid of are situations in which they give their best effort to do a good job and still fall short of other people's expectations. They protect themselves from these kinds of situations by not even trying to do well at anything at which they might be seen by others as incompetent. For them, living in the ministry model means attempting to do their best at something that would promote the welfare of another, even when their efforts might not be as good as someone else's.

Defiant kids like Jean are not frightened by the prospect of disappointing others like compliant and incompetent kids are. Instead, they are frightened of being disappointed or abandoned by someone they have grown to depend on. They protect themselves from this by not allowing themselves to depend on or trust anyone. For these kids, living in the ministry model means offering their friendship and trust to someone who has disappointed or hurt them in the past.

Resting and risk-taking will never be characteristic of a teen's life until he comes to understand and practice what it means to "fear the

Lord." For parents to lead their teen toward this, they must not only understand what it means themselves, but they must actively model it as well.

Modeling the Fear of the Lord

He who fears the LORD has a secure fortress,
and for his children it will be a refuge.   (Proverbs 14:26)

There I was racking my brain, trying to figure out what to do while my daughter sat up in her room in great despair—contemplating suicide for all I knew. And yet I felt paralyzed to do anything until I could be sure it was the right thing.

At times like these I find myself wishing that God had been just a little more specific in the Scriptures. I wanted a verse on exactly how to handle an adolescent daughter who felt betrayed by all her friends. But when I turn to the Scriptures with questions like these, I encounter mostly verses like Psalm 112:1-2, Psalm 128:1-4, and Proverbs 14:26—all assurances that the most significant thing I can do to impact my family and promote their well-being is to "fear the Lord."

Certainly, the only sufficient source of stability, strength, and security available to my teen when her world is falling apart is a relationship with Christ. However, the sense of pressure and panic I felt when I saw Christi in pain made me question whether I really believed Christ was sufficient for *me* when *my* family was falling apart. The fact that my first impulse when Christi was in pain was to put her out of pain, to quickly fix what made me feel like a failure as a man and as a father, revealed to me that I still depended on my own ability to prove that I was everything my world expected me to be (the father of a happy, well-adjusted daughter).

What started to become clear to me as I reflected that evening was that how I responded to my daughter (what words I used or what actions I took) wasn't nearly as important as where my center of dependency was as I responded. The critical thing was my own fear of the Lord, a real choice to believe God was sufficient to meet my deepest desires as a man no matter how well or how poorly Christi chose to deal with her disappointing circumstances. When this is not a reality in my own life, the probability is great that any response I make to my daughter's despair will only move her deeper into her own foolishness.

While only the Spirit of God can give a teen the faith to believe that God can and will provide what no one else ever has, Scripture holds parents responsible to provide an environment that encourages the development of this kind of faith in their kids. And according to the writers of the Psalms and Proverbs, the most important element in providing such a climate is the parents' modeling of what it means to fear the Lord.

As I walked up the stairs that night to talk to Christi, I felt a quiet confidence that I really could be of help to her. I still wasn't sure what I was going to say or do, but I knew that because of who God was I didn't have to get my daughter out of pain or make our conversation turn out a certain way. Because He was sufficient, I could rest in the knowledge that nothing crucial to my existence or my daughter's was at stake. I could risk getting more involved in her life knowing it would mean hearing about a lot of troubling circumstances I had no power to change, and yet I also knew that I didn't need to change them to be of real help.

At last I was ready to respond in a biblical way.

A BIBLICAL APPROACH TO RESPONDING TO AN ADOLESCENT'S DESPAIR

As I entered Christi's room that evening, I thought of perhaps a dozen different things I could have said or done that were still very biblical. A biblical response to a teen in despair does not consist of a certain set of magical words or actions. I believe, however, that a biblical response must always reflect a parent's understanding of what makes his teen tick, what causes the despair in his heart, and what can bring him real healing and relief in the midst of his pain. When parents have a biblical understanding of these three elements, they will respond in three important ways. First, they will take initiative to do more for their teen than just try to relieve his pain. They will try to enter his pain and understand it. Second, they will invite their teen to reflect with them on what to do about his despair. Finally, they will instruct him about the biblical route for satisfying the desires of his heart.

Entering a Teen's Pain

In order to be biblical in their responses, parents must try to promote a deeper relationship with Christ in their teen. When their only aim is to help their teen feel better, they are likely to alter the very set of circumstances that could drive her to seriously consider what a relationship with Christ has to offer. They are also likely to feel pressure and panic as they deal with their hurting teen because they'll assume responsibility for changing and controlling circumstances over which they have little control. *When parents understand that the seeds that will destroy their teen lie in her own heart, and not in her circumstances, they will shift their goals.* The teen's response to her circumstances, not the circumstances themselves, will become the parents' focus, and they'll be able to help her understand the things inside her that account for her despair.

To accomplish this, parents first need to help their teen articulate what she's feeling, especially about herself. They need to establish a climate that communicates acceptance of the teen no matter what feelings she expresses. As she's invited to talk freely about the feelings her circumstances are stirring up, her parents should encourage her to talk about the unfulfilled desires underneath her feelings, especially desires on the critical and crucial levels. As she talks, her parents should simply try to feel her despair with her. Once she's begun to clarify the deep desires that she can't get people to give her, she'll experience a growing sense of helplessness, something her parents simply must allow her to experience if they want her to pursue Christ. *Only when people become gripped with the reality of their inability to satisfy their deepest desires will they begin to thirst for God.*

Inviting a Teen to Reflect

Despair offers a teen one of her best opportunities to look within and get a glimpse of her unfulfilled desires, her ineffective plans for trying to get them fulfilled, the assumptions she's making about how she can get the world to meet them, how her assumptions affect the way she relates to people, and how the people and events in her world keep her plans from working and her desires from being fulfilled.

Parents should encourage their teen to reflect on all these things. While being careful not to assume a tone of rebuke or condemnation, they should challenge their teen's assumptions or expectations that the world can be manipulated to respect or love her in the way she most desires. Parents who talk openly at this point about some of their own despair and wrong assumptions can produce a climate that says, "We can relax because there's something broken about all of us. None of us will ever be good enough to get the world to give us what we most desire."

Pointing a Teen to Christ

In the end, a biblical response to a teen in despair directs him to the only place he can find fulfillment for his unmet desires. This, of course, involves teaching him what it means to fear the Lord. Parents must never give this kind of instruction in a sterile or condescending manner, but with the humility of one thirsty person telling another thirsty person where to find water.

Parents must be prepared, even when their teen is in great despair, for him to reject their instruction and continue trying to make his own foolish plan work. Parents have the responsibility to continually extend to their thirsty teen Christ's invitation to come and drink, with no guarantee of how their teen will respond. When he ignores their instruction and pursues his foolish ways, a second kind of parental response is in order. Now they must respond biblically, not only to their adolescent's desires, but also to the foolish purposes in his heart.

SUMMING IT UP

The more one comes to understand the importance the Bible puts on parenting, the easier it is to feel overwhelmed by the responsibility. One father recently shared with me the image he had of parenting his adolescent daughter through some difficult times. He visualized himself being dropped by God into the empty cockpit of a 747 while it was in flight. The members of his own family were the only passengers, and it was his job to land the jet with no more training or instructions than the command, "Keep it from crashing!"

Mercifully, God really does not put parents in such a critical situation. He never gives them the power to destroy their kids' lives.

Parents, even at their worst, do not have the power to rob their kids of the capacity to develop into loving, mature adults. (Even if through murder they rob them of their physical existence altogether, they cannot rob them of their eternal existence!)

How parents respond to the despair in their teen's heart is very important, but their kid's survival doesn't depend on their every action, as if one wrong response could ruin his life. A long-term pattern of wrong responses can be damaging of course, but never so devastating that God cannot provide enough help for the teen to heal and grow.

Rather than visualizing yourself as the unskilled pilot on a crash-course to disaster, imagine yourself being dropped with your teen into the front car of the most exhilarating and terrifying roller coaster in the world. Your job is to hold on tight to your teen until God brings the car safely to a standstill. At no time will the car be out of control from God's perspective, even though it will often seem so to you. In the end I think this image better captures what God expects from parents as they go through the despair of adolescence with their sons and daughters.

TEN

Responding to the Purposes in an Adolescent's Heart

I sat in my office with Jerome, a fourteen-year-old high school freshman. He had been suspended from school for being a bully and had locked his mother in the closet for several hours when she refused to take him to the hobby shop. His parents had asked me to help them determine how to respond to him in a way that would not only discourage this kind of behavior, but would also challenge the foolish purposes that lay beneath it.

When parents respond to their adolescent son or daughter only on the basis of the outward behaviors they observe, they run the risk of doing one of two things.

One, they may reinforce or strengthen the foolish purposes in their adolescent's heart. Suppose Jerome had behaved the way he did for the intended purpose of driving everyone who made him feel inferior out of his life. Since this is often the goal of a defiant adolescent, Jerome could have chosen this way to deal with the despair he felt as a result of the physical, intellectual, and social handicaps that made him appear inferior to his peers.

When Sheldon, Jerome's father, initially contacted me for help, he said his first impulse was to have nothing more to do with his son. He had already substantially distanced himself from Jerome in the wake of the boy's repeated outbursts of anger and defiance. After the most recent episode, Sheldon could have easily given in to the temptation to sever whatever emotional bonds still existed between the two of them, treating Jerome like a boarder who would be permitted to take his meals with the family only as long as he kept their rules. If this had been his parents' response, Jerome's foolish purposes would have accomplished exactly what they were designed to accomplish. He would have successfully driven out of his life the two people with the power to make him feel the "lowest," and his resolve to continue relating this way would have been strengthened.

Parents who respond only to the outward behavior of their teen run a second risk. They may encourage their kid to merely find new, and sometimes even more destructive, behaviors to accomplish the same foolish purposes. Suppose Jerome's purpose in choosing increasingly defiant acts was to make an impact on those around him in the only way he felt he had open to him. Whenever he was able to upset or hurt someone, he felt powerful and important. This was especially true when he could cause his parents to lose control and become emotionally unglued. All of the negative side effects of his behavior were worth it to Jerome because he felt like he mattered to someone, if only for a few minutes.

If this were Jerome's purpose, imagine the effect his parents' response of detaching themselves would have had on him. Once Jerome discovered that his defiant behavior no longer evoked any emotional response from them, and in fact was pushing them farther away instead of bringing them closer, he would more than likely have stopped his defiant behavior—especially if he thought continuing it would result in losing relationship with his parents altogether. Jerome's parents would probably have considered it a major victory when their strategy succeeded in modifying their son's behavior. Little would they suspect that the same cancer (the same foolish purposes) would surface in some other behavior sooner or later.

As life returned to "normal" in Jerome's family, Jerome would retain his longing to have some sense of impact in his world. His plan to attain it by finding a way to feel important or powerful would continue. In time Jerome would invent new behaviors that reflected his foolish purposes—behaviors that were either more acceptable to his parents (e.g., auto mechanics or weight lifting) or more hidden from them (e.g., sexual fantasy or vandalism). Both kinds of behavior would allow him to continue pursuing the same foolish purposes, but without the immediate threat of parental retribution. When and if they were as unsuccessful in providing Jerome with a sense of impact as were his old ones, he might eventually choose a third set of behaviors, a set that was self-destructive (e.g., suicide or substance abuse).

It is dangerous and risky to respond to an adolescent's behavior without taking into account the purposes in his heart that direct it. Such a response will almost certainly be compromised because *it calls the kid to do something about his actions, but nothing about the purposes behind them.*

HOW ADOLESCENTS VIEW THEIR PROBLEMS

As I listened to Jerome explain the problems he'd been having, I kept asking myself, "What's missing? What's wrong?" Here was a fourteen-year-old boy. An image bearer of God. Someone who had been created to seek God and love others. And yet, as I listened to him speak, I heard no evidence of any of it. There seemed to be no interest or intention on his part to pursue the things he was built to pursue.

Jerome seemed totally unaware that his behavior was a personal choice based on the purposes in his heart. He kept blaming his reactions on other people and not on himself. When they refused to give him what he wanted, he believed *he really didn't have a choice in how he responded.* He saw himself as a mere reactor to his environment. Until Jerome developed some sense of awareness or ownership of his choices, his parents' exhortations for him to change would be fruitless. After all, how can a person be expected to change something over which he believes he has no control?

But Jerome's lack of awareness of himself as a volitional being was only one of the missing elements that prevented him from moving toward health and maturity. A willingness or desire to subject his own purposes to God's purposes was another. As Jerome described his cruelty toward others, he seemed void of genuine concern for anyone but himself. Having fun was the primary purpose of all his activities. What God desired for his life or anyone else's seemed foreign and irrelevant to him. His plan for finding life was directed toward things that were self-exalting or self-indulgent, and away from things that required self-denial or self-sacrifice.

Jerome claimed to be a Christian and never missed a church activity. It is not unusual for kids from seemingly strong Christian homes and churches to possess no more sense of responsibility for their actions or duty to Christ than Jerome did. Very often, however, these kids can operate like this for years without anyone challenging them as long as their outward actions remain within the behavioral boundaries commonly accepted by the Christians around them.

Any biblical strategy for ministry to adolescents, whether it be through the church or through the family, must never shoot for anything short of getting to the very hearts and control centers of kids. Although a biblical strategy for youth ministry never ignores adolescents' outward actions, it does recognize that ultimately the kind of behavior God desires can flow only from a heart controlled by biblical purposes. David recognized that a person's outward actions become something God can take pleasure in only when the person's heart is subjected to His will. He wrote,

> O LORD . . .
> You do not delight in sacrifice, or I would bring it;
>> you do not take pleasure in burnt offerings.
> The sacrifices of God are a broken spirit;
>> a broken and contrite heart,
>> O God, [these] you will not despise. . . .
> Then there will be righteous sacrifices,
>> whole burnt offerings to delight you.   (Psalm 51:15-19)

The idea of generating a heart for God in an adolescent can be inconceivable to parents who haven't even found a good way to get him to put his dirty underwear in the right place. Accomplishing anything quite so noble as getting him to pursue God's purposes in his relationships can seem impossible. Nobody is in a better position to know how deep and pervasive a teen's selfishness is than his mom or dad. Nobody is in a better position to doubt whether it's possible to transform a consumer into a lover than a parent of an adolescent. As parents, it becomes a temptation to lower sights and shoot for simply surviving, and helping their children survive, those troubled years. *Parents are most apt to fall into this trap when they assume that the responsibility for producing these kinds of changes in their teens lies with them.* It is no wonder that parents who operate by this assumption sooner or later become consumed with disillusionment and guilt and give up. *It is a losing match anytime parents attempt to combat the depravity in their child's heart with their own parenting ingenuity and expertise.*

When I work with teens like Jerome, or even with ones like my own daughter, Christi, I would quickly give up in despair if I didn't depend on the promise in Ephesians 3:20-21:

> Now to him who is able to do immeasurably more than all we ask or imagine, according to his power that is at work within us, to him be glory in the church and in Christ Jesus throughout all generations, forever and ever! Amen.

I know I'm just not good enough as a counselor and parent to generate the deep kinds of changes needed in the hearts of the teens I work with. As I get involved with kids who operate with almost no sense of personal awareness or moral responsibility, I often become overwhelmed with the task that confronts me. Sometimes I wonder if I'm out of my mind to think that it's possible for troubled kids to become spiritually mature. In those moments I'm tempted to settle for handing out Band-Aids that will help kids get out of pain or stay out of trouble. And yet promises from God like the one above keep me from settling for this kind of ministry.

I believe God is at work in kids' hearts. And I believe He is summoning them to nothing less than a life of servanthood for Him. My goal is to provide the kind of environment in the relationship and responses I offer kids that makes them both aware of and accountable for why they do the things they do. When my strategy majors on getting them to just change their behavior to get out of trouble, or just change their circumstances to get out of pain, then I am actually making it easier for them to enter adulthood without grappling with the main issue of life: *Who are they* intending to serve through their actions?

THE TWO TASKS OF AN UNCOMPROMISED RESPONSE

When parents are confronted with the evidence of foolish tendencies in their teen, they have two tasks. First, they must strengthen the teen's sense of awareness and ownership of his purposes for the things he does. Second, they must call him to choose purposes that are directed at serving Christ, in whatever he does.

The order of these tasks is very important. It's impossible to ask somebody to give something away until he knows he owns it. *Before a kid will be in a position to give his whole heart to Christ, he must first come to see it as his own to give away or to do with as he pleases.* Most kids are unaware that they really own their own hearts, that they really are free agents who choose their purposes and the behaviors they believe will accomplish those purposes. Parents must first give their teen his heart (i.e., the sense of being in control of his own life) before they can ask him to give it up to Christ. And they must do this through uncompromised responses that strengthen the teen's sense of volitionality and summon him to a life of humility.

Task One: Strengthening a Teen to Be a Free Agent

> The righteousness of the upright delivers them,
> > but the unfaithful are trapped by evil desires.
>
> > > > > (Proverbs 11:6)

Kids have legitimate desires to feel safe in a hostile and unpredictable world. They want to feel significant in circumstances that constantly remind them of their limitations and inadequacies, to feel secure in someone's love while surrounded by people who are disappointing and failing them. However, these desires become illegitimate or evil when kids mistrust God's ability to fulfill them, and try to satisfy them on their own.

When kids do this, they end up attaching their desires to things or people in their world. When a girl attaches her desires to specific objects (cars, clothes, trips, status symbols), she becomes a materialist. When she attaches them to people, she becomes a manipulator. *And whatever a kid attaches her desires to takes on the illusion of having the* power to control her. She begins to feel compelled to do whatever it takes to keep from losing the objects or relationships she is depending on. When this occurs, she loses all sense of being a "free agent," someone who is free to pursue any goals she wants, using any behaviors she wants.

Jerome, for example, used his relationships with smaller or weaker people to provide him with a sense of power or esteem. Because of his intellectual, physical, and social handicaps, he concluded that he could never feel safe, significant, or loved around his peers or adult men like his father. He decided the only place he could experience these things was in relationships with younger kids on the bus and in the neighborhood as well as with women like his mother and sister. In these relationships he felt secure because his physical size and brutish behavior won respect and intimidation for him. To maintain his position of dominance in these relationships, Jerome developed a style of relating that was intimidating. Whatever he had to do to get his way in these relationships seemed like something he had to do, a reflex rather than a choice. And when others resisted him, he felt he had no choice but to respond by intimidating them even more with his forcefulness and anger. To choose not to relate this way would have meant choosing to risk losing the only thing that provided him with a sense of significance and security, a fate that seemed worse than death to an emotionally hungry fourteen-year-old boy. In light of the potential consequences of choosing a different way of relating, Jerome truly felt choiceless in the matter.

When responding to their adolescent, parents can automatically assume he is operating with little awareness of his own free agency. They can assume he feels ruled most of the time by whatever or whomever he has come to rely on for satisfaction, and that he believes he really has no other choice than to behave in whatever way is necessary to hang on to what is giving him a measure of fulfillment.

Parents must exert painstaking effort to cultivate a personal awareness in their teen of his ability to make choices as well as an awareness of the purposes behind the choices he makes.

A teen must know of his power to choose. Every action an adolescent takes actually represents a choice he is making. However, a recent study of high schoolers found that kids do what they really want to do only about 20 percent of the time. At least 80 percent of the time these kids have no sense of choice in what they are doing.

Parents can cultivate a sense of choice in their teen by using two main strategies. First, whenever they see her exercising her volitionality they can *call her attention to it*. Regardless of whether they agree or disagree with the content of her decisions and choices, it is important that they make her aware of them and affirm her in her ability to think and choose on her own. Parents should communicate their excitement with her ability to make her own decisions, and that they are especially pleased whenever she exercises it. They should be cautious, however, not to fall into a habit of communicating approval only when she makes the same decisions they would make. She may quickly pick up on this and conclude that the only way she can make her parents proud of her is by choosing what they would choose, which would erode her sense of volitionality rather than strengthen it.

A second strategy parents can use is to *create as many opportunities as possible for their teen to exercise his volitionality* within the moral boundaries established by God in the Bible. A teen has many options to pursue in making his choices—some of which concur with biblical teaching, some of which do not. *Biblically legitimate* choices include such things as dress (as long as it's modest), career (as long as it's honest), entertainment (as long as it's not immoral), etc. *Biblically illegitimate* choices include immodesty, dishonesty, immorality, etc.

God has given all people, including adolescents, the freedom to make both kinds of choices. He does warn them, however, to restrict their freedom to making choices that don't conflict with His Word because of the harmful consequences these choices inevitably bring to themselves and others. Because God has created people to be free agents, they naturally desire to make their own decisions, chart their own direction, and individually express their own will. Normally they restrict the exercise of their volitionality only when they believe that something crucial to them is at stake.

Volitional problems begin to arise when foolish people choose to believe either of two false propositions: that exercising their freedom to make biblically legitimate choices threatens what is crucial to their well-being as a person; that exercising their freedom to make biblically illegitimate choices threatens nothing that is crucial to their well-being.

Kids usually come to believe the first proposition even before they reach adolescence. They start to feel obliged to be whatever kind of person is most rewarded or least assaulted by the people in their world—especially the people closest to them. The kind of person they've become by the time they reach adolescence seems to be the product of other people's choices and not their own.

One high school girl I worked with felt this way. Molly grew up believing she had to conform totally to what her mother wanted her to be or do. If she deviated from her mother's wishes, she believed she would deeply hurt her mother and expose herself to everyone (especially her parents) as the terrible person she perceived herself to be. To keep this from happening, she let her mother pick her friends, select all her clothes, decide how she would spend her time, and choose what college she would attend. The choices she felt she could make without risking total annihilation of herself as a person were very few.

When an adolescent doesn't permit herself to express her volitionality in biblically legitimate ways, pressure builds up. She starts to feel caged in. She experiences a loss of concentration and motivation in the things she does. Eventually she feels driven to look for hidden ways to express her individualism, or to experience the thrill of personal choice. She looks for ways she can be the kind of person *she wants* to be without the significant people in her life even knowing.

For Molly this involved practicing two secret activities: binging on great quantities of food, and drinking alcohol. Both were activities she knew her parents would disapprove of if they ever found out. Whenever she was home alone, she would consume large amounts of food and alcohol that were stored in the house. She would eat and drink until she became nauseous and then vomit everything up. When she was eating and drinking in this way she experienced two things: the thrill of doing something that was entirely her own choice, and a sense of revenge as she defiantly did something she knew would shock and hurt her parents. Afterward, Molly always felt physically ill and emotionally overwhelmed with guilt. She took great precautions to keep her parents from finding out about her secret acts of defiance.

When an adolescent like Molly chooses to find a secret outlet to express her volitionality, she frequently chooses activities that abuse or punish her own body. Perhaps in a single act she is both declaring her freedom to choose for herself and then punishing herself for how "bad" she feels about doing such a thing. *If a teen experiences a personal sense of choice only when she makes illegitimate choices like these, in the end she loses desire to be a free agent.* She comes to fear that if she really did make more of her choices, the person she is in secret would somehow show. Others would see it and her life would be ruined.

Adolescents usually can avoid falling into these traps only with lots of help from their parents. Every parent's goal should be to provide as much freedom and opportunity as he can for his child to exercise his volitional capacities in legitimate ways. Of course, when a child is still a preteen, he is not yet allowed to exercise his freedom of choice in all the areas the Bible allows. Because of his maturity level, his parents still reserve the right to make many of these choices for him (e.g., when he dates, when he gets his driver's license, etc.). However, it is imperative that as the child reaches adolescence his parents encourage him to make more and more legitimate choices for himself until, at the age of twenty-one, he has been imparted all the freedom and responsibility for making all his own choices.

As I worked with Jerome's parents, this became a real challenge to them. We attempted to draw up a list of the various opportunities in a given week in which Jerome could make legitimate choices for himself. Our list turned out to be very short. Jerome lived in a rural area where he had no friends his age. Since he didn't drive, and his parents were too busy on the farm to chauffeur him, he could not spend time with friends when he wanted to. He had no means of earning his own money either, so he was dependent on his parents' decisions about what to buy or not to buy for him. Since he was assigned a number of farm chores both before and after school each day, he had almost no discretionary time he could spend in the way he wanted. Because of learning difficulties, he also had to spend almost every spare minute studying. At school Jerome chose to go out for football but was not allowed to stay on the team because of health problems. He was not allowed to take most of the classes his friends were taking because his grades were too low.

The longer we talked about Jerome's life, the more we began to see how void it was of opportunities for him to choose. Once his parents realized how destructive this was, they started to deliberately create opportunities for Jerome to get practice at making his own choices. They instituted an allowance and gave Jerome freedom over how to spend it. They gave him a voice in which chores he wanted to do around the farm and made sure he had free time to use as he saw fit. They made arrangements for him to get into town to see his friends when he asked. They helped him pursue some activities he expressed interest in at the "Y." They also bought him a motorized bike he could use to get around the area on his own.

However, this was only the beginning of their work in instilling in their son a sense of ownership over his life. Next they had to help him become aware of his purposes behind the choices he made.

When parents attempt to cultivate in their teen a personal awareness of his ability to make choices, they're trying to help him see that *his choices are really his own.* When they attempt to cultivate in him a personal awareness of his purposes for the choices he makes, they're trying to help him see that *his choices are self-serving.* Helping an adolescent recognize the self-centered nature of his own purposes is a prerequisite to growth in the adolescent toward maturity and Christlikeness.

Parents get their best opportunities to expose their teen's inner purposes when he makes his requests or decisions known to them. It is necessary, then, for parents to be equipped with some basic strategies for responding uncompromisingly to the requests and decisions of their adolescent.

Responding to an adolescent's requests. If we could go back in time with Jill, Jerome's mother, and relive the conversation she had with her son the morning he locked her in the closet, we would have heard it begin with a request: "Mom, will you take me to the hobby shop today?"

Any healthy way she might have responded to his request might have triggered the same reaction in Jerome. An uncompromised response, however, would have delayed any decision about his request until she was able to first clarify two things: (1) the full details of the request; and (2) Jerome's intention in making the request.

Some nondefensive questions could have gotten Jerome to clarify both of these. "Now, explain to me what exactly you want me to do," Jill could have asked. "What makes getting to the hobby shop today so important?" "How would you feel if we waited until your suspension from school was over before we went?"

An uncompromised response on Jill's part, then, would have required her to distinguish between the nature of the object or privileges that were being requested (was what he was asking for intrinsically harmful to him?) and the nature of the purpose for the request (was it strictly self-serving?). Depending upon the nature of these two factors, Jill could then determine an appropriate response to her son's request. The matrix in figure 16 can guide parents as they make this determination.

FIGURE 16
UNCOMPROMISED RESPONSES TO AN ADOLESCENT'S REQUESTS

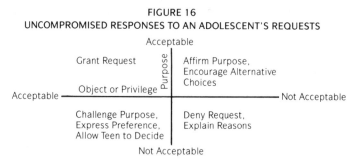

Moving counterclockwise on the matrix, notice the four scenarios parents might face. First, the object or privilege their teen is requesting, as well as the teen's purpose for requesting it, are both acceptable. In this case it is appropriate to grant the request.

Second, the object or privilege being requested is acceptable, but the purpose is not. In this case the parents should challenge the adolescent's purpose (explain to him what is self-serving and destructive about his reason for making the request), and express their desire for him to pursue a different kind of goal. In the end the parents are wise to allow their teen to decide for himself whether his request should be granted, based on his own evaluation of his purposes.

Third, both the object or privilege being requested and the purpose of the request are unacceptable. In this case the only appropriate response for the parents is to deny the teen's request and carefully explain the reasons why. It is imperative that they point out to him not only the harmful nature of his request, but also the harmful nature of his underlying purposes.

Finally, the purpose for the request is acceptable but the object or privilege being requested is not. In this case it is important that the parents call attention to the nature of the teen's purpose and take time to affirm him for his intentions. They should carefully explain the reason why the object or privilege he is requesting is not acceptable, and then encourage him to think of other ways he might accomplish the same purposes.

Had Jill used this strategy for responding to Jerome's request, she would have faced the fourth type of scenario. Jerome's purpose for wanting to go to the hobby shop was to purchase an item to give to someone on his bus as a replacement for something he had broken. There was something constructive about this purpose that Jill could have affirmed, even though she still may have wanted to deny Jerome's request for a day or two to give him the full impact of his suspension from school. Even if Jill had affirmed him for the good idea and encouraged him to think of another option, Jerome still might have decided to react by trying to force his will on his mother. In that case his purposes and actions would have become altogether unacceptable, and Jill would have had the responsibility to sternly warn him of the consequences if he chose to persist.

Responding to an adolescent's decisions. Parents have the opportunity to make their teen aware of his purposes not only when he states his requests, but also when he announces his decisions. Oftentimes he doesn't express them in words and may, himself, be totally unaware of a decision he's made. That's why parents should always be on the lookout for indications that their adolescent has made a decision (e.g., a sudden change in the teen's behavior, plans, or preferences). They should then invite him to talk about the decision and the events and thought processes that led up to it. Parents shouldn't force their teen to talk about his decisions. However, if he resists they should always consider the possibility that they are doing something to make him feel uncomfortable about being open in their presence.

When a teen *is* willing to talk with her parents about a decision she has made, they should always encourage her to think about the purpose she had for making it. Had Molly's parents noticed a decision she'd made to not call one of her friends again, and got her talking about it, they could have helped her recognize her purpose behind it. She had decided never to call Mary again in order to protect herself. Her mother didn't like Mary, and Molly was afraid of losing her mom's approval and experiencing a widening of the "gap." If her parents had known this, they could have talked with her about some of the foolish assumptions she was making about life, and about the way she was depending on her own compliant style of relating to get her deepest desires fulfilled.

Parents should not expect these kinds of conversations to carry a lot of weight with their teen at first. Chances are that early on she'll find them "weird" and confusing, and she'll possibly even feel attacked. However, as parents are able through numerous conversations like these to show their teen a general pattern in the reasons she does the things she does, she'll start to feel more ownership over her life and understand her actions as part of a self-chosen course toward what she thinks will bring her real satisfaction.

Ultimately, parents want their teen to seek God's help to change the whole direction and focus of her life. A kid will never even consider doing this until she gets an honest look at the foolishness and selfishness in her own heart and the purposes she has chosen for her life. Once she has, she will be in a position to consider the radical call Christ makes for her to serve God and others.

Task Two: Summoning a Teen to Be a Servant

> Humility and the fear of the LORD
> bring wealth and honor and life. (Proverbs 22:4)

According to the writer of Proverbs, a fool's goal is to exalt himself (Proverbs 30:32-33). Since every kid emerges into adolescence already operating as a fool, his natural bent is to pursue whatever will enhance his sense of safety, significance, or love. A parent's most difficult task is to summon his son or daughter away from this kind of life to a life of self-denial and self-sacrifice.

If a kid is allowed to pursue self-exaltation, he faces disastrous consequences. Jesus promised that those who try to find their own life will lose it (Luke 9:24). Parents call their teen toward a life of servanthood when they help him get a taste of two things: the consequences of choosing foolish purposes for his life and the benefits of choosing wise purposes.

The consequences of choosing foolish purposes.

A servant cannot be corrected by mere words;
  though he understands, he will not respond.
  (Proverbs 29:19)

Although parents may excel at putting into words what their teen is feeling and at making him aware of the kind of goals he's pursuing, he may not be convinced that he needs to make a drastic change in direction until he's had the opportunity to experience the consequences of some of his own foolish choices.

There are two types of consequences that parents can make sure their teen experiences: *natural* and *engineered.* Both are essential in giving the teen an authentic taste of the outcome of foolish living.

Natural consequences occur as a direct result of behavior or choices. Jerome's getting suspended from school or Molly losing friends she refuses to call are examples of natural consequences. When a kid makes foolish choices and pursues foolish purposes, his parents should allow him to experience the natural consequences. *The pain such consequences bring can be one primary thing God uses to get a kid to reevaluate and change the foolish strategies he lives by.*

When a teen is experiencing a natural consequence of one of his choices, parents should use it as an opportunity to get more involved with him, to invite him to reflect with them on what he's experiencing, and to share his pain. And they should help him connect his pain to a choice he has made. *Building this bridge between the purposes in a teen's heart and the disappointment he experiences in the world is essential to helping him become disillusioned with his own foolishness.* Without this kind of help from parents, a teen will frequently fail to notice any relationship at all between the painful consequences of his choices and the foolishness of the choices themselves. He can continue to believe that his foolish strategy is really a source of life.

Natural consequences alone, however, can almost never convince adolescents to repent of their foolishness because they often lack the immediacy and severity that is required to challenge adolescents in their stubbornness (Proverbs 13:19). When teens make biblically illegitimate choices (going outside the boundaries God and their parents have erected for them), the immediate consequences they experience are frequently pleasurable instead of painful. The actual destructive consequences of these choices (e.g., the choice to engage in premarital sexual intercourse) may not occur for several weeks, months, or even years. Because of this delay, kids can easily become deluded into believing that a choice to violate God's moral boundaries is no big deal.

Also, when natural consequences occur immediately, they are often not severe enough to communicate to the teen the seriousness of what he's chosen to do. A sexually promiscuous teen may in the short term experience some increased emotional and relational difficulties, but these may not be severe enough to convince him of how destructive premarital sex really is. The natural consequences of sin are often too unreliable to sufficiently deter adolescents from sinning.

Parents are thus responsible to engineer consequences for their adolescent's foolish choices whenever the natural consequences are not adequate to challenge his foolishness. Parents need to build an association in their adolescent's mind between his foolish purposes and the actual significance God attaches to them. To do this, engineered consequences should be designed to give a kid an immediate sample of the *ultimate* consequences foolishness reaps: a loss of the freedom he deeply desires to impact the world and experience relationship in the way he chooses. Engineered consequences should always be designed to prevent a kid from successfully using his foolish strategies to satisfy these desires.

Although a teen's wrong strategies will never be able to win for him the pure kind of impact and relationship it takes to totally fulfill him, they can win him a perverted kind of impact and relationship that temporarily satisfies.

Jerome, for example, achieved a perverted form of impact by successfully intimidating those who were weaker than he was. Molly acquired a perverted form of relationship by pleasing people with her performance. In neither case was the quality of what the teens experienced anything close to what they longed for, but it was enough to keep them tenaciously clinging to their foolish styles of relating.

The less these strategies are allowed to work for kids like Jerome and Molly, the more willing these kids will be to let go of them. An uncompromised response by their parents will involve engineering the kinds of consequences that will make it as difficult as possible for their kids' styles of relating to be effective at winning the perverted forms of relationship and impact they've learned to be satisfied with.

Parents usually need to do some extensive reflection to design and engineer these kinds of consequences for their teens. The following questions can guide parents in this process.

- What needs and desires in your teen are most likely being met through his foolish behaviors or choices?

As Jerome's parents and I reflected on this question, it became obvious to us that Jerome's greatest need at the present time was to experience some sense of significance in a world that constantly reminded him of his limitations and inadequacies. His problem behaviors were accomplishing this for him to a limited degree. He was reaping a form of attention and respect from others whenever he bullied them into giving him what he wanted. Nothing Jerome had legitimately chosen had provided him with a healthy sense of impact or mastery over his world, so he made an illegitimate choice to gain "mastery" of those physically smaller or weaker than he. As we attempted to design a response to this foolish strategy, we first had to trace his behavior to the problem thinking that lay beneath it.

- What kinds of foolish assumptions could be leading your teen to try to get his needs met this way?

Jerome's parents needed to be reminded that the goal of their response was not just to get their son to change his problem behaviors, but to challenge his foolish assumptions about life. As we speculated about what kinds of foolish assumptions could account for Jerome's behavior, I encouraged Sheldon and Jill to try to state them in two or three sentences. After a lot of discussion, these were the sentences they thought captured the essence of Jerome's foolish assumptions:

Life depends on me being the kind of person who can make others do what I want them to do. When I can get people to respond to me this way, there must be something valuable or significant about me. If I didn't behave this way I wouldn't be the kind of person people would see as valuable or significant.

Once Sheldon and Jill put Jerome's problem thinking into words like these, they were ready to respond in an uncompromising way. To think of their son entering adulthood with this kind of formula for life was quite alarming. The consequences would be devastating. It was important for them to give him a taste of these consequences in hopes of driving his foolishness out of him before he reached adulthood.

•What kind of response to the problem behavior in your adolescent will challenge instead of reinforce the foolish assumptions in his heart?

Most parents have a tendency to respond automatically to their adolescent in ways that reinforce his foolishness. The detached parent, for example, tends to respond to problem behavior in his teen by lowering his involvement with him and expecting even less from him. Sheldon's first impulse was to respond in this way. It would have reinforced in an already defiant teen the belief that he was the kind of person who really wasn't worth anybody's time and effort.

Parents of teens like Jerome can begin to challenge their kids' foolish assumptions by getting more involved with him and letting him know that they see him as a person capable of making a very significant (and legitimate) impact.

For Sheldon this meant responding to the "shove-Mom-in-the-closet" episode in ways that were quite unnatural to him. First, it meant increasing his involvement with his son. Earlier Sheldon had taken away one by one all the activities he and Jerome did together as punishment for his misbehavior. (Withdrawing relationship like this is never appropriate discipline of a teen.) This added to the unfulfilled desires in Jerome that fueled his misbehavior, since it robbed him of healthy ways to feel significant. To increase involvement with Jerome, Sheldon reinstituted these activities and let his son know they were a priority to him. *Increasing involvement in response to ugly behavior in a teen is one of the best methods parents can use to give their kids a taste of*

God's grace. It ought to be part of every consequence parents engineer.

Second, in response to Jerome's defiant behavior, Sheldon took a strong stand, something he'd previously neglected to do out of fear of getting into more fights with his son. Sheldon's normal way of responding to such events was to lose his temper and yell, take away some privileges, and walk off, never to bring up the subject again. This time Sheldon chose to take his son on a field trip. He asked a police sergeant at the local jail to take Jerome on a guided tour and explain to him what happens to people who try to use abusive behavior to get their way. Even some of the prisoners assisted in showing Jerome where he could bunk if he ever came for a stay.

After the tour, Sheldon shared these words with his son while they were still in the parking lot of the jail.

> Jerome, I brought you here today for one reason. I wanted to show you how much I love you. I love you so much that I am committed to doing whatever it takes to keep you from ever having to end up at a place like this. Son, the way you've been going, this is exactly where you're going to end up. Because I am so committed to not let that happen, the next time you get abusive with anyone I will call the sergeant and and make arrangements for you to be arrested. I want you to experience what kind of life you're headed for. By the way, Son, how you've been acting—that's partially my fault too. I've been failing you in some big ways as a dad. But that's going to change too. I plan to be a whole lot more involved in your life. I hope we can work at being real friends again. Is there anything you want to say to me?

Sheldon's response was designed to give his son fair warning of the consequences of his foolishness. It was designed to assure Jerome that he would no longer be free to experience anything but painful consequences if he chose to continue in his abusive behavior. This response, combined with increased involvement by his parents, began to challenge Jerome's notion that the only way he could feel significant was to be somebody who was defiant.

Helping a teen taste the consequences of his foolishness puts him in a position to ask, "If being this kind of person doesn't get me anywhere, what do I do? What kind of person do I have to be to find life?" An uncompromised response by the parents at this time can help the teen answer this question by giving him a taste of what life can be like when he's the kind of person whose purposes are wise.

The benefits of choosing wise purposes.

> [He] gives grace to the humble.
> The wise inherit honor,
>> but fools he holds up to shame.   (Proverbs 3:34-35)

A life of humility rarely sounds attractive to kids. It doesn't make sense to them to humble themselves in order to be exalted. It makes no sense that in order to find satisfaction for their deepest desires, they must choose not to pursue self-fulfillment. And yet this is the kind of choice God calls wise and promises will lead to honor and life.

There is little chance that a teen would ever choose to live this way unless someone helps her get a taste of what being a servant of Christ is all about. Parents can help do this by adopting three practices that will give her a taste of the benefits a life of servanthood can yield.

Model for your teen self-denial and self-sacrifice. In chapter 6, I defined self-denial as a decision to allow one's desires to go unfulfilled by others, something that's possible only when one is trusting Christ to fulfill them when and how He chooses. I defined self-sacrifice as a second decision to take whatever risks are necessary to promote this kind of trust in Christ in others. Both elements were involved in the new way Sheldon chose to respond to his son.

When parents consistently demonstrate godly self-denial and self-sacrifice in their relationships (especially with their family), their kids start to get a clearer picture of what it means to be a servant. They get a picture of a person who has strength, dignity, and a deep sense of satisfaction in the way he lives his life.

Teach your teen about self-denial and self-sacrifice. Kids are rarely exposed to any approach to life that doesn't advocate being self-serving in both purpose and style of relating. Therefore, parents must teach their kids about both the ministry and consumer models of living (see chapter 6). Because the ministry model is so foreign to the culture kids live in, it is vital for parents to show their kids many real-life examples of people who chose the ministry model, perhaps through biblical and biographical materials. Parents who expect an immediate response to this kind of teaching will experience great disappointment. Servanthood will only start to make sense to kids after repeated exposure to the idea through a variety of means over a number of years. This was clearly the method the Apostle Paul used to summon Timothy to a life of servanthood (2 Timothy 3:10-15).

Invite your teen to join you in doing things that require self-denial and self-sacrifice. There is probably no better way to help a person sample the ministry model than to invite him to participate in a ministry endeavor that requires self-denial and self-sacrifice. When parents can get their teen involved, even for a few short minutes, in doing something that makes him forget about his own needs long enough to care about someone else's, it will give him a taste of what it means to lose his life for Christ's sake. This can often be the first step to opening a teen's mind and heart to a whole new way of life.

SUMMING IT UP

Perhaps the sentences in the New Testament that best capture the essence of parenting a teen are found in Colossians 1:28-29:

> We proclaim him, admonishing and teaching everyone with all wisdom, so that we may present everyone perfect [mature] in Christ. To this end I labor, struggling with all his energy, which so powerfully works in me.

For a parent to follow Paul's pattern of ministry with people, he must have as his end "to present his teen mature in Christ," to help him enjoy and trust the person of Christ as the center of his dependence in life. When this becomes a parent's long-term objective, two things will always be true.

First, parenting will always be a struggle. Even the godliest parent will have to labor hard to provide unconditional involvement and uncompromised responsiveness for his kids on a consistent basis. This kind of parenting requires high energy levels that often surpass what a parent has in his own flesh to expend. This is why he must take heart in a second truth: God promises to provide the power he needs to practice biblical parenting.

Paul labored with people "struggling with all Christ's energy, which so powerfully worked in him" in order to present them mature in Christ. When you step out to do the same thing with your own teens, you can have the confidence that Christ will likewise give you the energy you need. You will struggle. At times you will hurt. But committing yourself to learning to love your kids in a whole new way will take you on a journey you will never regret—an adventure into the power and grace of the gospel, into the very heart of God.

Afterword

Worship is almost inevitable when we face life honestly. A clear picture of the way things really are provides a dark background against which the grace of God sparkles brilliantly. And when the sparkle blinds us, there's nothing else to do but worship.

When we feel God's grace, we have a desire to make it known to others. And nowhere do we have a more important opportunity to be gracious (in the richest sense of the word) than with our kids.

After reading Kevin's book, it may be particularly important to keep that central idea in mind. Let me explain why.

If you're like me, you may feel somewhat overwhelmed by all that the book provoked you to think about. You've seen your family in several of the illustrations and wondered if the solutions that worked there will work for you. Perhaps you've sensed in a new way the pain that your kids feel and you long to reach into their hearts with tender support. Maybe you've seen things in yourself that need corrective attention.

But you're still not sure what to do. It all seems so complicated. You may be tempted (as I am) to scrap it all and return to some form of a "love-'em, spank-'em, and-get-on-with-life" philosophy. That approach served previous generations who didn't understand, and therefore didn't worry, about such things as hidden motives and emotional scars. Or you may respond to the book by thinking so hard about everything Kevin said that parenting will become a complicated burden stripped of all naturalness and joy.

I hope neither you nor I will yield to those temptations. Consciously building all our efforts to parent on the foundation of grace — both God's grace to us and our reflection of that to our kids — may help us richly profit from the excellent but occasionally difficult ideas in Kevin's book.

We must agree with Kevin that there is more to effective parenting than laying down God-honoring rules, trying to enforce them fairly, and doing our best to keep communication lines open with teenagers who chat endlessly with friends and speak in one-word sentences to us. There's more to it than requiring our kids to sit still (and awake) during early-morning devotions or, failing in that, to scream biblical truths at them during times of uncontrolled conflict.

Who we are as people, how we deal with feelings like hate, frustration, and pressure, and what we are insisting happen in both ourselves and our kids are important. We cannot ignore these kinds of concerns as we continue on in our busy lives, too preoccupied and too scared to look beneath the surface at what really may be going on in our families.

Kevin provides clear categories to help us think more richly about ourselves and our kids. But we're still likely to get tripped up as we take a hard look at life as it really is at home. Honesty comes hard because what is true about our homes will convince us that we're not able to control what matters most to us. And giving up control (or realizing we never had it) scares us to death. We want to know we can do what is needed to make everything we care about turn out as we want.

But giving up control is precisely what grace demands. To *receive* God's grace, we must admit we're licked. There's simply nothing we can do to become better people or to make others better.

As terrifying as it is to admit that (to admit it deeply, not merely to acknowledge it as religious truth), doing so presents us with an unparalleled opportunity. When we present ourselves before God naked and deformed and helpless, we are then affected in our very natures by His continued involvement. He doesn't back away in disgust. He sticks with us; He makes it clear He's for us, even though we're a mess and have no idea how to clean ourselves up.

Receiving God's grace makes us want to extend it to others. *Extending* grace to our kids begins when we realize that, like us, they can't improve the quality of their lives. All they can do is present themselves honestly before God as they are, unimpressive and morally unclean, filthy. It is our grace to them that the Holy Spirit often uses, enabling them to be honest and to want to bring themselves as they are before God.

Although our kids are unable to make themselves good, they are still responsible for how they live. Our job as parents includes bringing consequences to bear when their actions reflect a clear commitment to have things their way at others' expense. At the same time, we must stay involved with them in a way that says, "I really like you, and no matter what you do, I believe in you; you are a treasured bearer of God's image who can become the wonderful person God made you to be." Our attitude, whether we're grounding them for two weeks or buying them a car, makes all the difference in the world.

I recall a recent time in our family when one of our sons was involved in things that were simply wrong. As I drove for an hour to meet him, I prayed for one thing: "Lord, let me demonstrate to my son the grace You've given to me." Never have I more richly felt the thrill of both receiving and extending grace. The time together made a significant difference in both our lives.

More than anything else, I want our sons to remember keenly those moments when they saw in me, unexpectedly, something of the wonder of grace. I want them to feel less deeply those times when my eyes blazed with anger and my tongue sliced into them with rejecting force. Extending grace is the special privilege of parents. Both good times and bad provide opportunity to embody grace in an up-front relationship, but the bad ones give grace a chance to reach more deeply inside.

Involvement when it's pushed away, a tender spirit in response to meanness, a warm resolve to do good to someone who's breaking your heart, discipline administered firmly (not hatefully) even at times when it will likely provoke vicious defiance in your teen, quiet hope that continues to believe in someone after repeated failure—all this and more, much more, is involved in grace.

Becoming a gracious person matters more than understanding internal dynamics or having regular devotions or spending quality time with your kids. Those things matter, but without a love fueled by grace they add up to nothing.

The central point of Kevin's book is a good one to repeat as I finish my comments: *The key to becoming a more effective parent is to become an increasingly godly person.* And because godliness is more a matter of the heart than a set of prescribed activities, becoming a godly man or woman requires some awareness of emotions we wish weren't there, our real motives as we interact with our kids, and whatever else we'd prefer not to notice.

As we become aware of who we are, the grace of God will compel us to worship with willing, grateful hearts. He is still for us. We're not cast off. Our lives can matter. And as the realization of grace seizes our deepest parts, we will want with all our heart, soul, mind, and strength, to extend to others the grace we have received. A parent committed to extending grace to his kids because God's grace tastes so good to him is a godly, mature parent. He may not be able to follow every detail of Kevin's thinking in this book, but if he gets the main point, no matter. His kids will be in line for rare blessing.

As they see grace in our dealings with them, perhaps our children will come to deeply believe that everything they want is available in a Savior who forgives them for being everything they shouldn't be. The effect of that kind of belief is humble, God-honoring maturity, the character that every Christian parent longs to see develop in his kids.

That's been Kevin's prayer as he wrote the book and mine as I add my remarks.

LARRY CRABB

If you and your family have benefited from the principles of *Parenting Adolescents*, you'll enjoy these titles as well:

PARENTING ADOLESCENTS VIDEO SERIES.

Worthwhile whether you have teens in crisis or you just want to improve your parenting skills, this small group video series uses dramatic vignettes, film clips, and interviews with parents and their children to demonstrate new ways to guide your teen toward maturity, responsibility, and Christlikeness—without relying on simplistic formulas.

Hosted by Jim Hancock, and featuring key insights and principles from Kevin Huggins, author of *Parenting Adolescents*, the video segments are fast paced and provocative. You'll find the balance of drama, teaching, and encouragement a profound help as you learn more about yourself—and just how effective you can be as a parent.

Parenting Adolescents Small Group Video Package
(Includes eight 15-minute segments on two video cassettes, one discussion guide, and one copy of book; SPCN 9900735846) $119.00

PARENTING TEENS WITH LOVE AND LOGIC

When kids hit their teen years, parenting takes on a whole new dimension. As teenagers struggle toward independence and autonomy, some dicey issues emerge.

That's where love-and-logic parenting comes in. Love means giving your teens opportunities to be responsible and empowering them to make their own decisions. Logic means allowing them to live with the natural consequences of their mistakes—and showing empathy for the pain, disappointment, and frustration they'll experience.

When you parent with love and logic, it's a win-win situation. You'll win because you'll learn to love in a healthy way and effectively guide your teens. And your teens will win because they'll learn responsibility and acquire the tools they'll need to cope with the real world.

Parenting Teens With Love and Logic by Foster W. Cline and Jim Fay, M.D.
(Hardback; ISBN 0891096957) $16.00

PARENTING WITHOUT PRESSURE

All children have parenting needs—even those adolescents who claim they don't want *any* parenting! But how often do you find your attempts to be a good parent deteriorating into a power struggle with your child?
There *is* a better way!

Parenting Without Pressure is an approach that involves your whole family in managing conflict and resolving differences. And it helps prepare your kids for independence. It leaves you in control, but brings your children into dialogue about the parenting process.

Since 1987, social workers, school counselors, court systems, and therapists have recommended Teresa Langston's Parenting Without Pressure workshops. Now her book can help you stop nagging and start relating to your children with love, respect, and healthy detachment. Why fight when you can parent without pressure?

Parenting Without Pressure by Teresa Langston
(Oversize paperback; ISBN 0891097503) $12.00